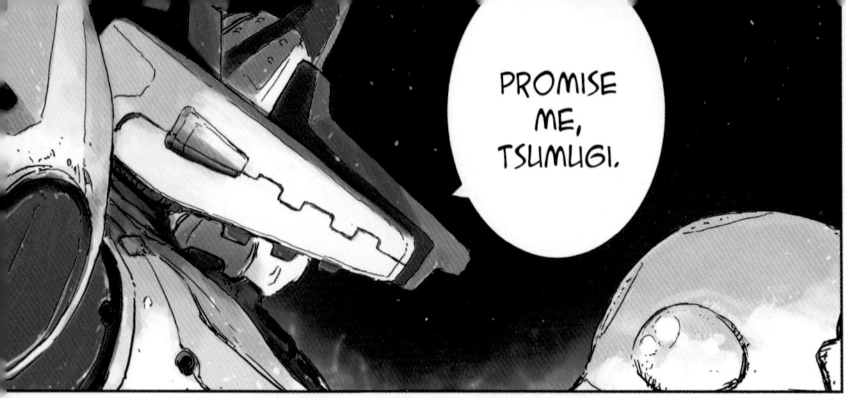
PROMISE ME, TSUMUGI.

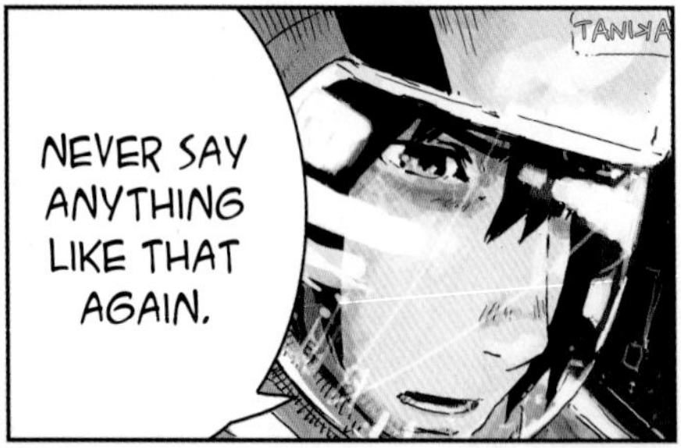
NEVER SAY ANYTHING LIKE THAT AGAIN.

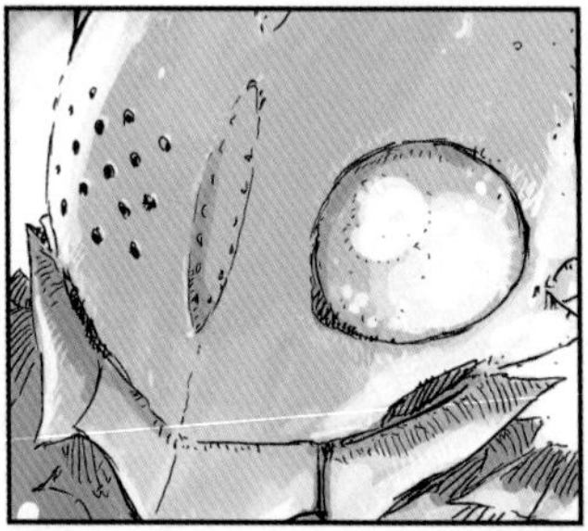

#60 The Semiautonomous Conversion Organ's Placement

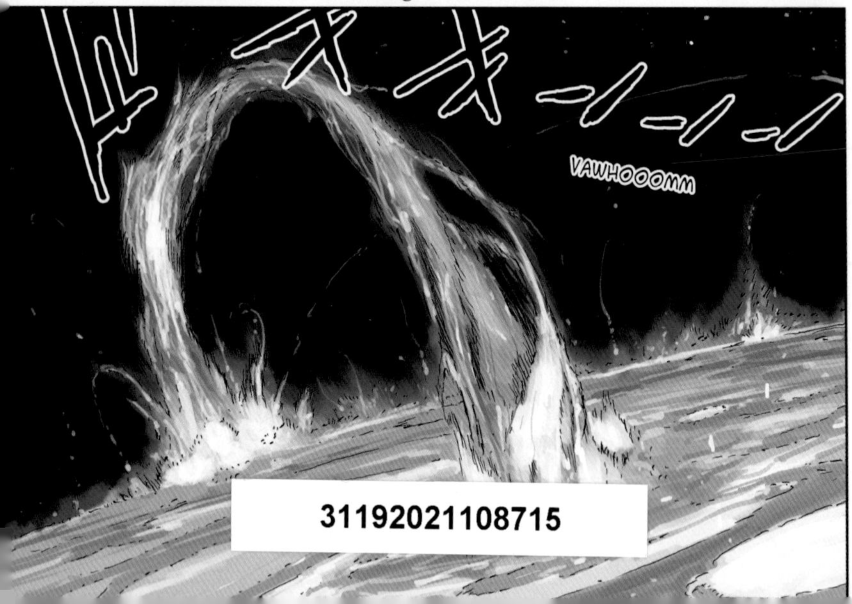
VAWHOOOMM

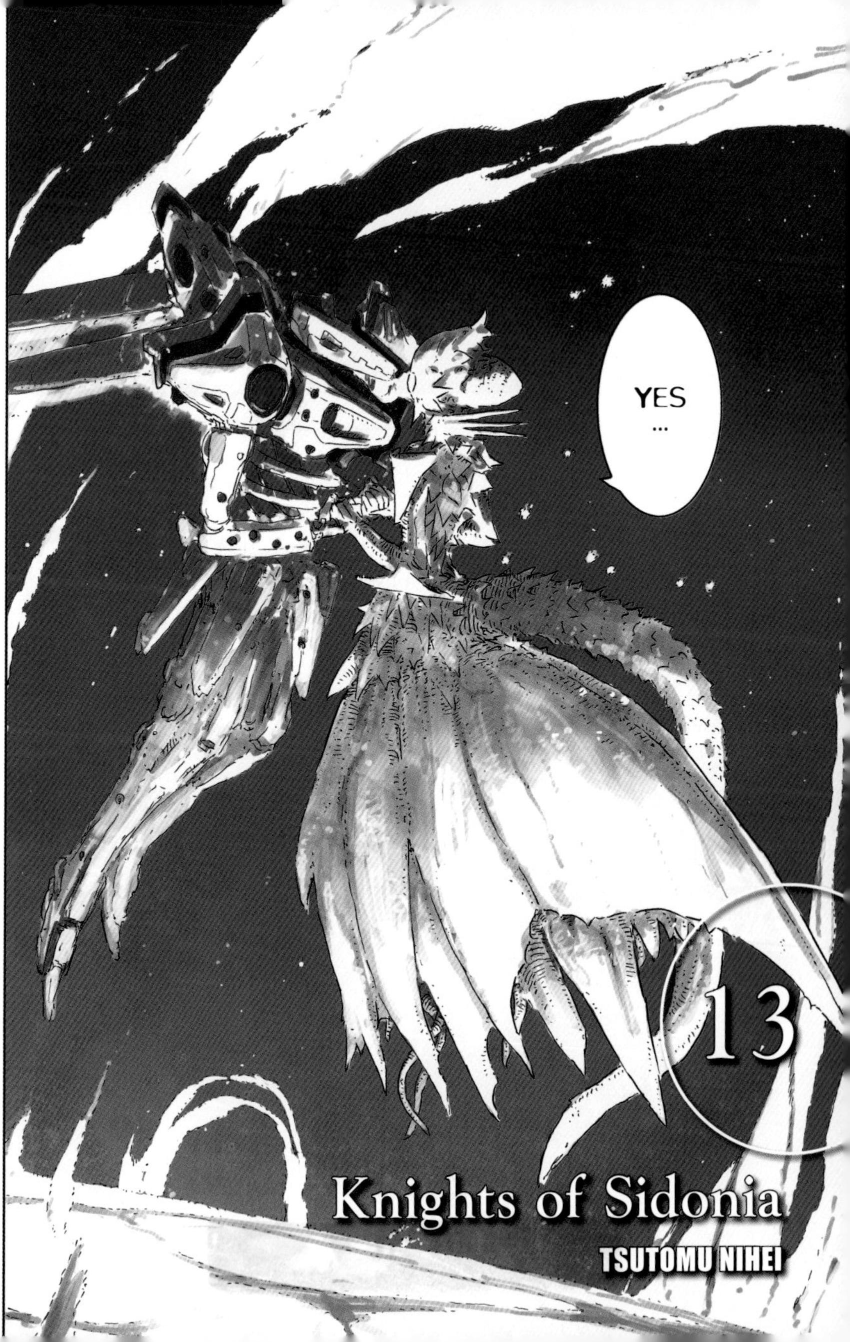
YES
...
13
Knights of Sidonia
TSUTOMU NIHEI

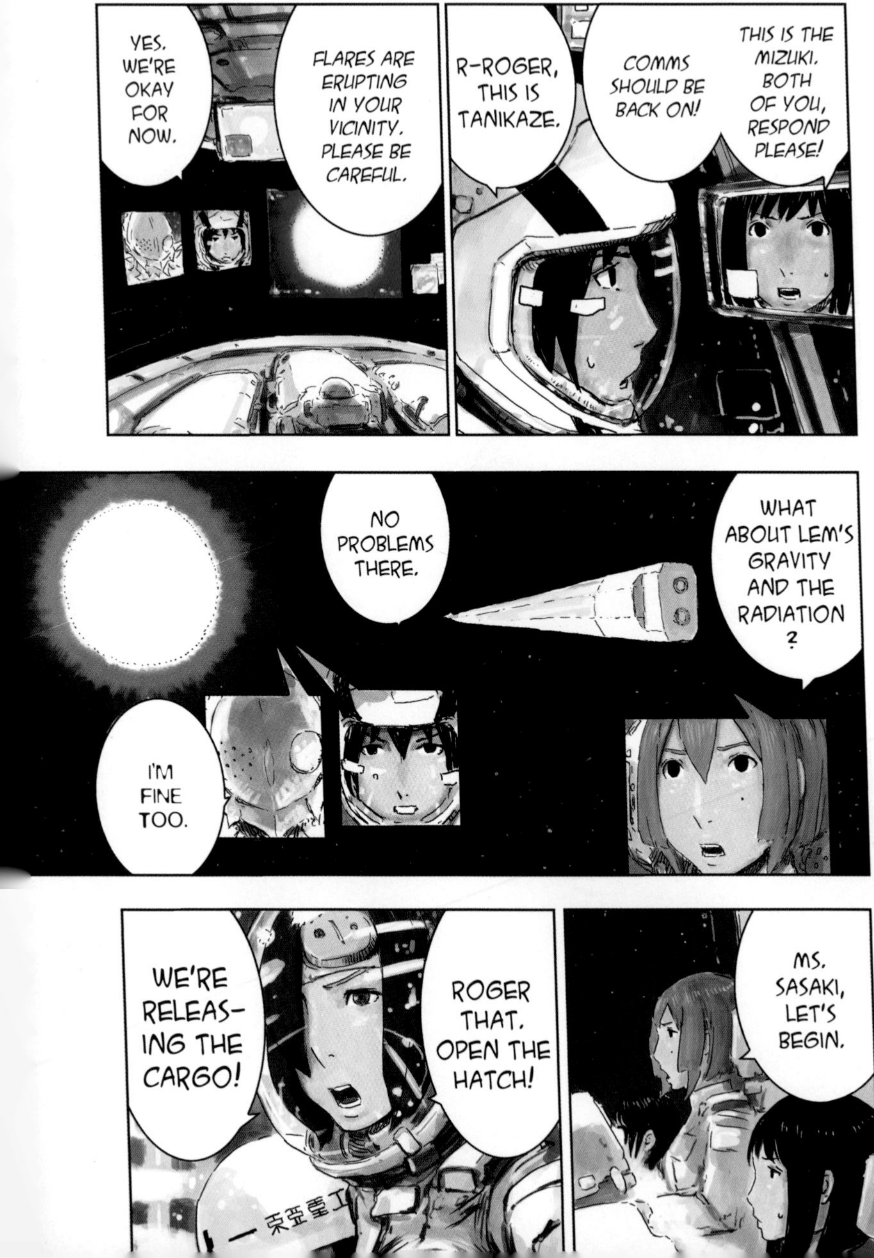
THIS IS THE MIZUKI. BOTH OF YOU, RESPOND PLEASE!
COMMS SHOULD BE BACK ON!
R-ROGER, THIS IS TANIKAZE.
FLARES ARE ERUPTING IN YOUR VICINITY. PLEASE BE CAREFUL.
YES. WE'RE OKAY FOR NOW.
WHAT ABOUT LEM'S GRAVITY AND THE RADIATION?
NO PROBLEMS THERE.
I'M FINE TOO.
MS. SASAKI, LET'S BEGIN.
ROGER THAT. OPEN THE HATCH!
WE'RE RELEASING THE CARGO!

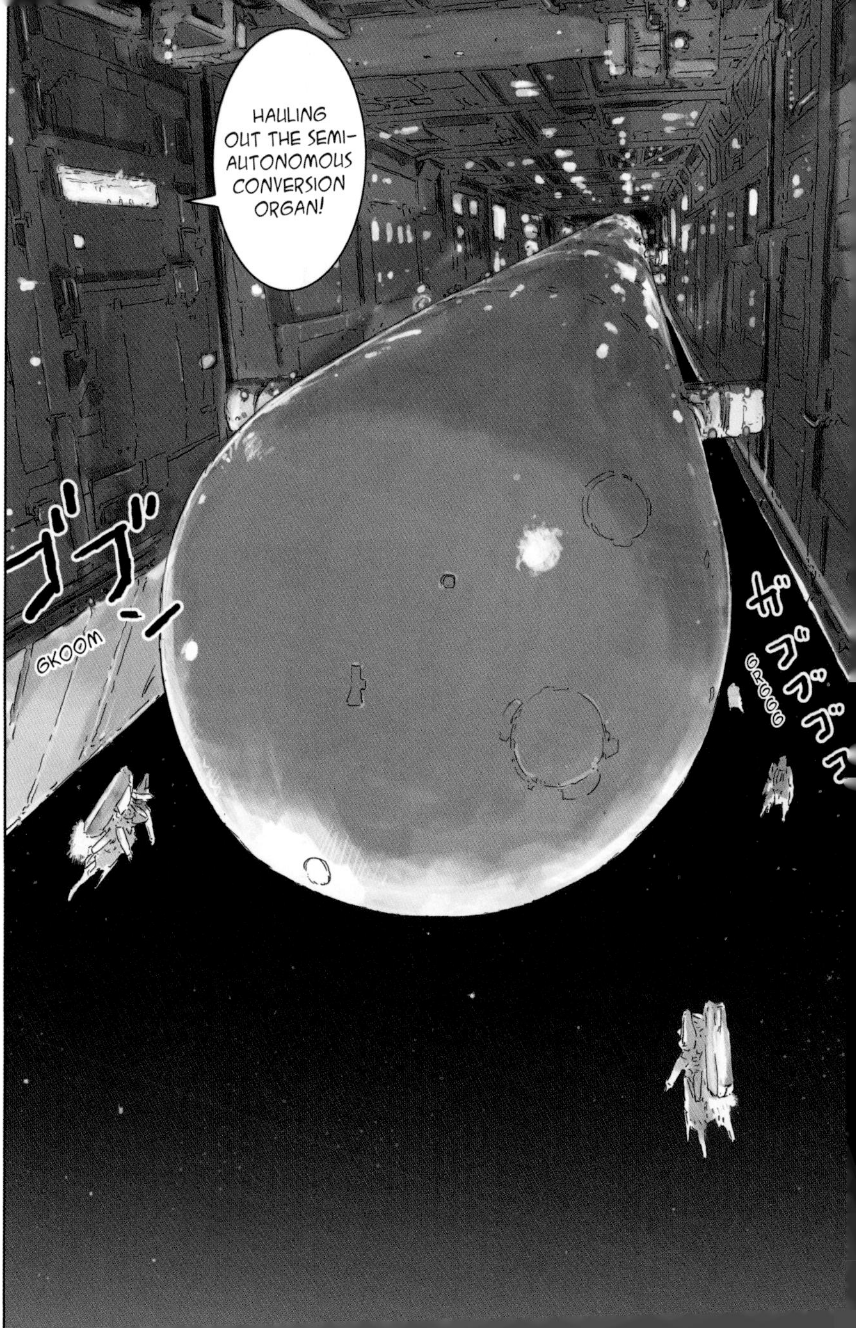
HAULING OUT THE SEMI-AUTONOMOUS CONVERSION ORGAN!
GROOO
GKOOM

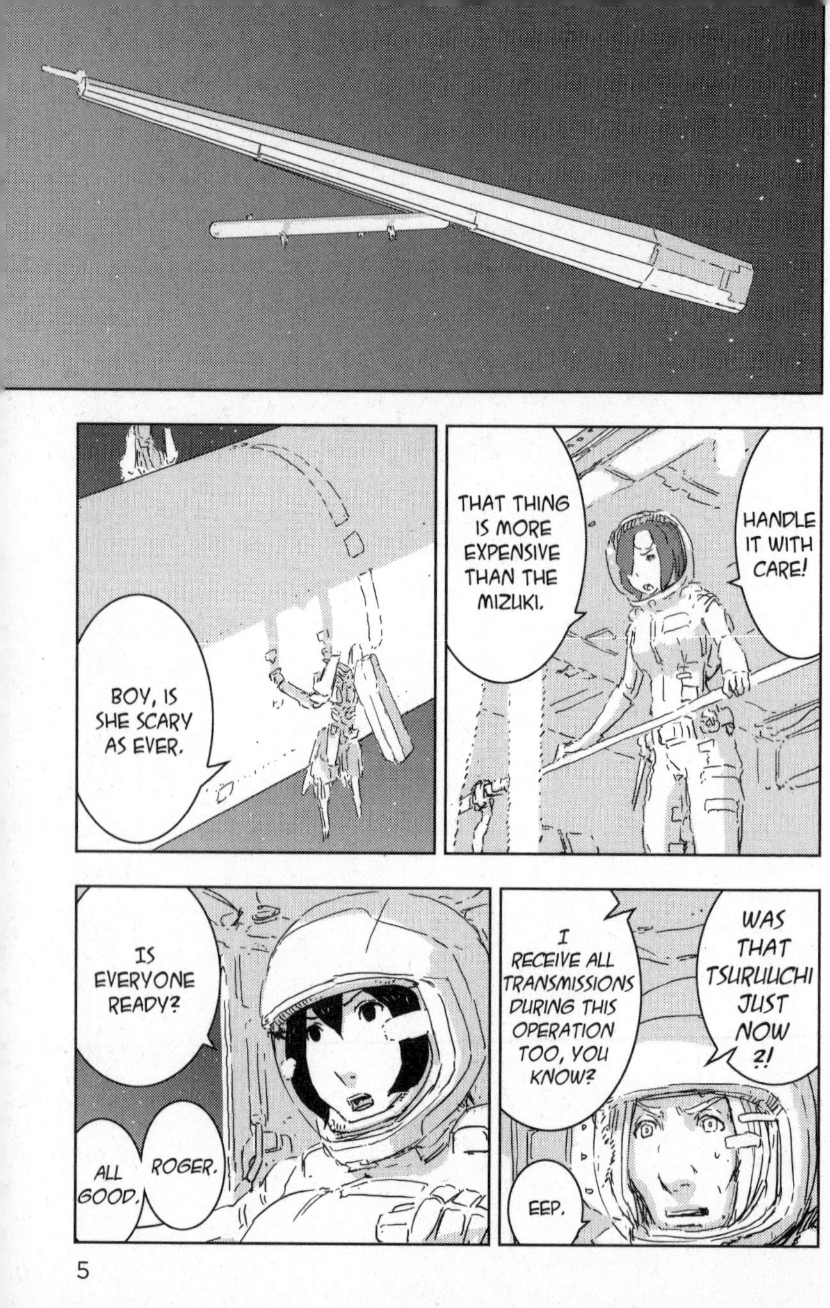
HANDLE IT WITH CARE!
THAT THING IS MORE EXPENSIVE THAN THE MIZUKI.
BOY, IS SHE SCARY AS EVER.
WAS THAT TSURUUCHI JUST NOW ?!
I RECEIVE ALL TRANSMISSIONS DURING THIS OPERATION TOO, YOU KNOW?
EEP.
IS EVERYONE READY?
ROGER.
ALL GOOD.

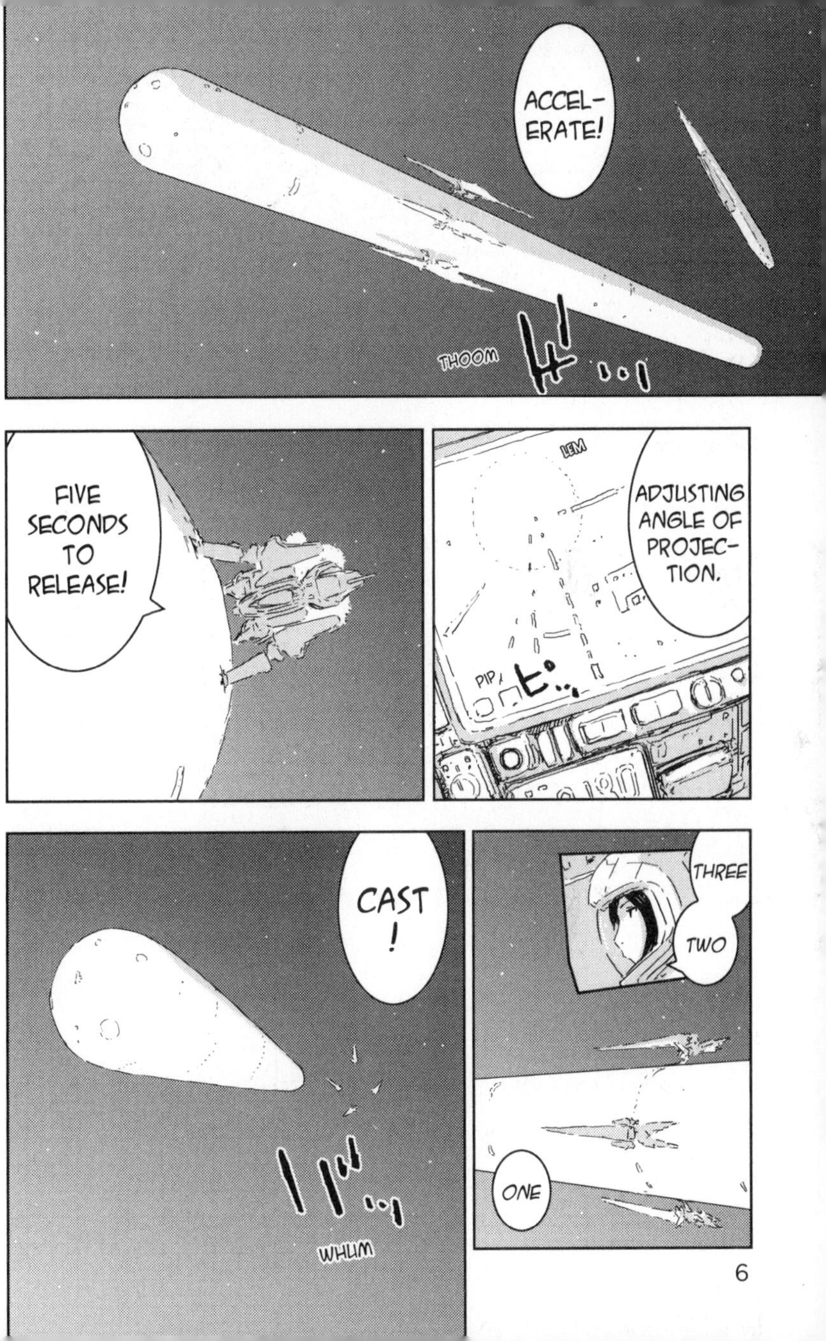
ACCEL-
ERATE!
THOOM
LEM
ADJUSTING ANGLE OF PROJEC- TION.
PIP
FIVE SECONDS TO RELEASE!
THREE
TWO
ONE
CAST !
WHUM

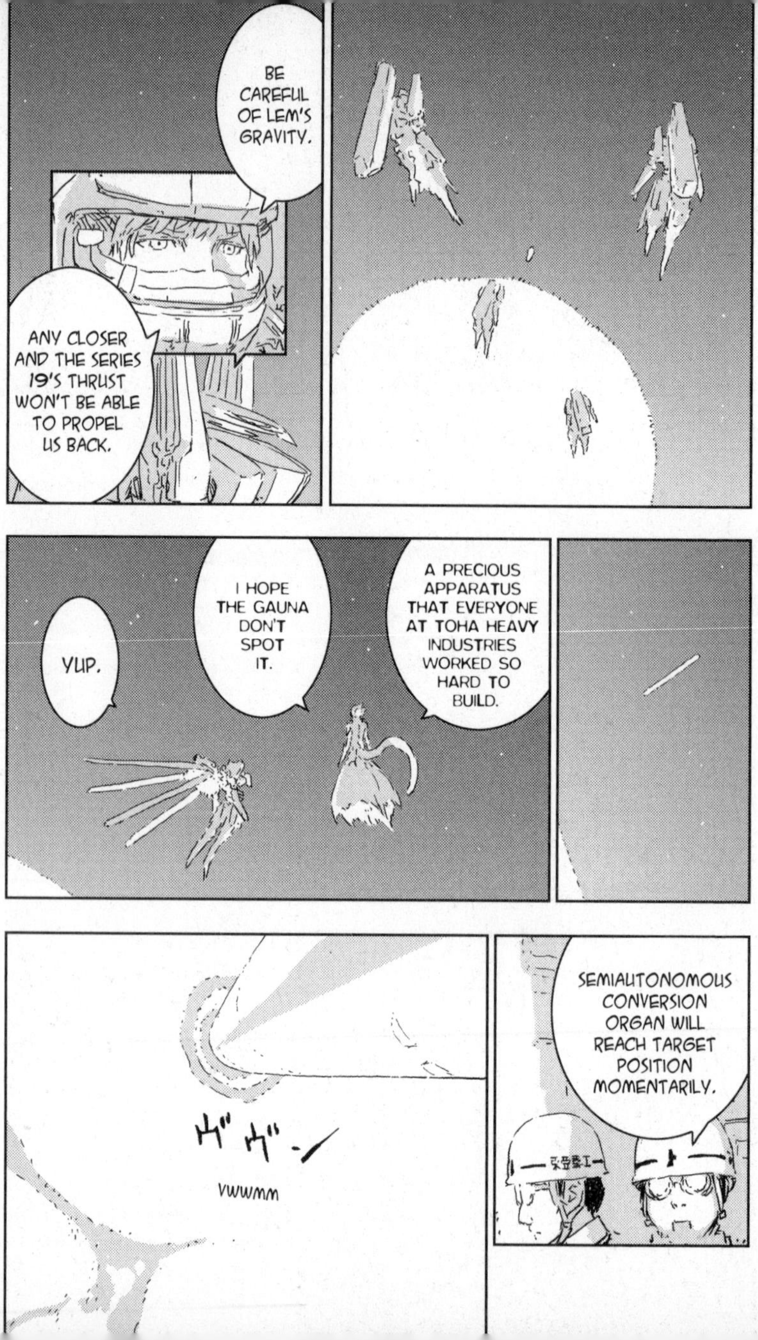
BE CAREFUL OF LEM'S GRAVITY.
ANY CLOSER AND THE SERIES 19'S THRUST WON'T BE ABLE TO PROPEL US BACK.
A PRECIOUS APPARATUS THAT EVERYONE AT TOHA HEAVY INDUSTRIES WORKED SO HARD TO BUILD.
I HOPE THE GAUNA DON'T SPOT IT.
YUP.
SEMIAUTONOMOUS CONVERSION ORGAN WILL REACH TARGET POSITION MOMENTARILY.
VWWMM

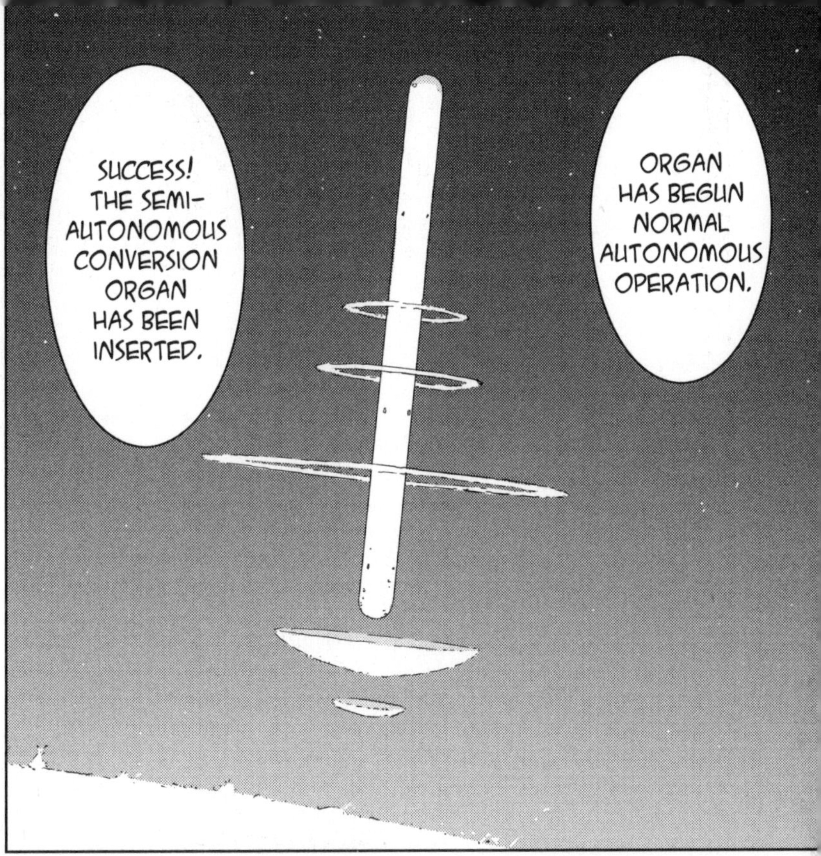
ORGAN HAS BEGUN NORMAL AUTONOMOUS OPERATION.
SUCCESS! THE SEMI-AUTONOMOUS CONVERSION ORGAN HAS BEEN INSERTED.

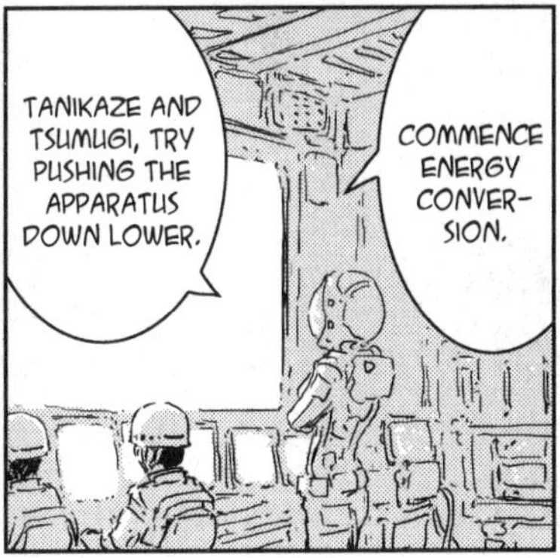
COMMENCE ENERGY CONVER-SION.
TANIKAZE AND TSUMUGI, TRY PUSHING THE APPARATUS DOWN LOWER.

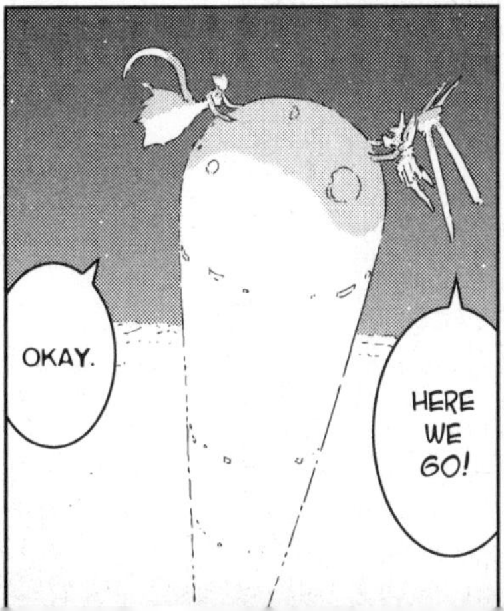
HERE WE GO!
OKAY.

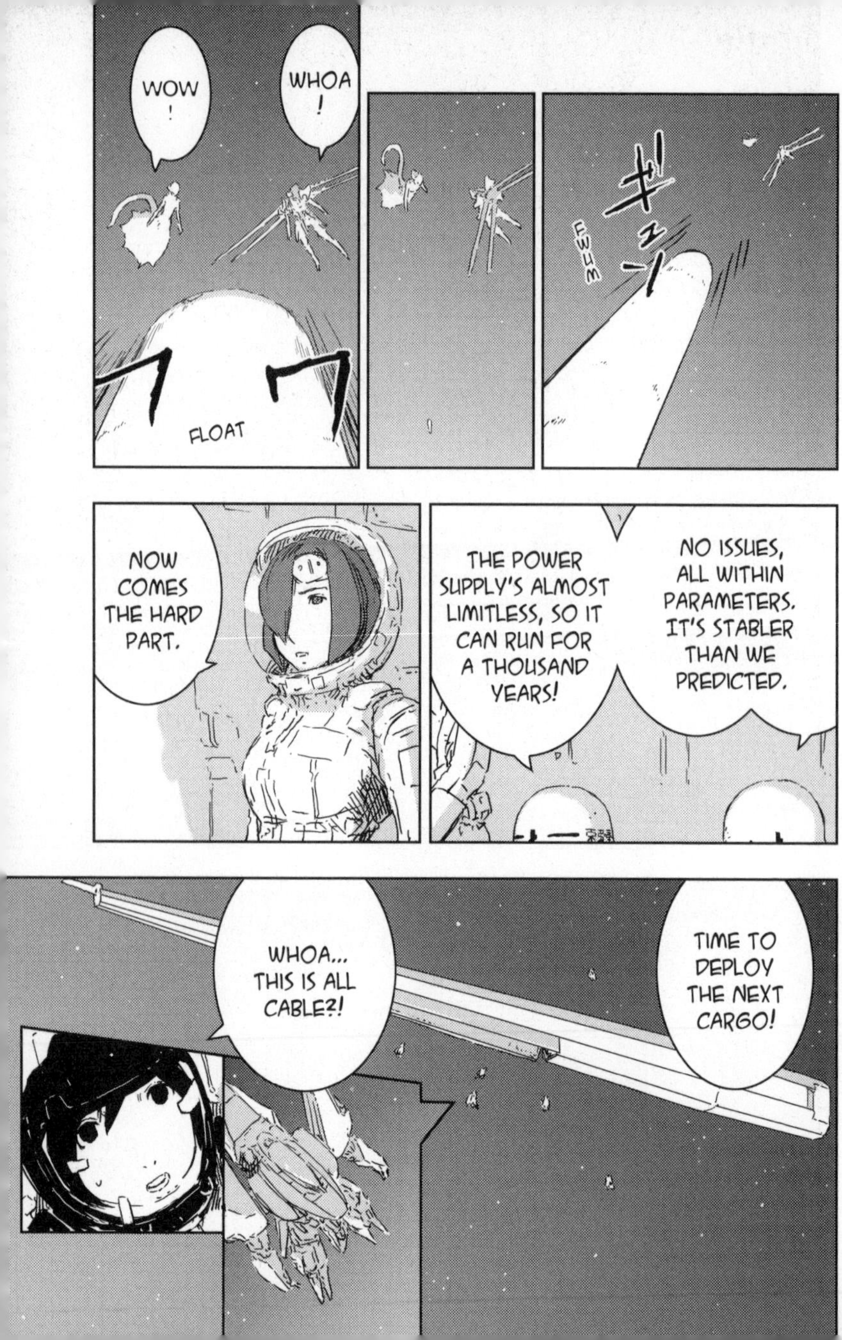
ギュン
FWUM
WHOA!
WOW!
FLOAT
NO ISSUES, ALL WITHIN PARAMETERS. IT'S STABLER THAN WE PREDICTED.
THE POWER SUPPLY'S ALMOST LIMITLESS, SO IT CAN RUN FOR A THOUSAND YEARS!
NOW COMES THE HARD PART.
TIME TO DEPLOY THE NEXT CARGO!
WHOA... THIS IS ALL CABLE?!

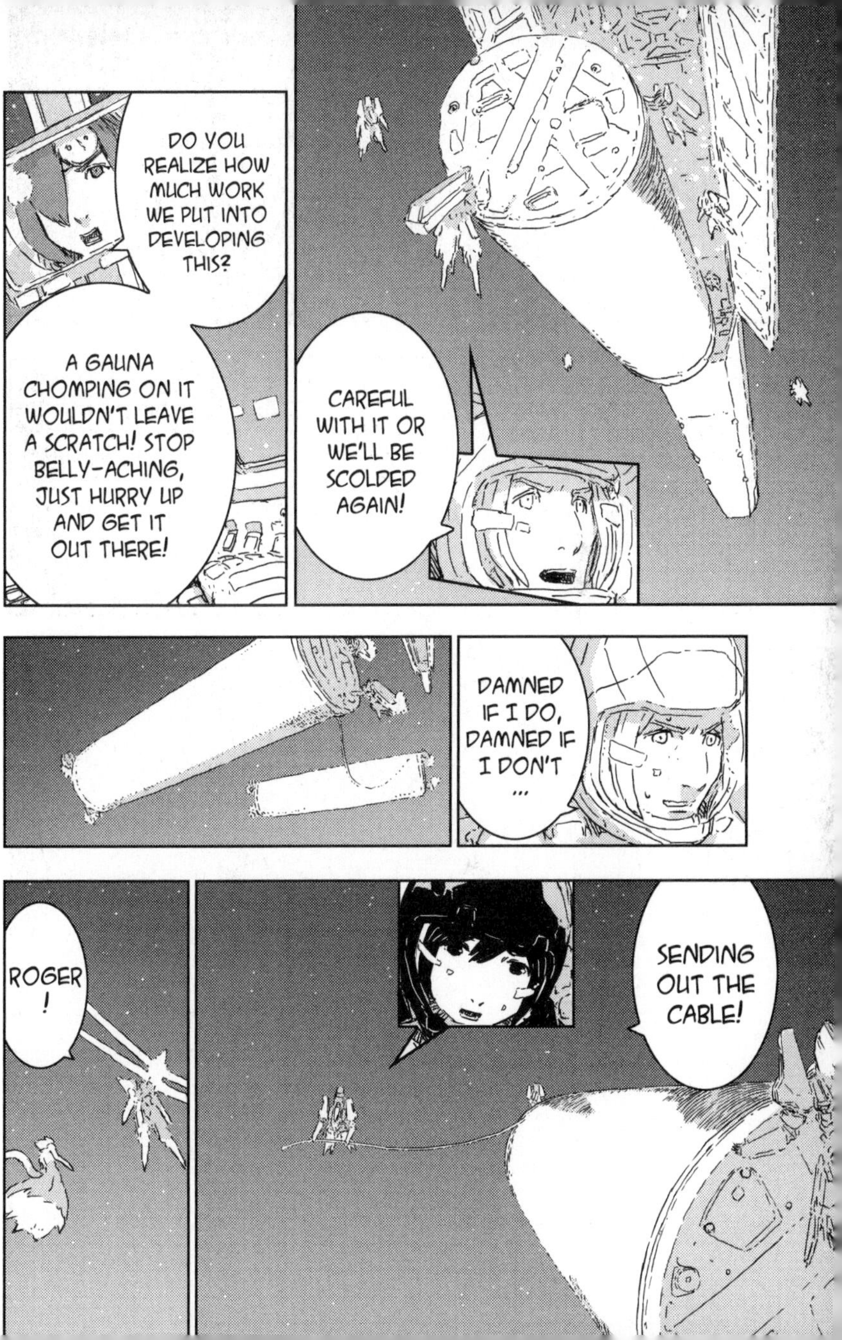
CAREFUL WITH IT OR WE'LL BE SCOLDED AGAIN!
DO YOU REALIZE HOW MUCH WORK WE PUT INTO DEVELOPING THIS?
A GAUNA CHOMPING ON IT WOULDN'T LEAVE A SCRATCH! STOP BELLY-ACHING, JUST HURRY UP AND GET IT OUT THERE!
DAMNED IF I DO, DAMNED IF I DON'T ...
SENDING OUT THE CABLE!
ROGER!

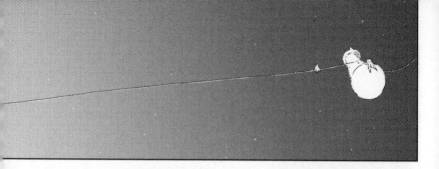

IT WON'T BE STABLE UNLESS IT'S EXTENDED OUT STRAIGHT.
TAKE IT NICE AND SLOW.
I'VE GOTTEN HOLD OF IT!
ALL RIGHT. ACTIVATING STABILIZER.
TANIKAZE, DRAW IT OUT SLOWLY.
TRANSPORT SQUAD, REMAIN ON STANDBY OVERHEAD.

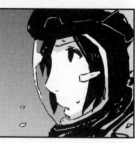

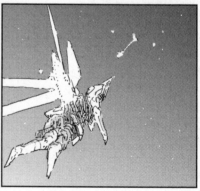

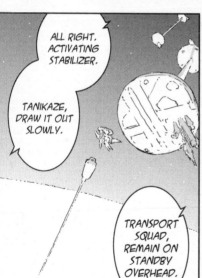

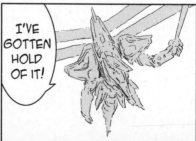

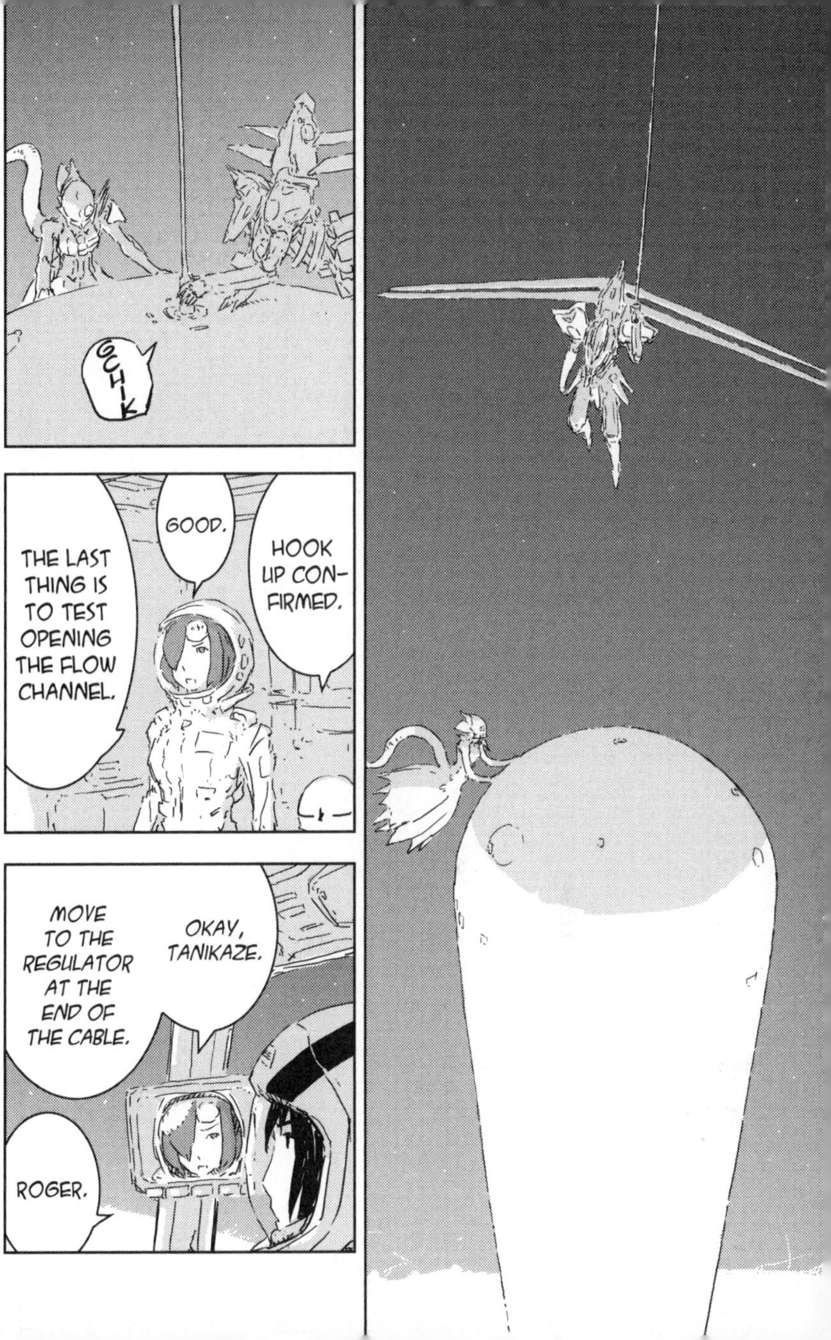
GCHIK
HOOK UP CON-FIRMED.
GOOD.
THE LAST THING IS TO TEST OPENING THE FLOW CHANNEL.
OKAY, TANIKAZE.
MOVE TO THE REGULATOR AT THE END OF THE CABLE.
ROGER.

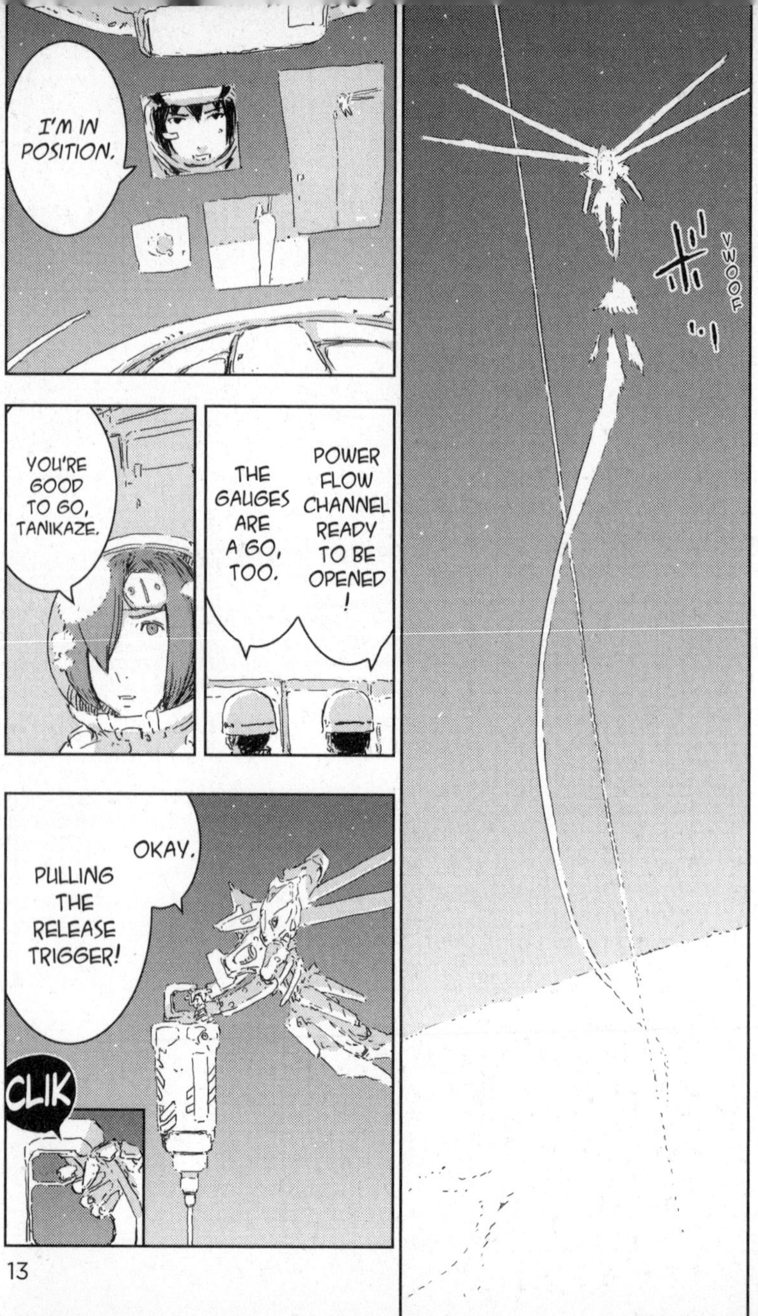
VWOOF
I'M IN POSITION.
POWER FLOW CHANNEL READY TO BE OPENED!
THE GAUGES ARE A GO, TOO.
YOU'RE GOOD TO GO, TANIKAZE.
OKAY.
PULLING THE RELEASE TRIGGER!
CLIK

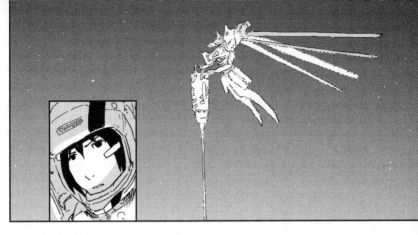

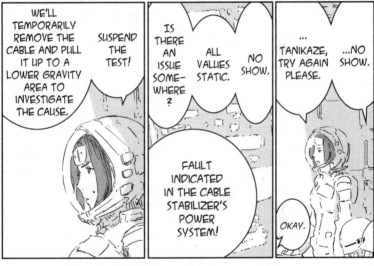

...NO SHOW.
...TANIKAZE, TRY AGAIN PLEASE.
OKAY.
NO SHOW.
ALL VALUES STATIC.
IS THERE AN ISSUE SOMEWHERE?
FAULT INDICATED IN THE CABLE STABILIZER'S POWER SYSTEM!
SUSPEND THE TEST!
WE'LL TEMPORARILY REMOVE THE CABLE AND PULL IT UP TO A LOWER GRAVITY AREA TO INVESTIGATE THE CAUSE.
TSUMUGI, REMOVE THE CABLE FROM THE CONVERSION ORGAN.
IT WON'T COME OUT.
I CAN'T UNLOCK THE SAFETY MECHANISM.

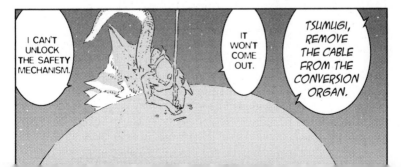

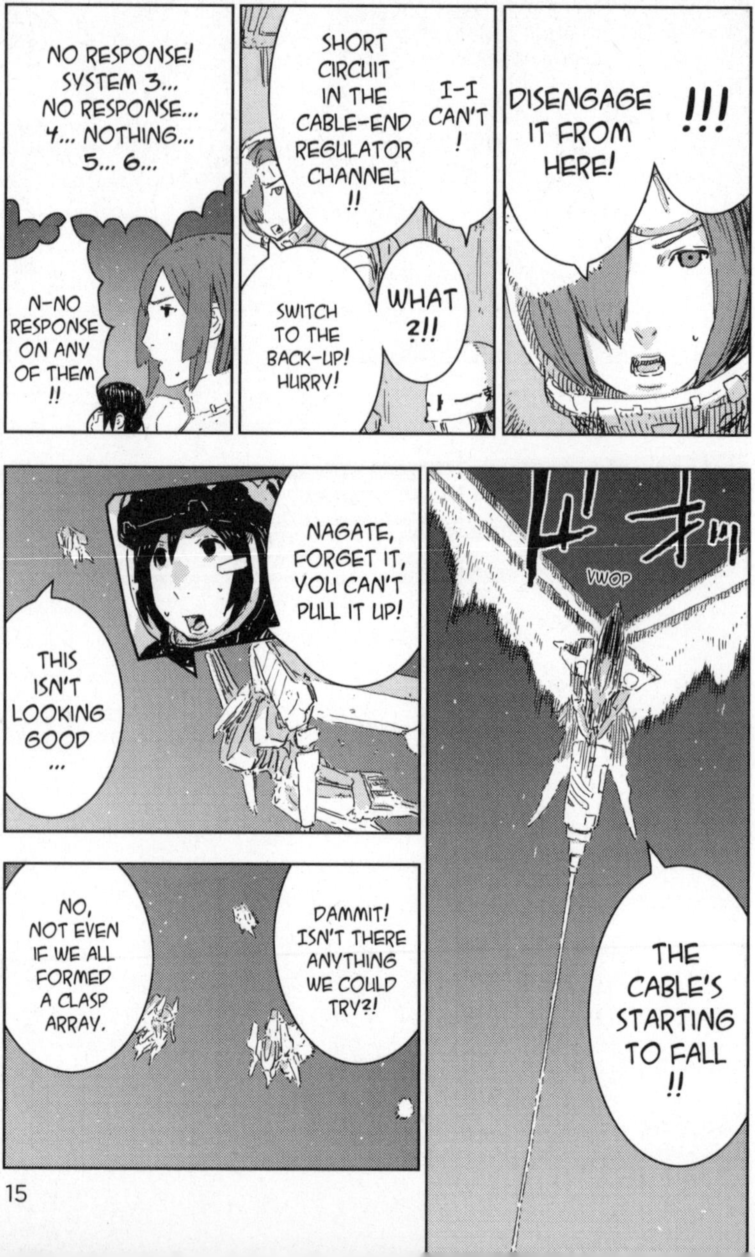
DISENGAGE IT FROM HERE!
!!!
SHORT CIRCUIT IN THE CABLE-END REGULATOR CHANNEL !!
I-I CAN'T !
WHAT ?!!
SWITCH TO THE BACK-UP! HURRY!
NO RESPONSE! SYSTEM 3... NO RESPONSE... 4... NOTHING... 5... 6...
N-NO RESPONSE ON ANY OF THEM !!
VWOP
THE CABLE'S STARTING TO FALL !!
NAGATE, FORGET IT, YOU CAN'T PULL IT UP!
THIS ISN'T LOOKING GOOD ...
DAMMIT! ISN'T THERE ANYTHING WE COULD TRY?!
NO, NOT EVEN IF WE ALL FORMED A CLASP ARRAY.

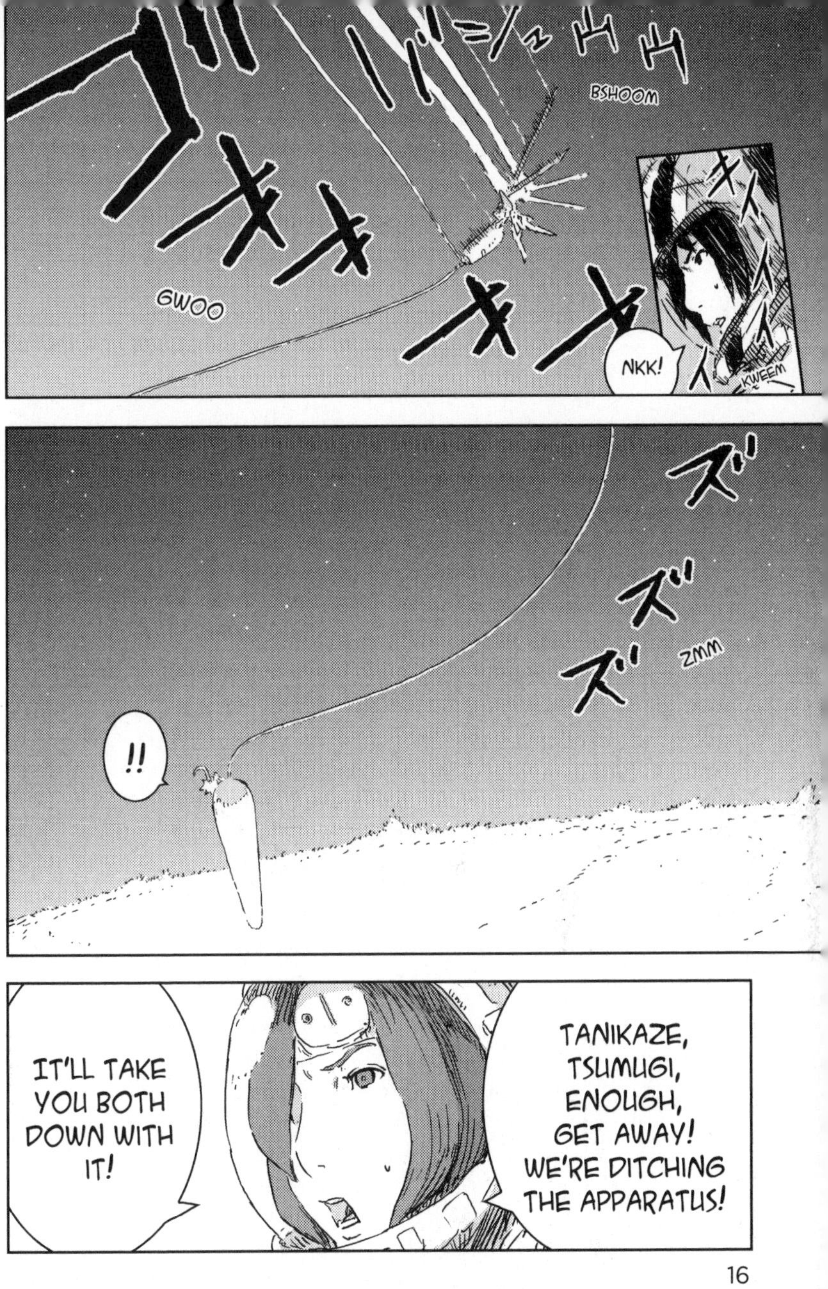
KWEEM
NKK!
BSHOOM
GWOO
ZMM
!!
TANIKAZE, TSUMUGI, ENOUGH, GET AWAY! WE'RE DITCHING THE APPARATUS!
IT'LL TAKE YOU BOTH DOWN WITH IT!

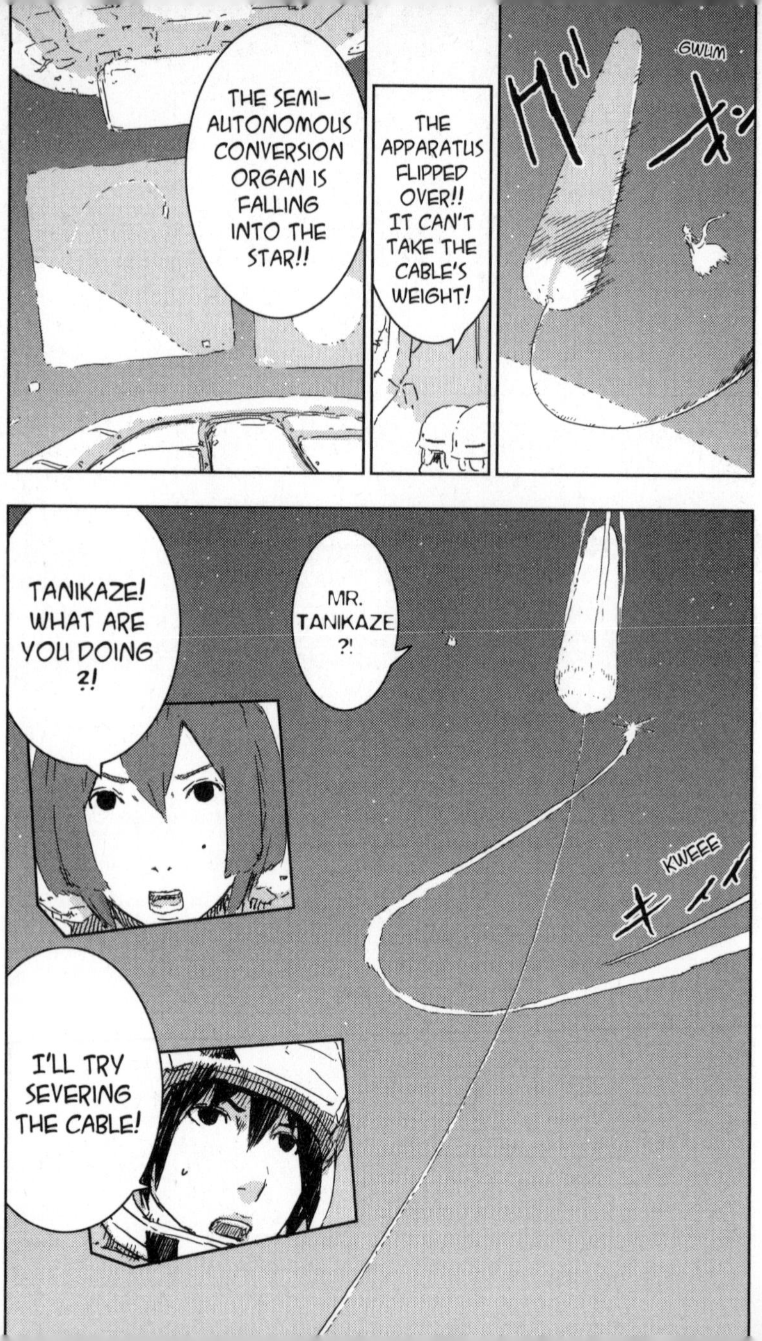
GWUM
THE APPARATUS FLIPPED OVER!! IT CAN'T TAKE THE CABLE'S WEIGHT!
THE SEMI-AUTONOMOUS CONVERSION ORGAN IS FALLING INTO THE STAR!!
KWEEE
MR. TANIKAZE ?!
TANIKAZE! WHAT ARE YOU DOING ?!
I'LL TRY SEVERING THE CABLE!

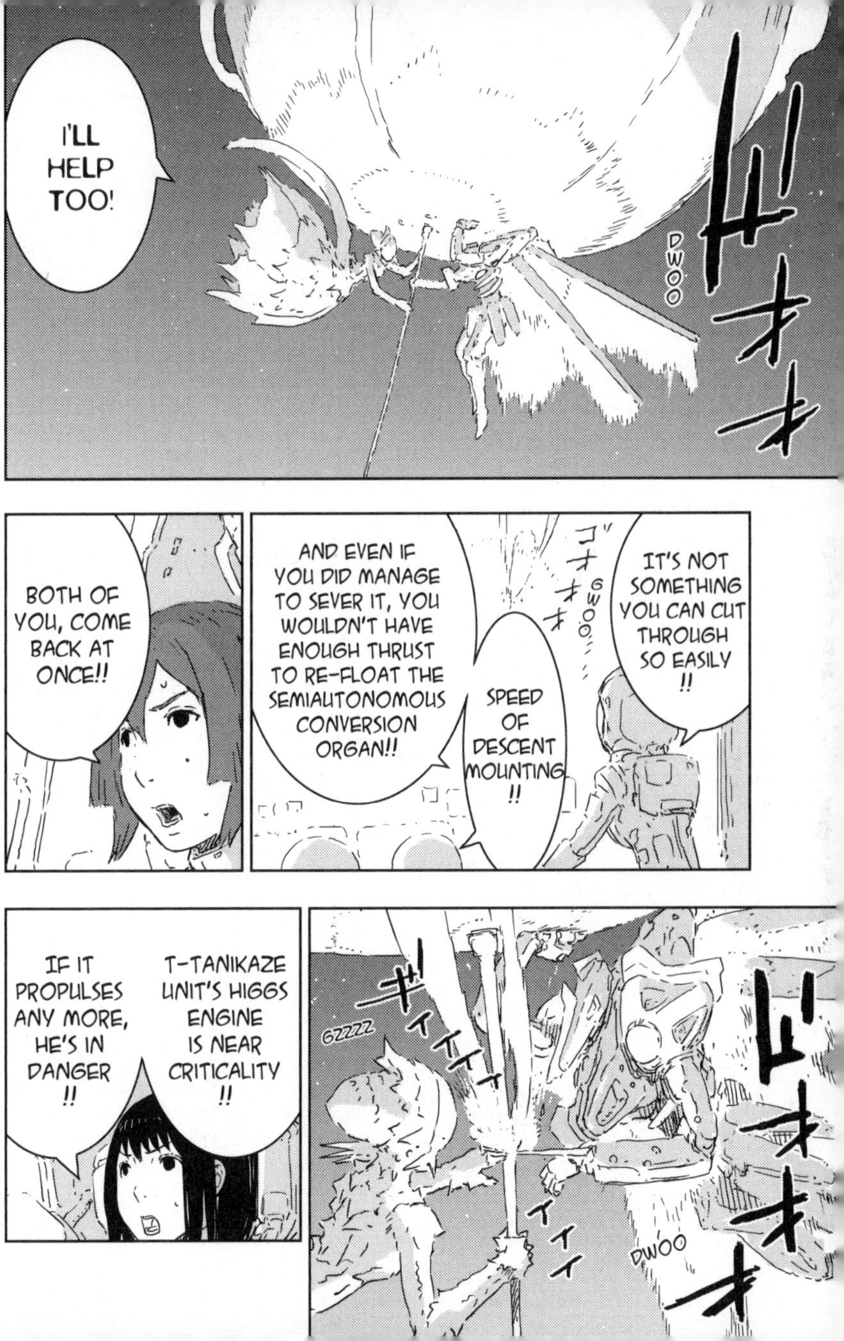
I'LL HELP TOO!
DWOO
IT'S NOT SOMETHING YOU CAN CUT THROUGH SO EASILY!!
GWOO
SPEED OF DESCENT MOUNTING!!
AND EVEN IF YOU DID MANAGE TO SEVER IT, YOU WOULDN'T HAVE ENOUGH THRUST TO RE-FLOAT THE SEMIAUTONOMOUS CONVERSION ORGAN!!
BOTH OF YOU, COME BACK AT ONCE!!
DWOO
GZZZZ
T-TANIKAZE UNIT'S HIGGS ENGINE IS NEAR CRITICALITY!!
IF IT PROPULSES ANY MORE, HE'S IN DANGER!!

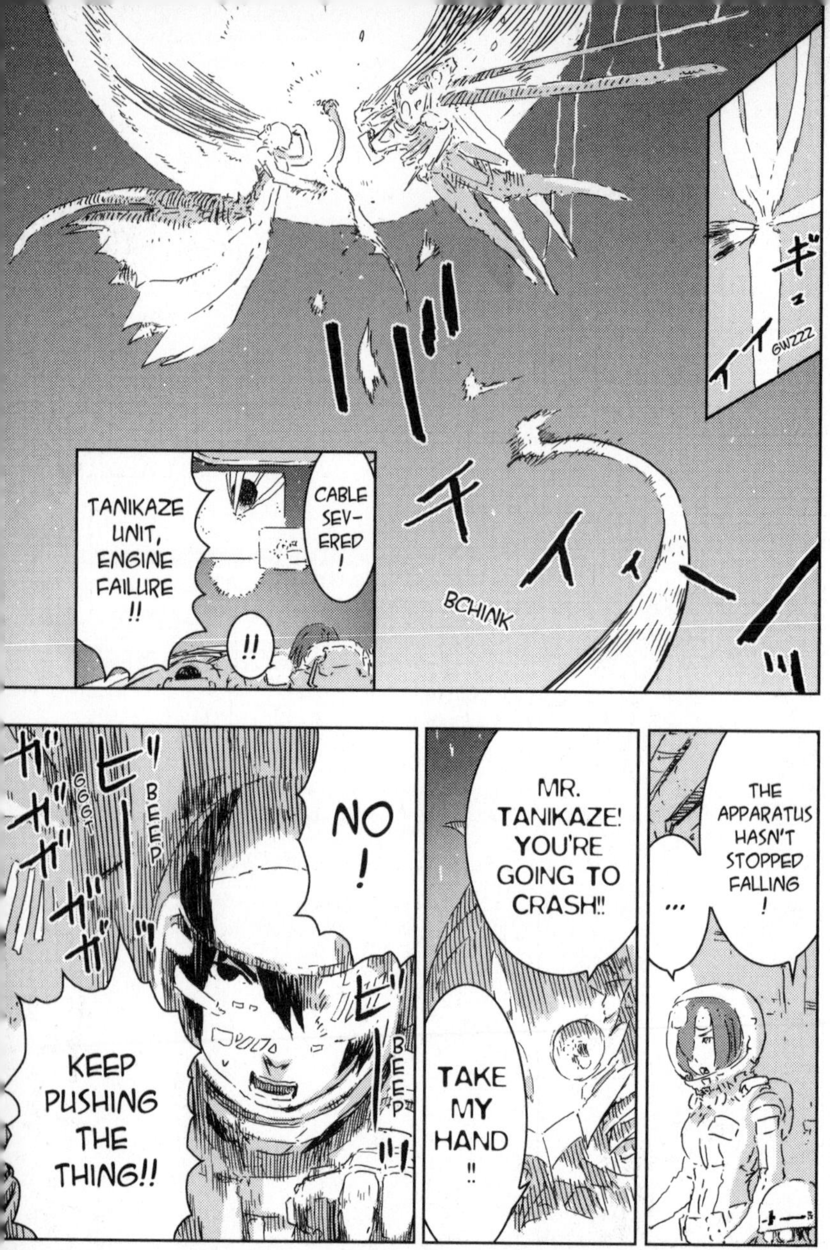
GWZZZ
BCHINK
CABLE SEV-ERED!
TANIKAZE UNIT, ENGINE FAILURE!!
!!
THE APPARATUS HASN'T STOPPED FALLING!
...
MR. TANIKAZE! YOU'RE GOING TO CRASH!!
TAKE MY HAND!!
NO!
BEEP
GGGT
KEEP PUSHING THE THING!!
BEEP

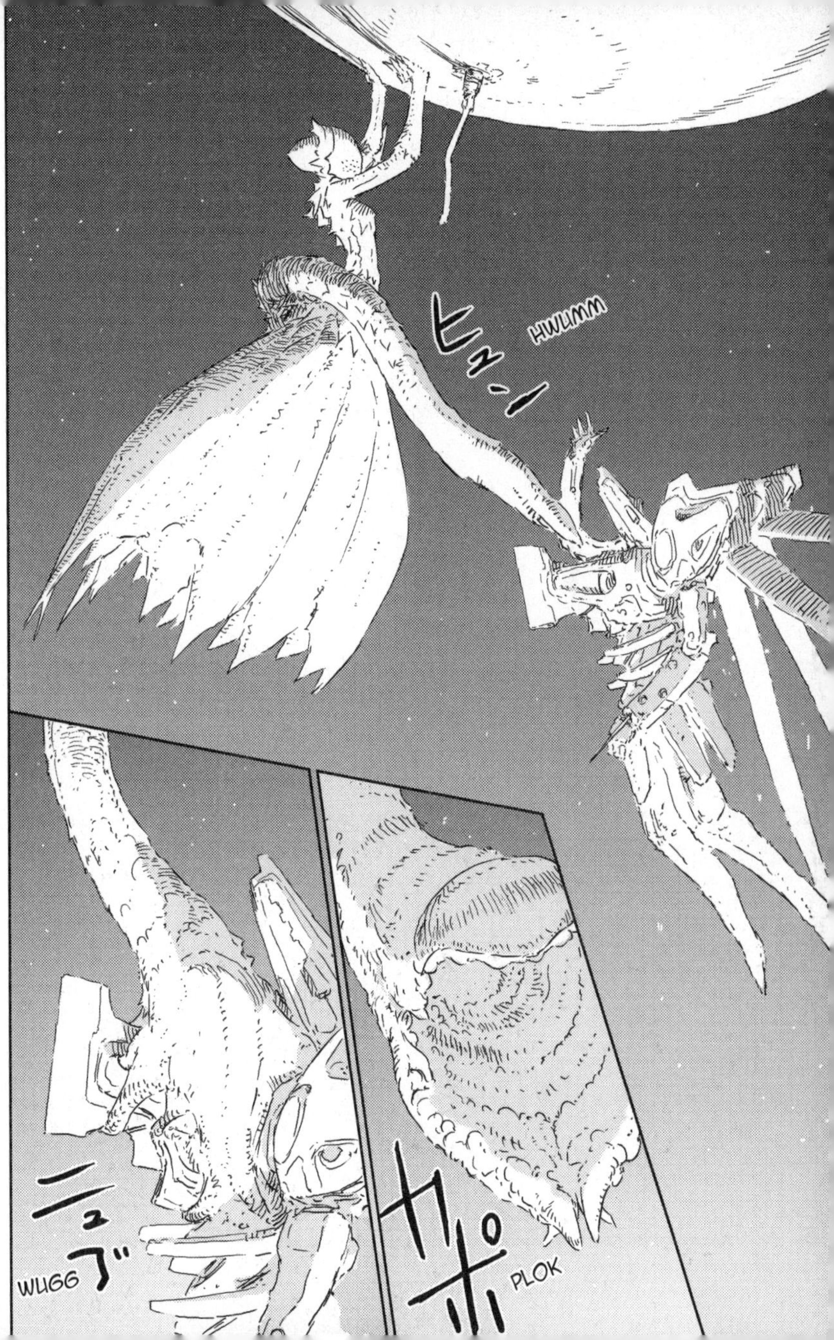
ヒュン
HWUMM
カポ
PLOK
ニュブ
WUGG

TANIKAZE UNIT AND THE CABLE ARE FALLING INTO LEM!

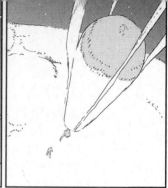

ズ
・・・
ズ
・・・

HANG IN THERE, TSUMUGI !!

TSU-MUGI ...

UP-SYY YY~

21

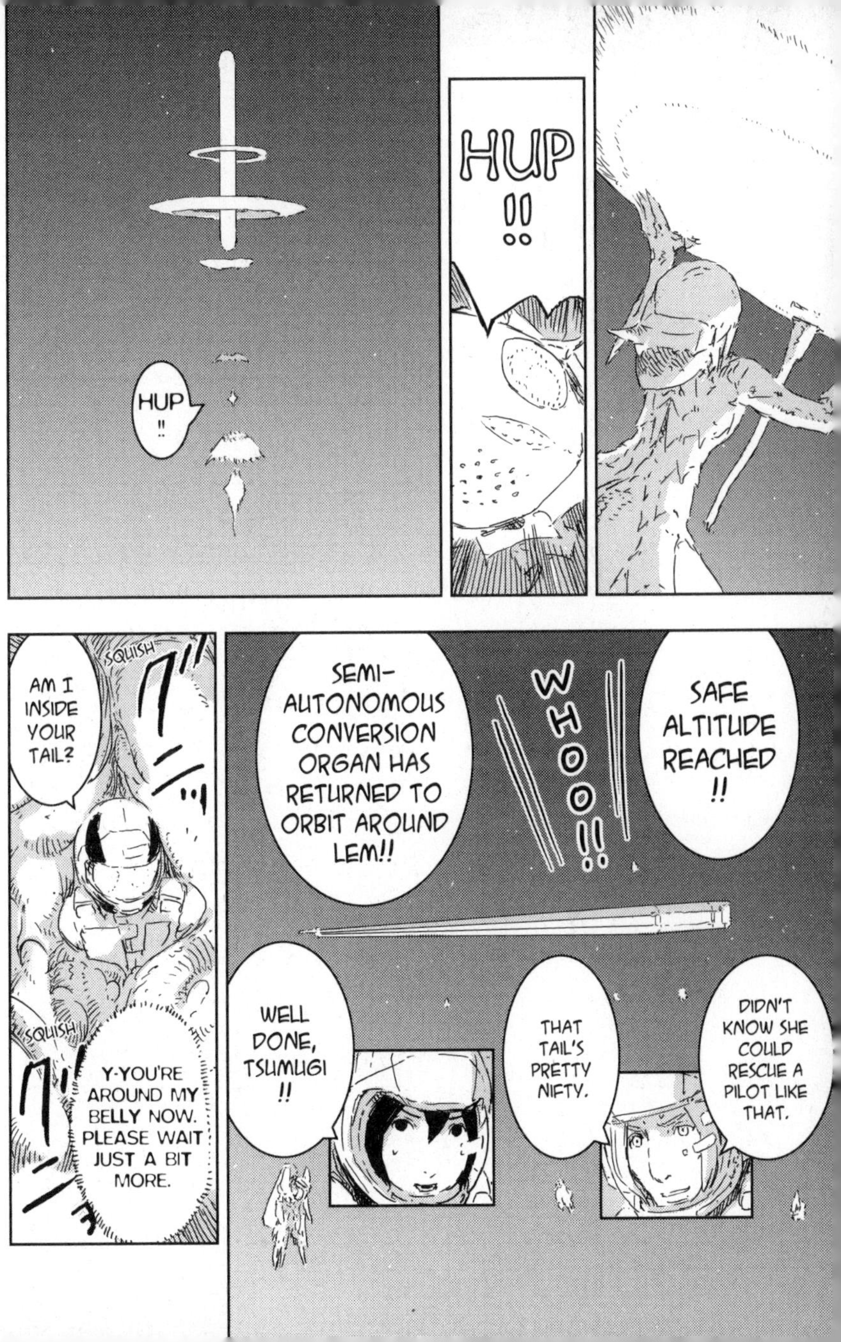
HUP!!
HUP!!
SAFE ALTITUDE REACHED!!
WHOOO!!
SEMI-AUTONOMOUS CONVERSION ORGAN HAS RETURNED TO ORBIT AROUND LEM!!
DIDN'T KNOW SHE COULD RESCUE A PILOT LIKE THAT.
THAT TAIL'S PRETTY NIFTY.
WELL DONE, TSUMUGI!!
SQUISH
AM I INSIDE YOUR TAIL?
SQUISH
Y-YOU'RE AROUND MY BELLY NOW. PLEASE WAIT JUST A BIT MORE.

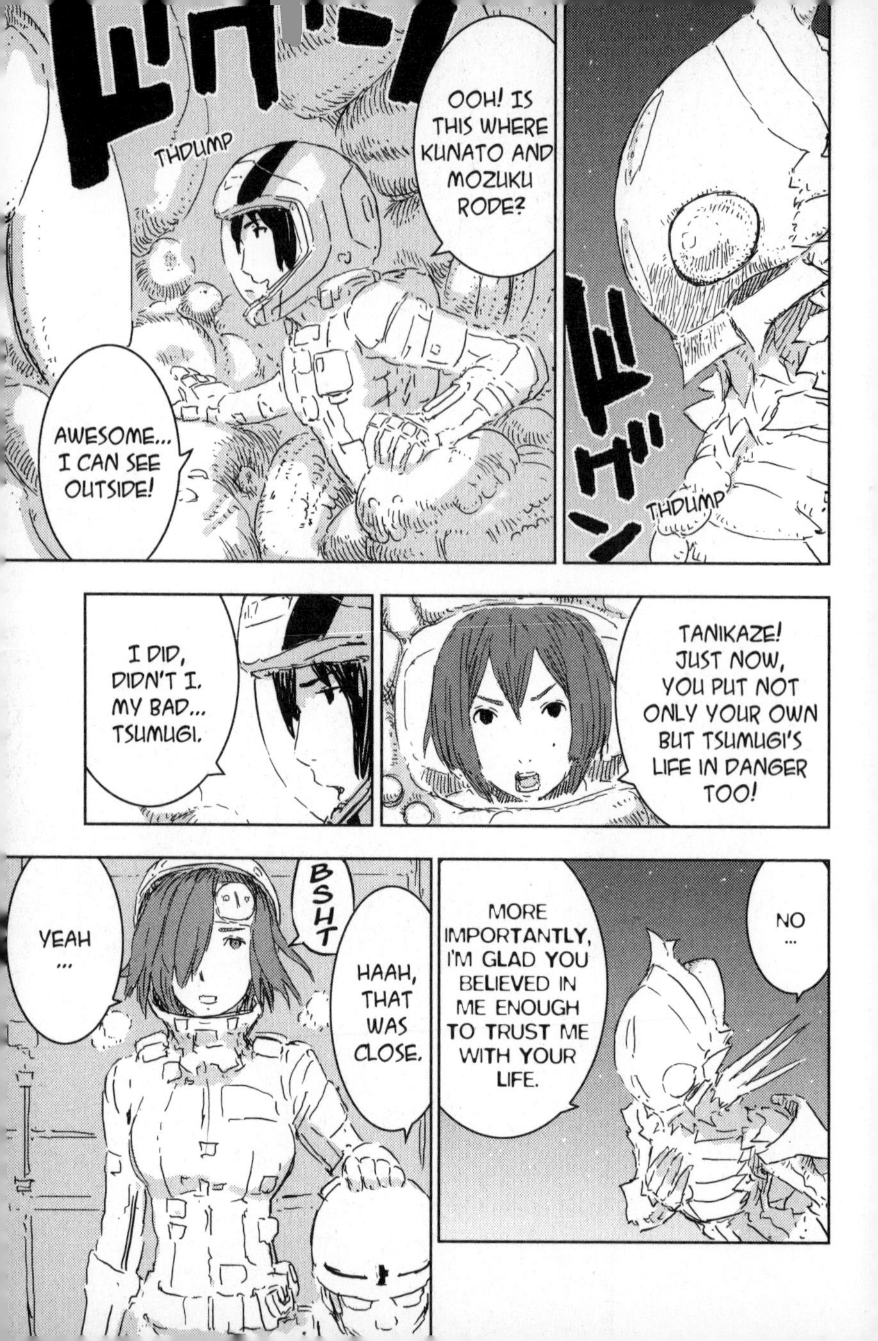
THDUMP
OOH! IS THIS WHERE KUNATO AND MOZUKU RODE?
THDUMP
AWESOME... I CAN SEE OUTSIDE!
TANIKAZE! JUST NOW, YOU PUT NOT ONLY YOUR OWN BUT TSUMUGI'S LIFE IN DANGER TOO!
I DID, DIDN'T I. MY BAD... TSUMUGI.
NO ...
MORE IMPORTANTLY, I'M GLAD YOU BELIEVED IN ME ENOUGH TO TRUST ME WITH YOUR LIFE.
BSHT
HAAH, THAT WAS CLOSE.
YEAH ...

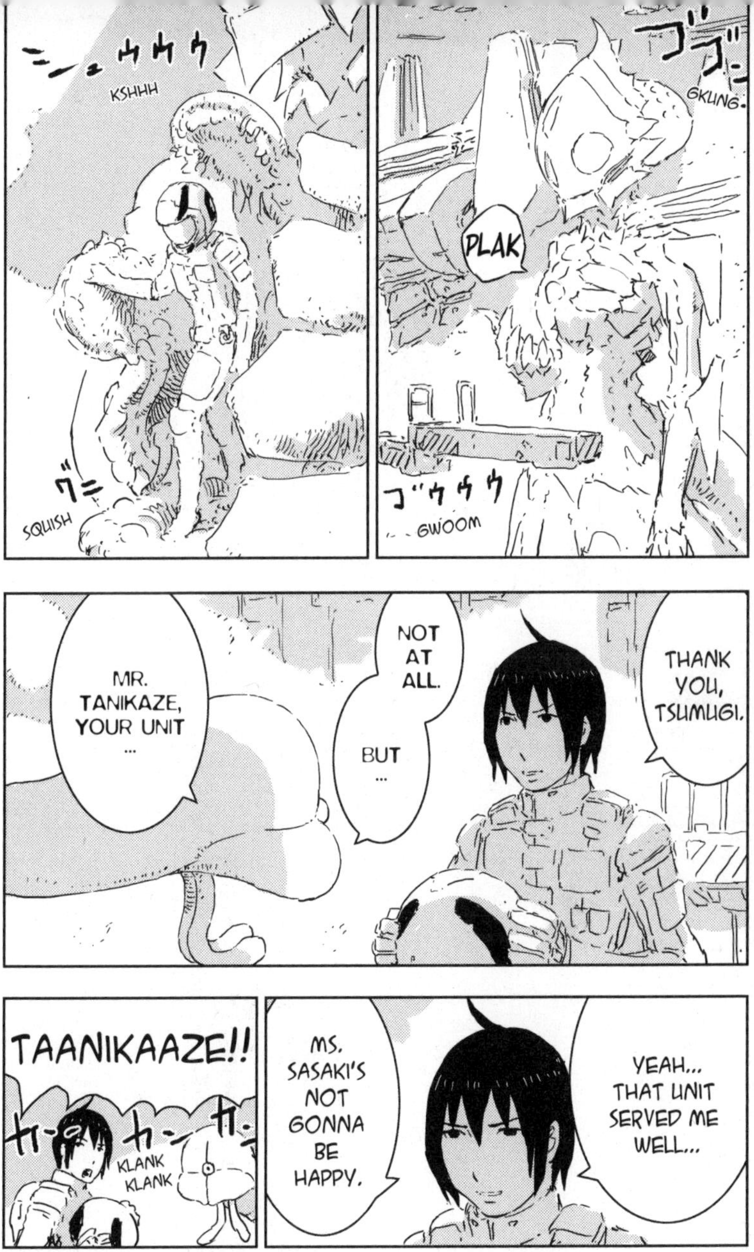
GKUNG
PLAK
GWOOM
KSHHH
SQUISH
THANK YOU, TSUMUGI.
NOT AT ALL.
BUT ...
MR. TANIKAZE, YOUR UNIT ...
YEAH... THAT UNIT SERVED ME WELL...
MS. SASAKI'S NOT GONNA BE HAPPY.
TAANIKAAZE!!
KLANK KLANK

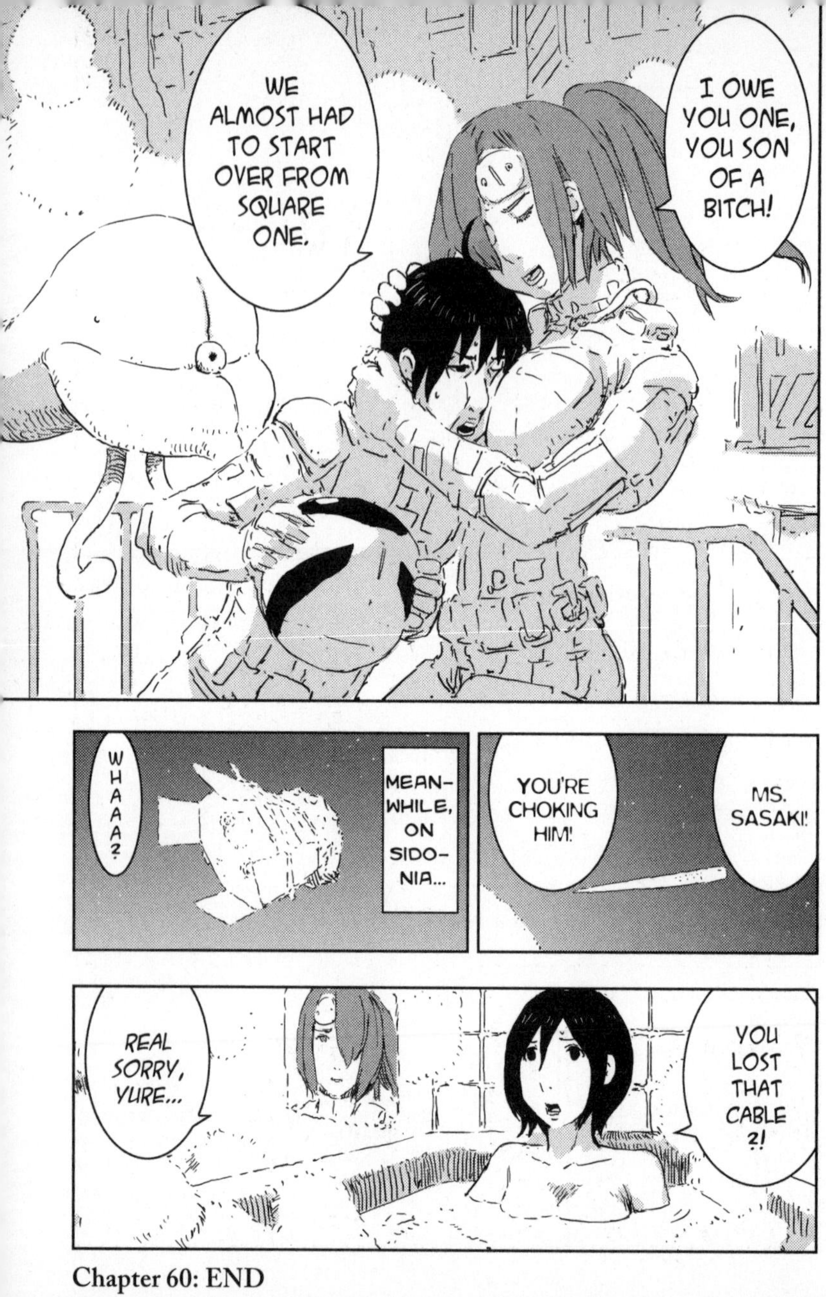
I OWE YOU ONE, YOU SON OF A BITCH!
WE ALMOST HAD TO START OVER FROM SQUARE ONE.
MS. SASAKI!
YOU'RE CHOKING HIM!
MEAN-WHILE, ON SIDO-NIA...
WHAAAA?
YOU LOST THAT CABLE?!
REAL SORRY, YURE...

Chapter 60: END

シドニアの騎士

KNIGHTS OF SIDONIA

Chapter 61: The New Pilots' Maiden Battle—Part One

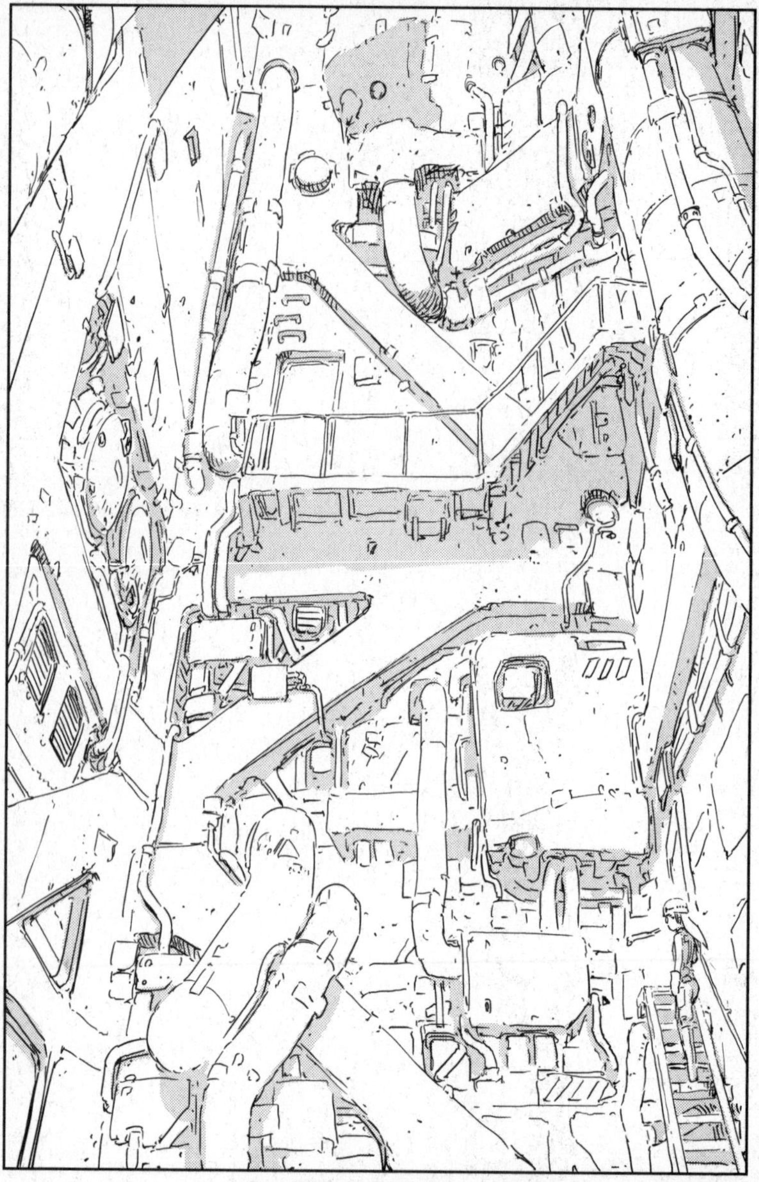

One Hundred Sights of Sidonia Part Forty-Six:
Toha Heavy Industries Employee Housing

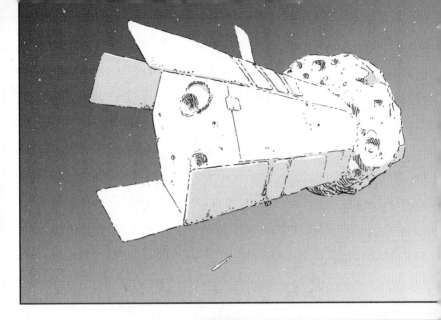

MIZUKI DOCKING COMPLETE！

ブン

KUNNG

ゴ K R R R R

ブブブゴゴ

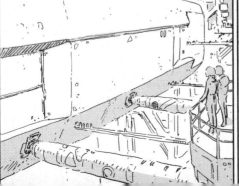

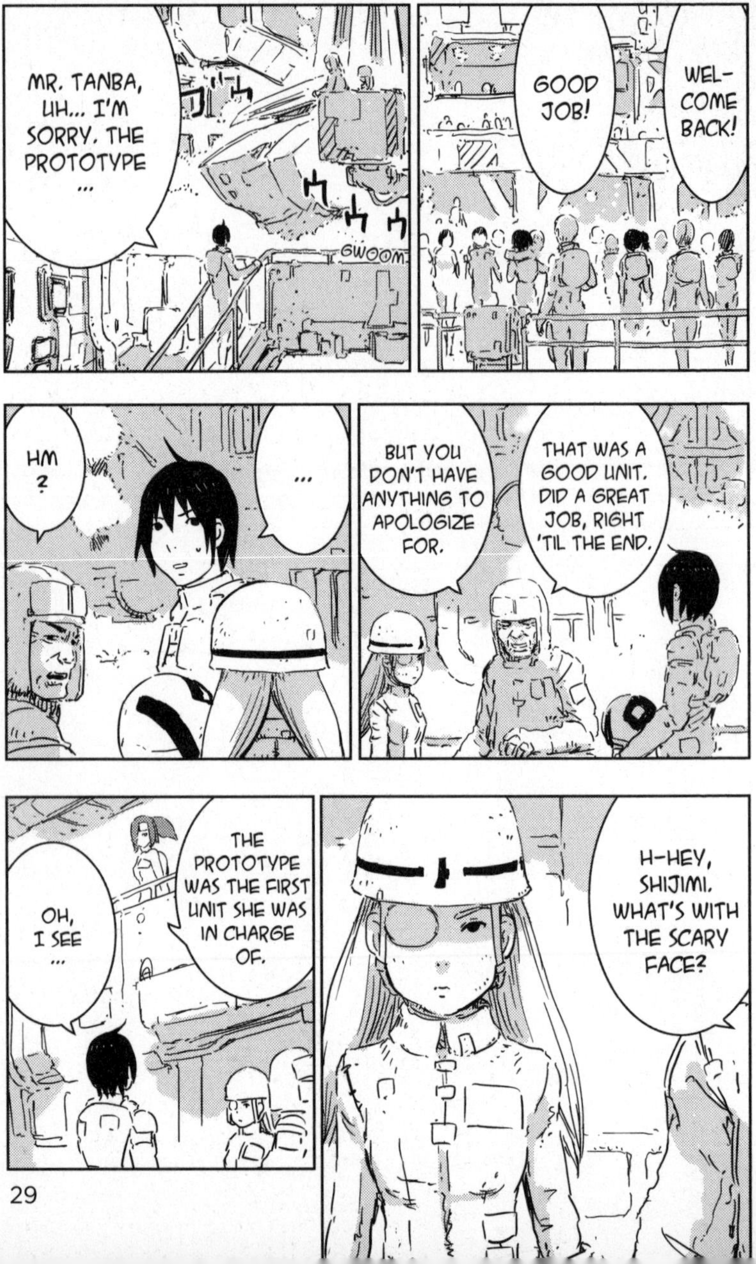
WEL-COME BACK!
GOOD JOB!
MR. TANBA, UH... I'M SORRY. THE PROTOTYPE ...
GWOOM
THAT WAS A GOOD UNIT. DID A GREAT JOB, RIGHT 'TIL THE END.
BUT YOU DON'T HAVE ANYTHING TO APOLOGIZE FOR.
...
HM ?
H-HEY, SHIJIMI. WHAT'S WITH THE SCARY FACE?
THE PROTOTYPE WAS THE FIRST UNIT SHE WAS IN CHARGE OF.
OH, I SEE ...

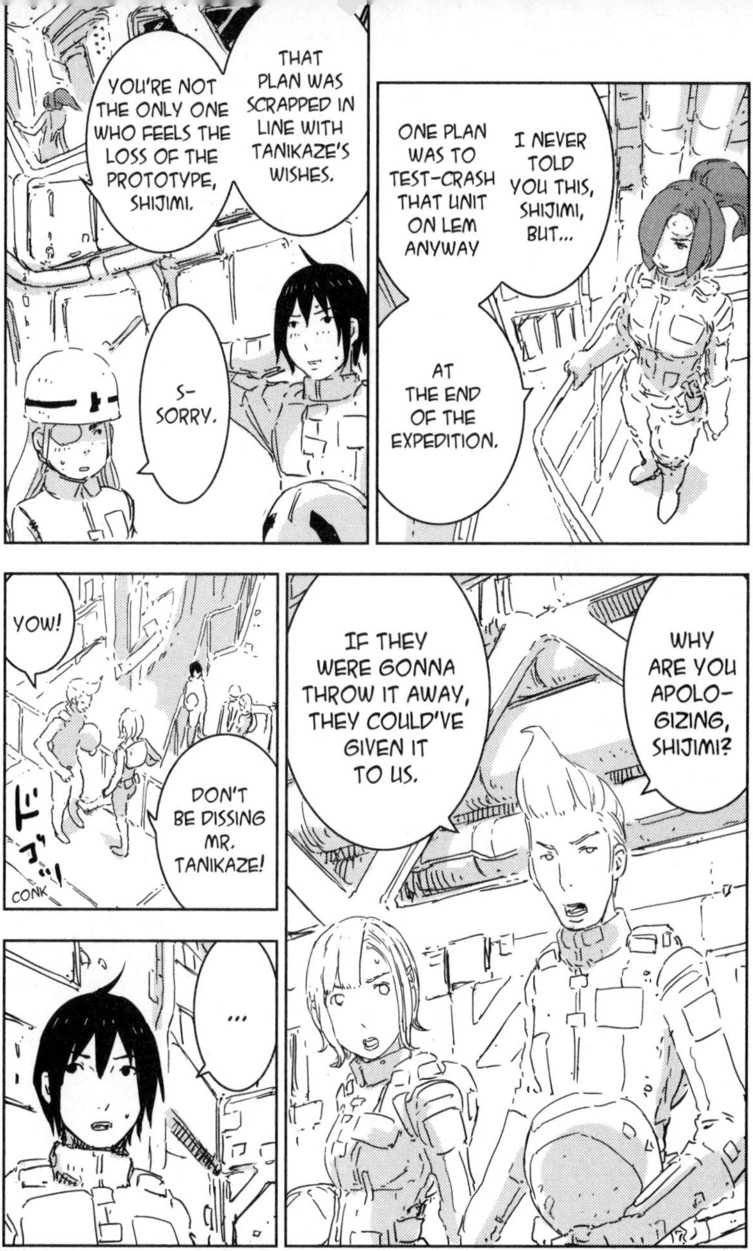
I NEVER TOLD YOU THIS, SHIJIMI, BUT...
ONE PLAN WAS TO TEST-CRASH THAT UNIT ON LEM ANYWAY
AT THE END OF THE EXPEDITION.
THAT PLAN WAS SCRAPPED IN LINE WITH TANIKAZE'S WISHES.
YOU'RE NOT THE ONLY ONE WHO FEELS THE LOSS OF THE PROTOTYPE, SHIJIMI.
S-SORRY.
WHY ARE YOU APOLOGIZING, SHIJIMI?
IF THEY WERE GONNA THROW IT AWAY, THEY COULD'VE GIVEN IT TO US.
DON'T BE DISSING MR. TANIKAZE!
CONK
YOW!
...

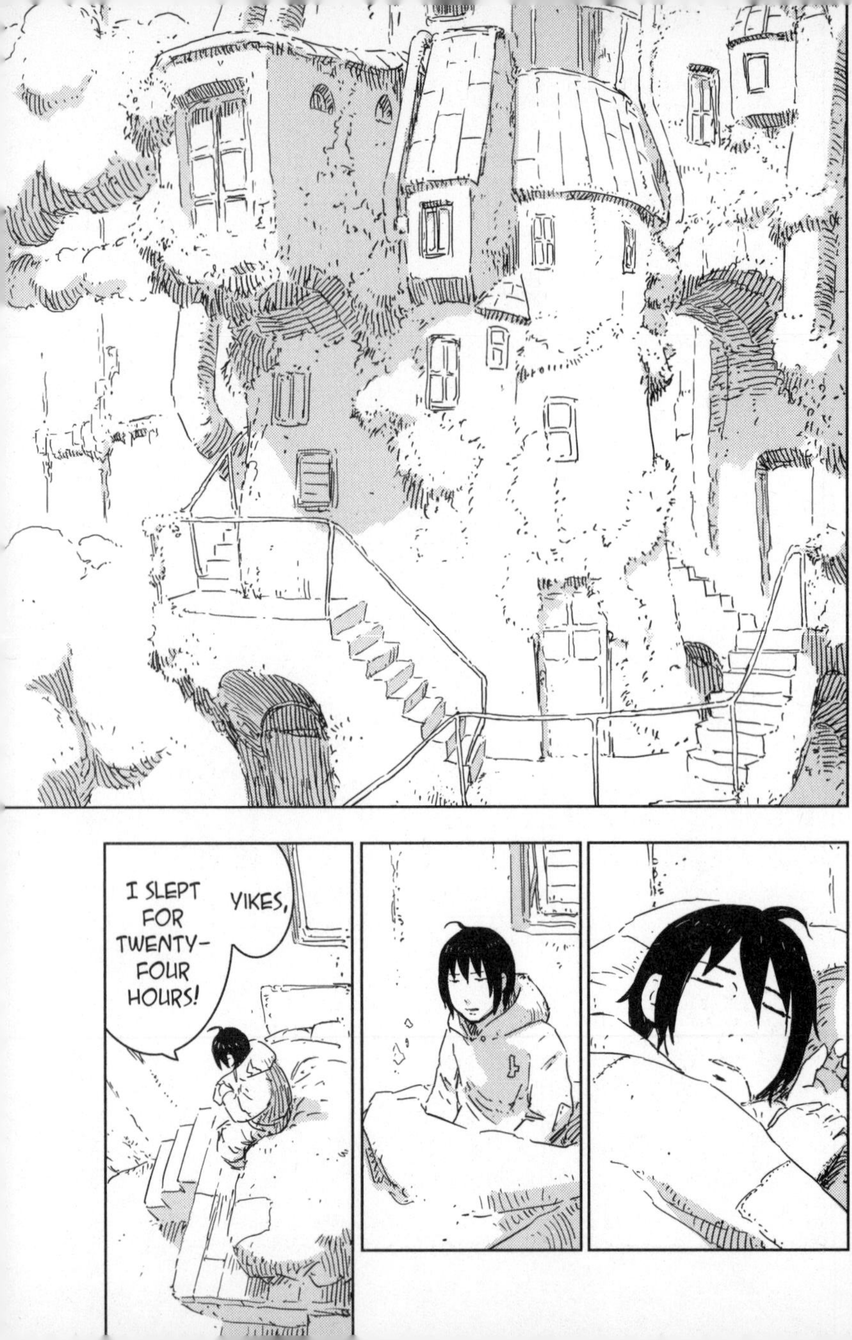
YIKES, I SLEPT FOR TWENTY-FOUR HOURS!

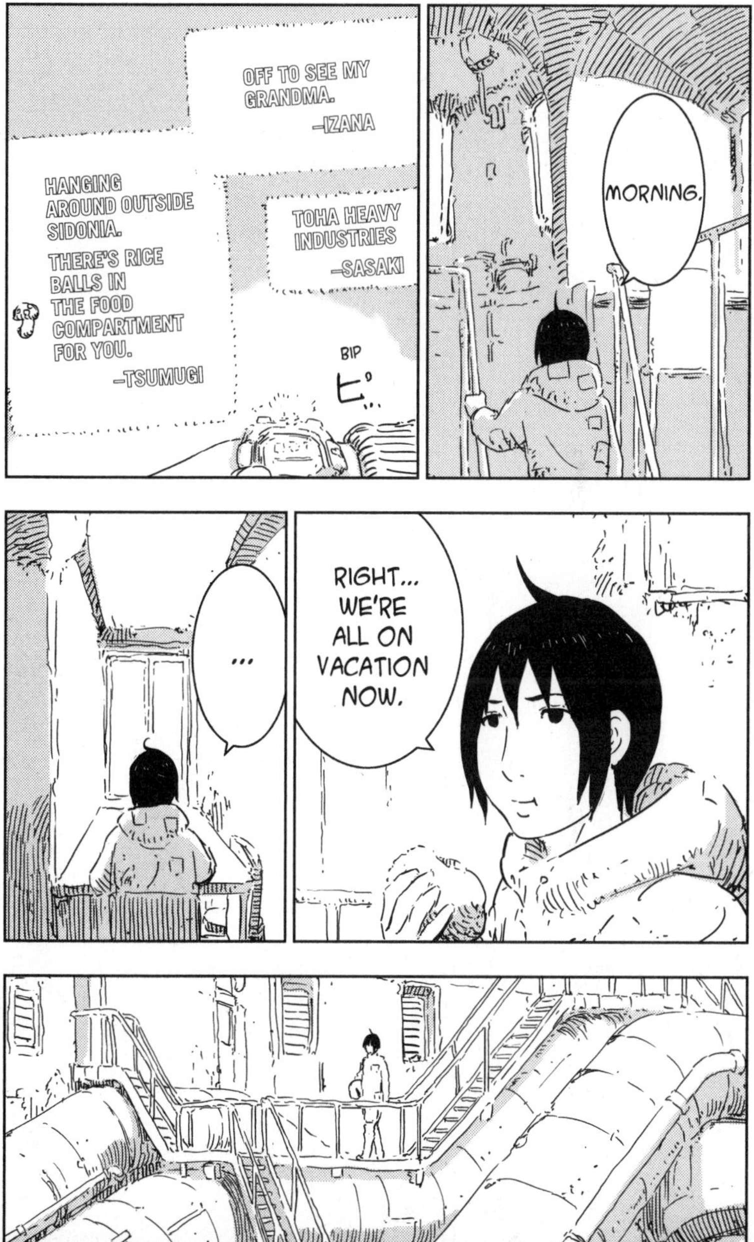
MORNING.
OFF TO SEE MY GRANDMA. —IZANA
TOHA HEAVY INDUSTRIES —SASAKI
HANGING AROUND OUTSIDE SIDONIA.
THERE'S RICE BALLS IN THE FOOD COMPARTMENT FOR YOU. —TSUMUGI
BIP
ピ
RIGHT... WE'RE ALL ON VACATION NOW.
...

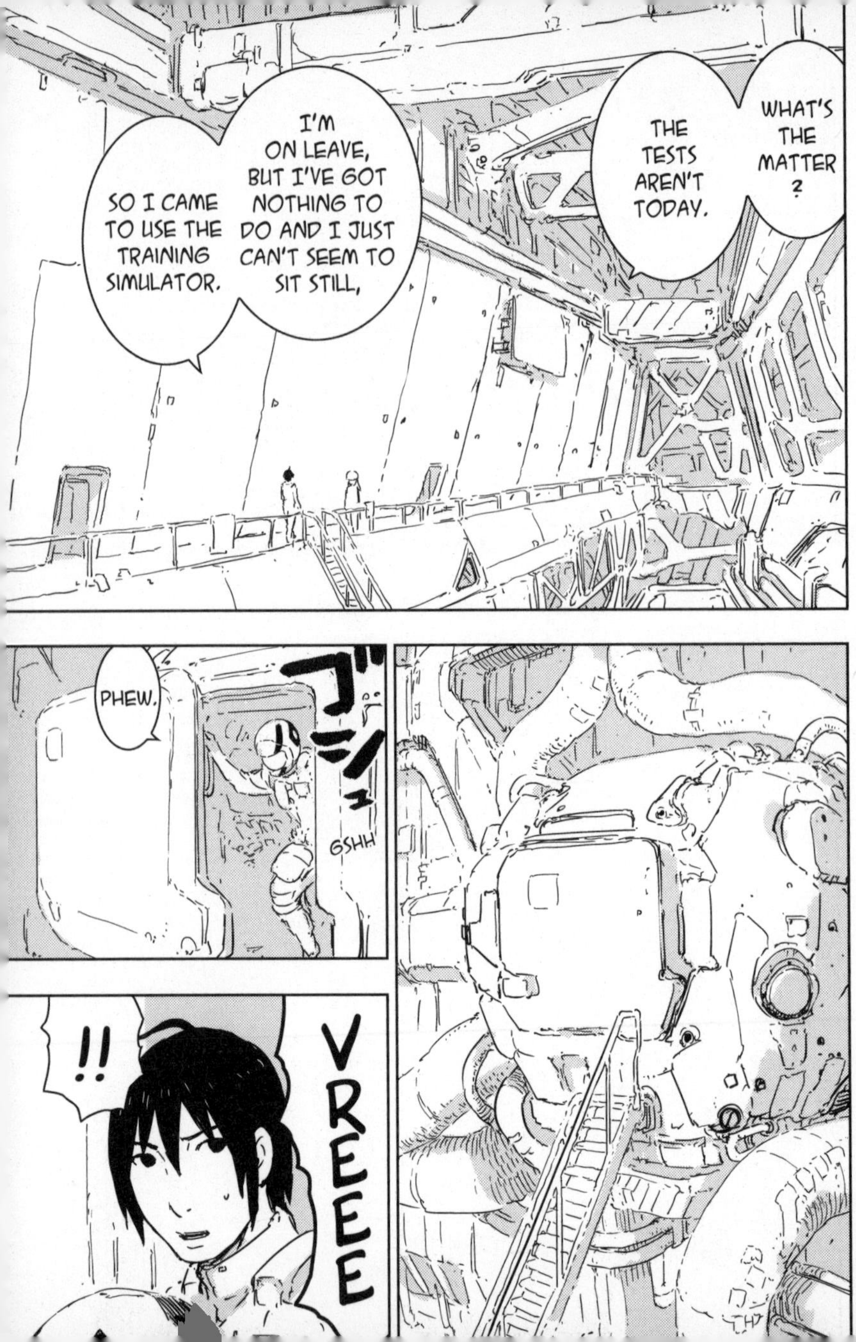
WHAT'S THE MATTER?
THE TESTS AREN'T TODAY.
I'M ON LEAVE, BUT I'VE GOT NOTHING TO DO AND I JUST CAN'T SEEM TO SIT STILL,
SO I CAME TO USE THE TRAINING SIMULATOR.
PHEW.
ゴシュ
GSHH
!!
VREEE

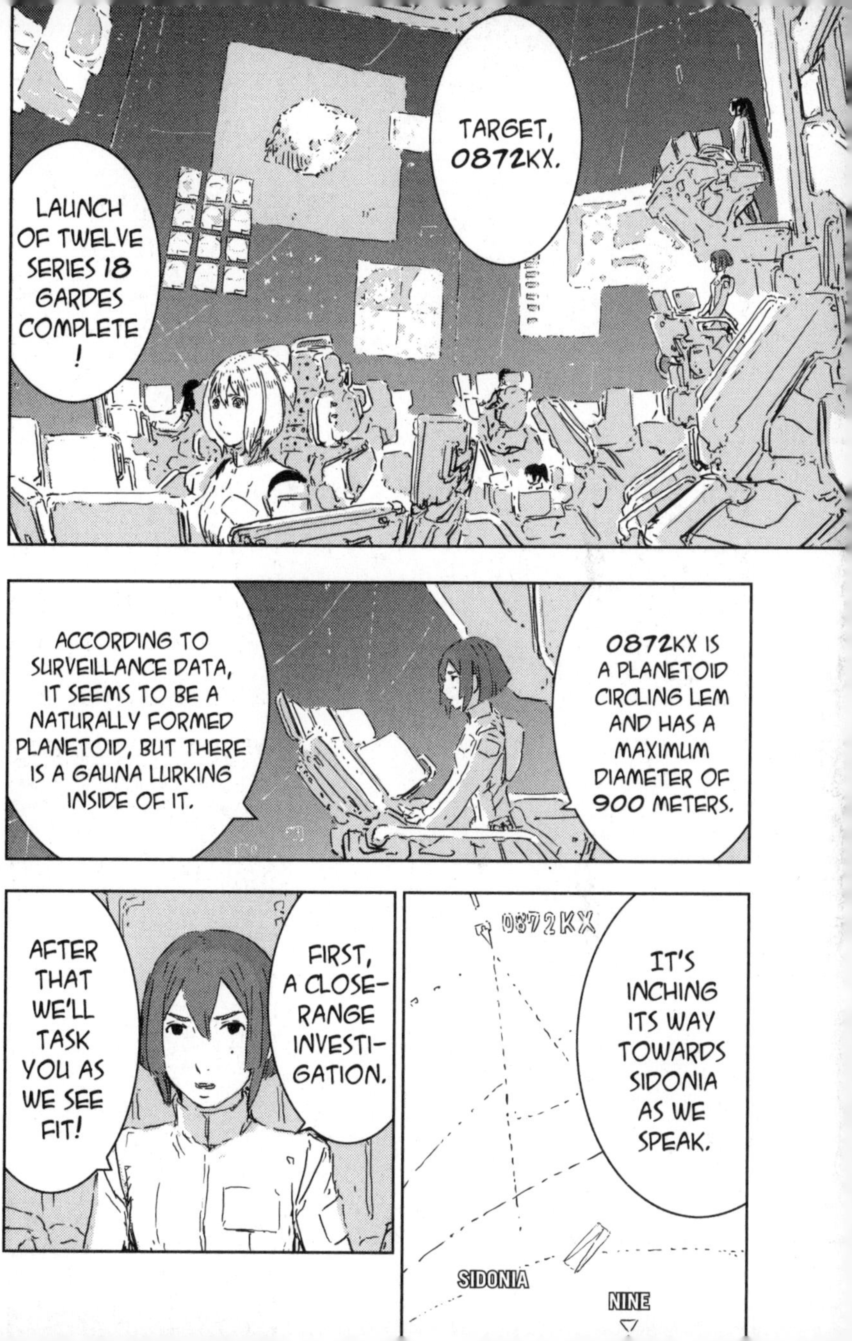
TARGET, 0872KX.
LAUNCH OF TWELVE SERIES 18 GARDES COMPLETE!
0872KX IS A PLANETOID CIRCLING LEM AND HAS A MAXIMUM DIAMETER OF 900 METERS.
ACCORDING TO SURVEILLANCE DATA, IT SEEMS TO BE A NATURALLY FORMED PLANETOID, BUT THERE IS A GAUNA LURKING INSIDE OF IT.
0872KX
IT'S INCHING ITS WAY TOWARDS SIDONIA AS WE SPEAK.
SIDONIA
NINE
FIRST, A CLOSE-RANGE INVESTIGATION.
AFTER THAT WE'LL TASK YOU AS WE SEE FIT!

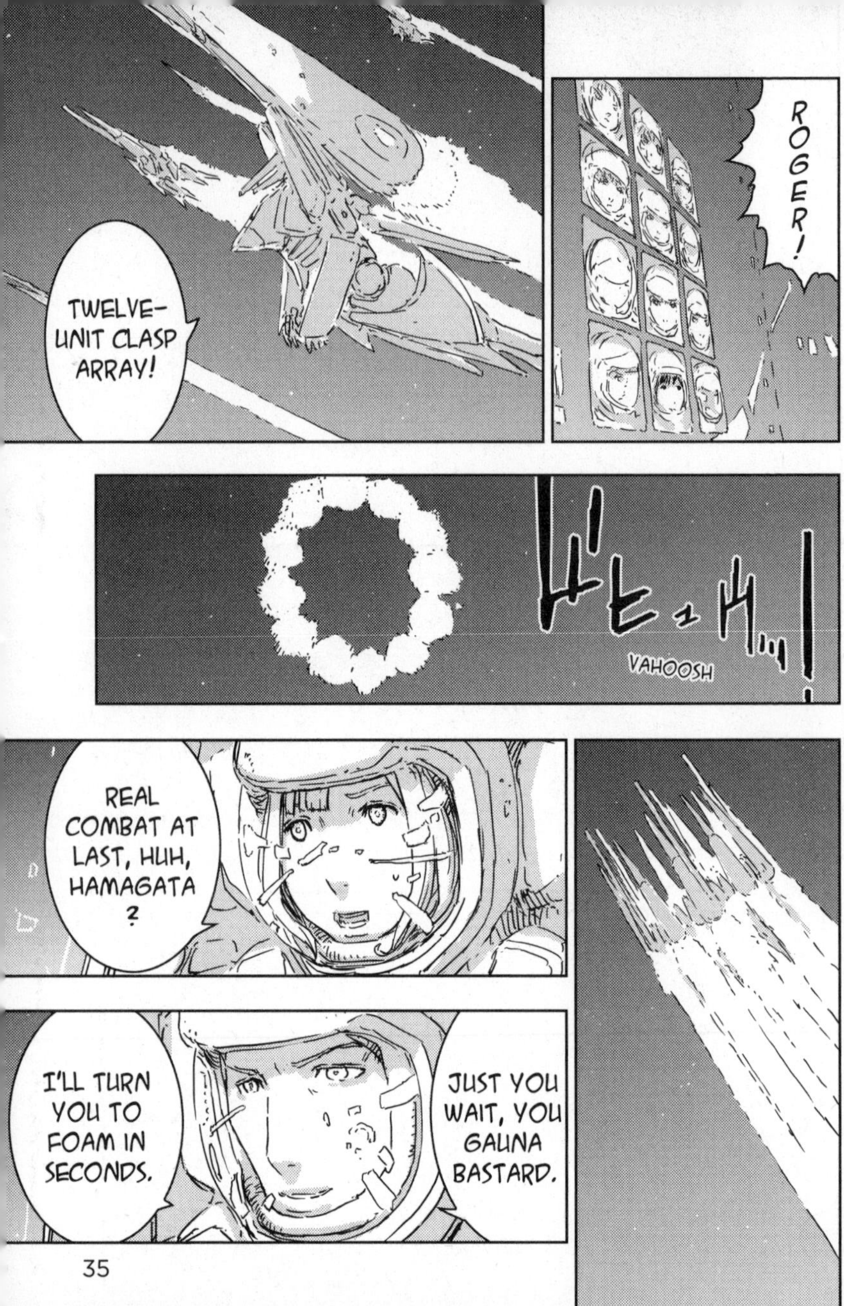
ROGER!
TWELVE-UNIT CLASP ARRAY!
VAHOOSH
REAL COMBAT AT LAST, HUH, HAMAGATA?
JUST YOU WAIT, YOU GAUNA BASTARD.
I'LL TURN YOU TO FOAM IN SECONDS.

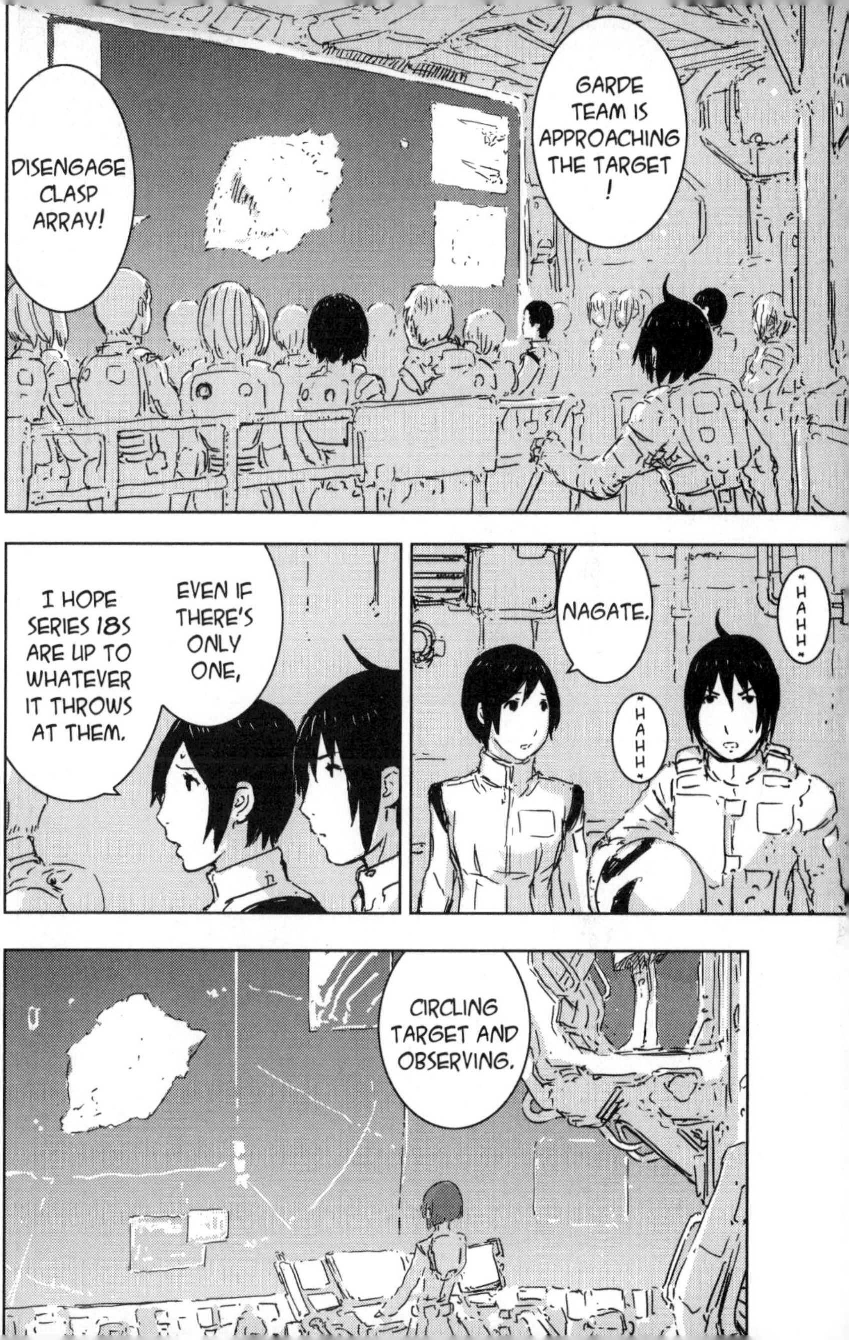
GARDE TEAM IS APPROACHING THE TARGET!
DISENGAGE CLASP ARRAY!
"HAHH"
NAGATE.
"HAHH"
EVEN IF THERE'S ONLY ONE,
I HOPE SERIES 18S ARE UP TO WHATEVER IT THROWS AT THEM.
CIRCLING TARGET AND OBSERVING.

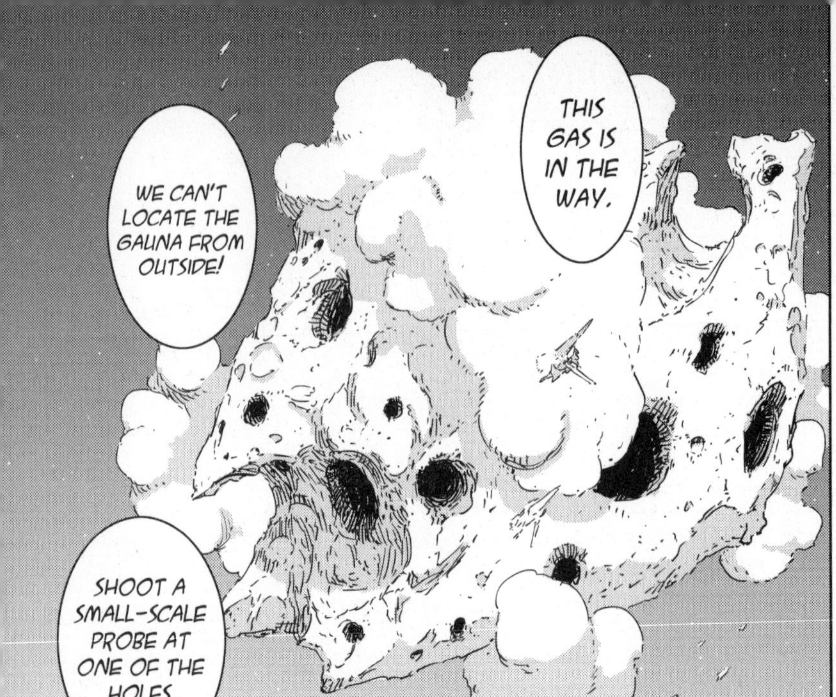
THIS GAS IS IN THE WAY.
WE CAN'T LOCATE THE GAUNA FROM OUTSIDE!
SHOOT A SMALL-SCALE PROBE AT ONE OF THE HOLES.

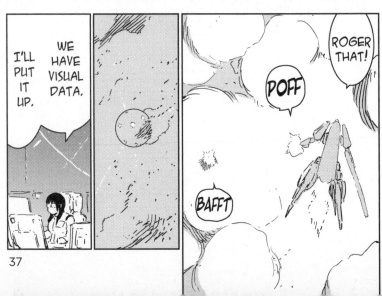

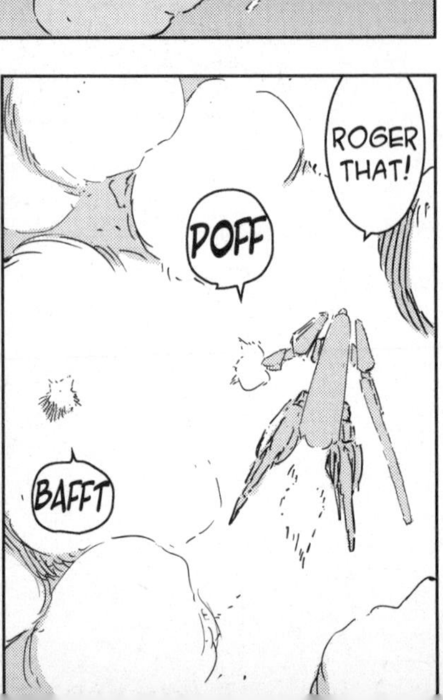
ROGER THAT!
POFF
BAFFT

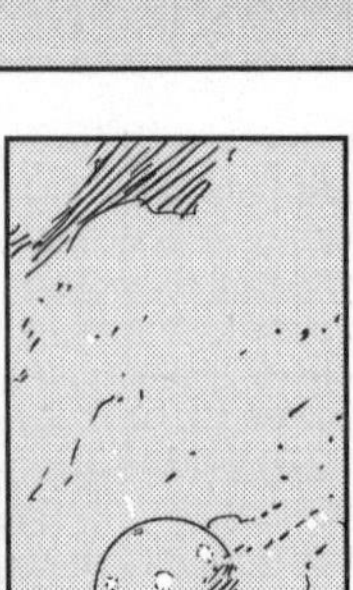

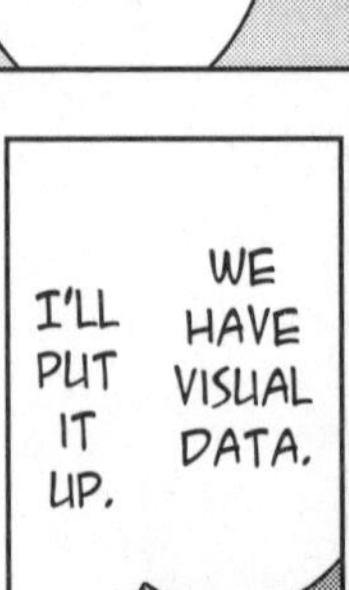
WE HAVE VISUAL DATA.
I'LL PUT IT UP.

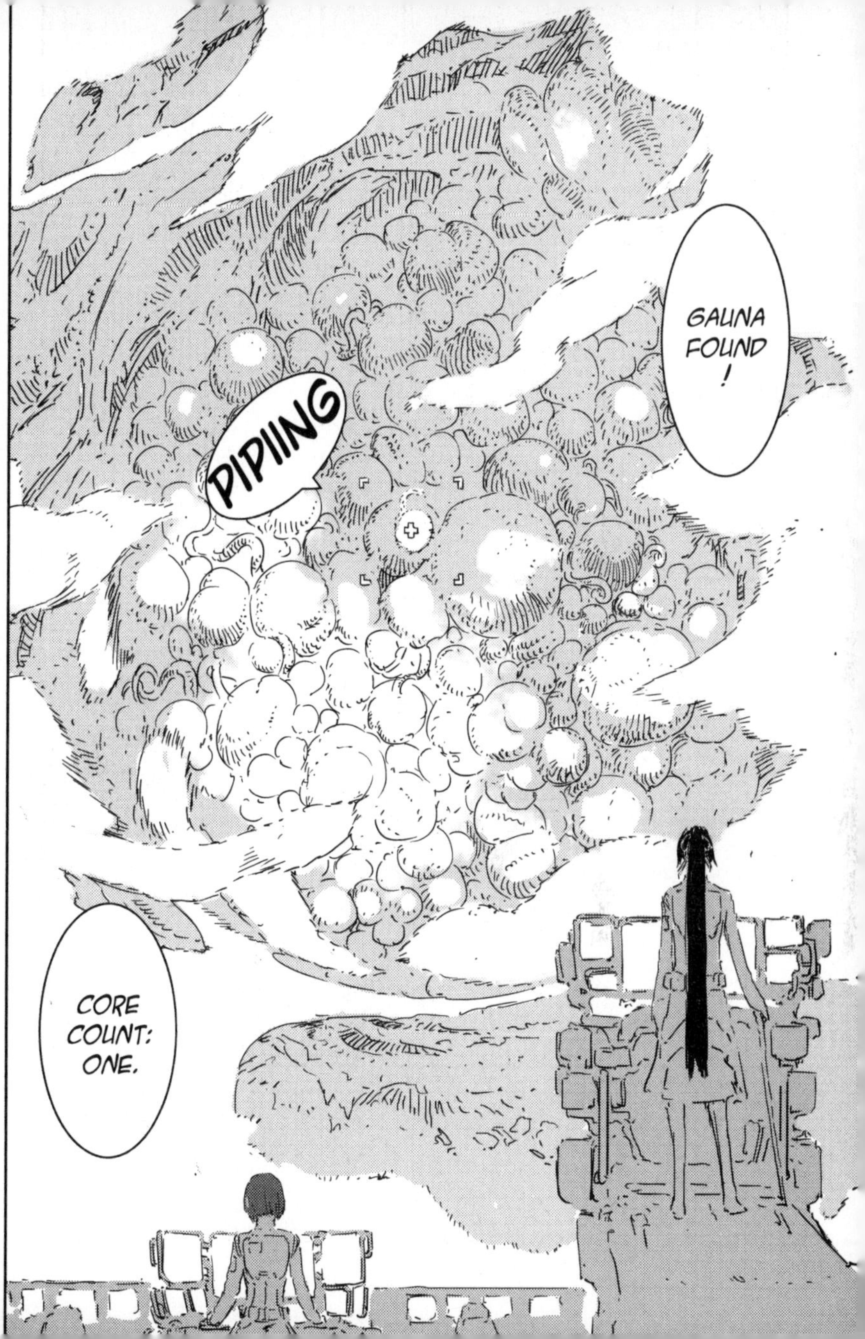
GAUNA FOUND !
PIPIING
CORE COUNT: ONE.

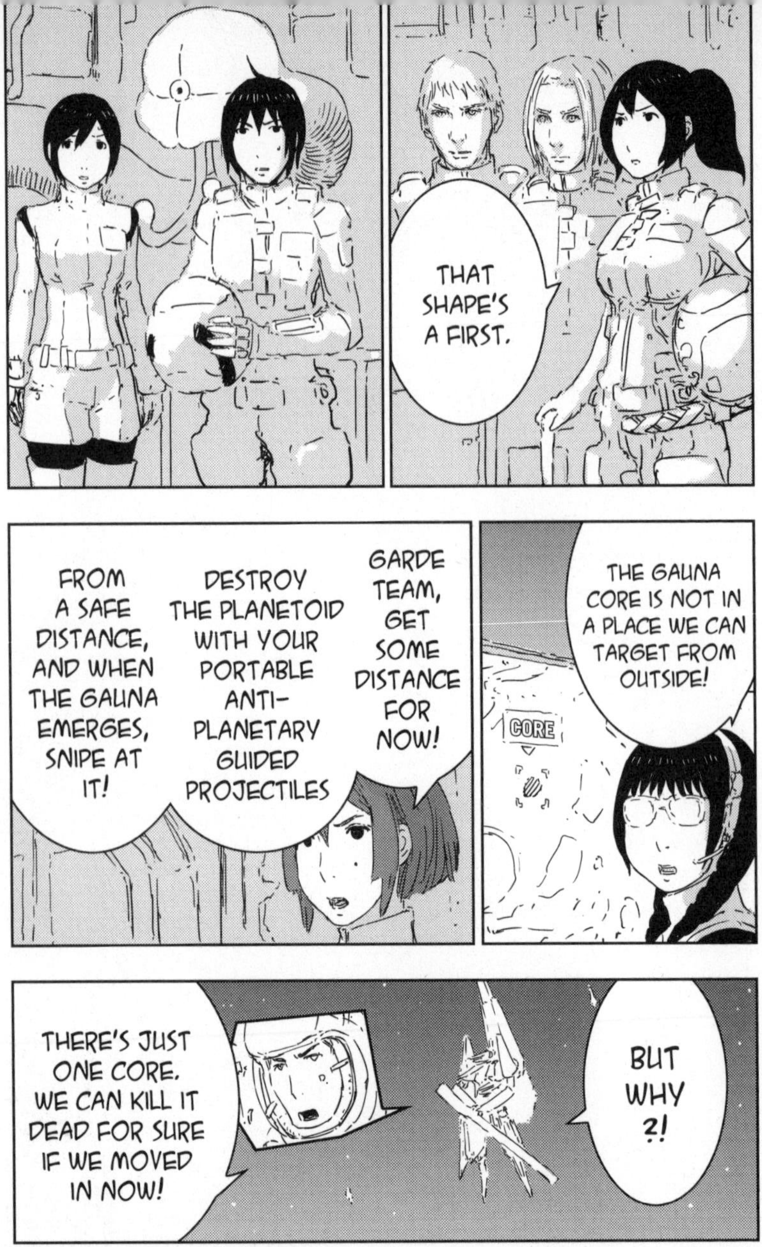
THAT SHAPE'S A FIRST.
THE GAUNA CORE IS NOT IN A PLACE WE CAN TARGET FROM OUTSIDE!
CORE
GARDE TEAM, GET SOME DISTANCE FOR NOW!
DESTROY THE PLANETOID WITH YOUR PORTABLE ANTI-PLANETARY GUIDED PROJECTILES
FROM A SAFE DISTANCE, AND WHEN THE GAUNA EMERGES, SNIPE AT IT!
BUT WHY?!
THERE'S JUST ONE CORE. WE CAN KILL IT DEAD FOR SURE IF WE MOVED IN NOW!

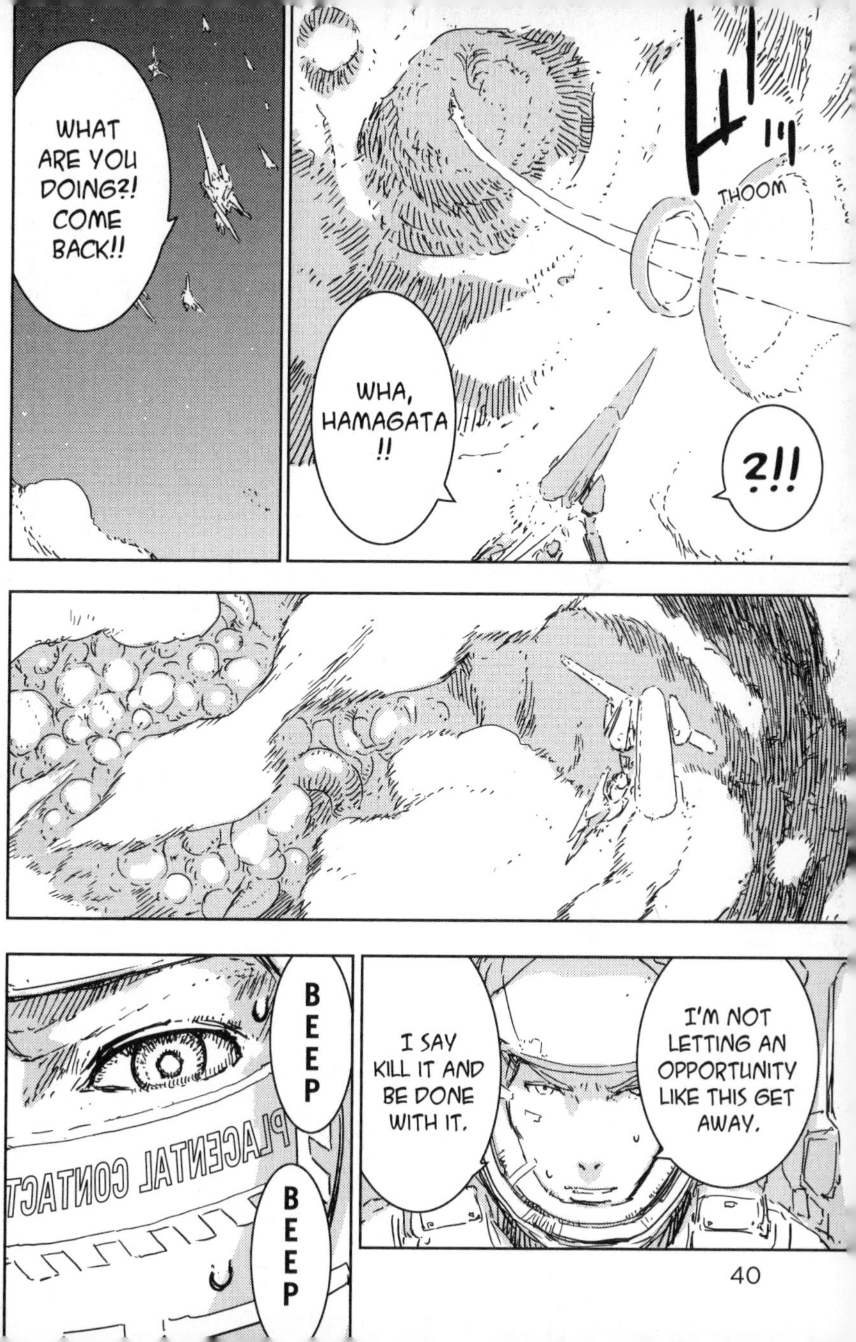
THOOM
?!!
WHA, HAMAGATA !!
WHAT ARE YOU DOING?! COME BACK!!
I'M NOT LETTING AN OPPORTUNITY LIKE THIS GET AWAY.
I SAY KILL IT AND BE DONE WITH IT.
BEEP
BEEP
PLACENTAL CONTACT

TH- THERE'S PLACENTA ON MY BACK!! GET IT OFF, PLEASE!!

HA- MA- GA- TA!

GAAHH!!

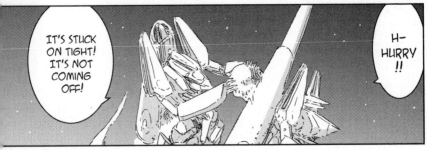

IT'S STUCK ON TIGHT! IT'S NOT COMING OFF!

H- HURRY !!

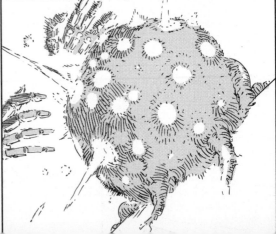

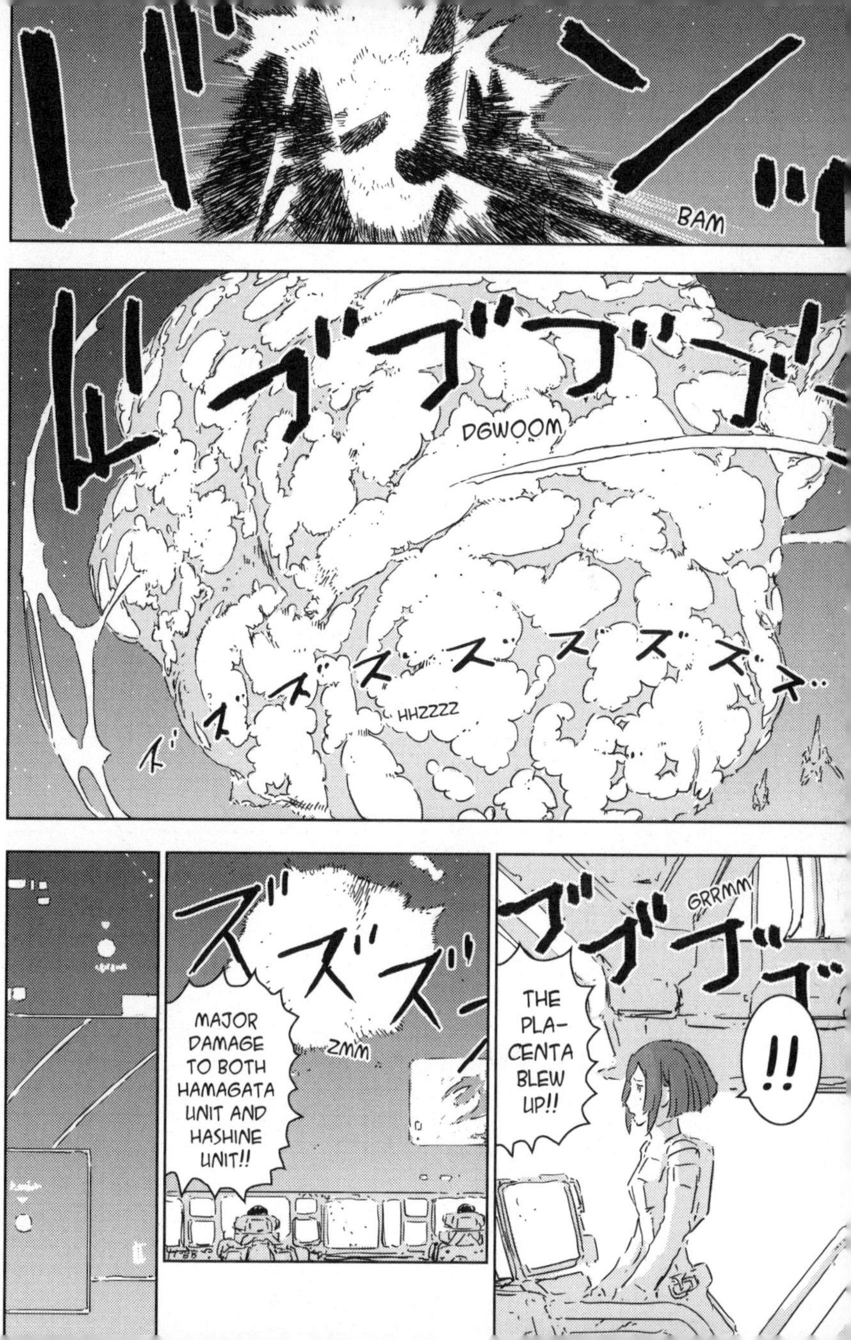
BAM
DGWOOM
HHZZZZ
GRRMM
!!
THE PLA-CENTA BLEW UP!!
MAJOR DAMAGE TO BOTH HAMAGATA UNIT AND HASHINE UNIT!!
ZMM

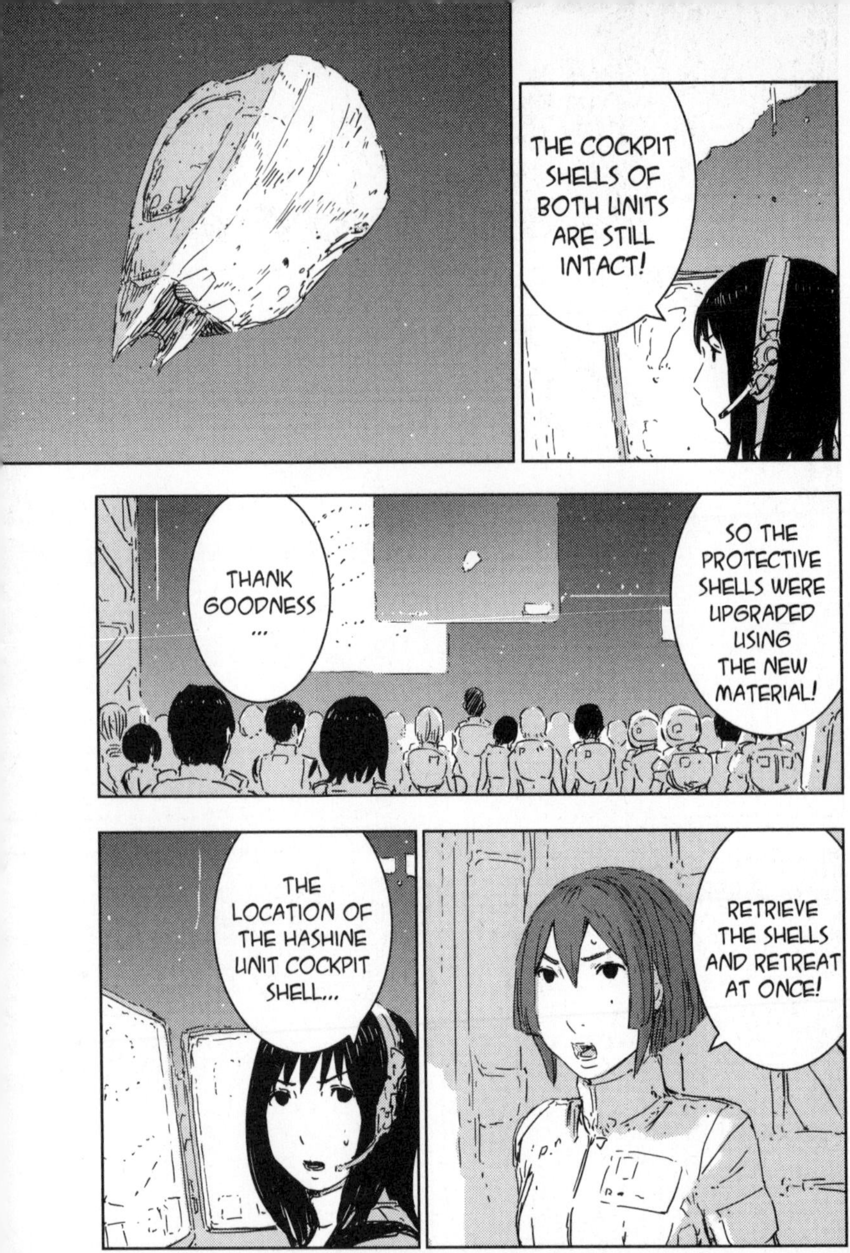
THE COCKPIT SHELLS OF BOTH UNITS ARE STILL INTACT!
SO THE PROTECTIVE SHELLS WERE UPGRADED USING THE NEW MATERIAL!
THANK GOODNESS ...
RETRIEVE THE SHELLS AND RETREAT AT ONCE!
THE LOCATION OF THE HASHINE UNIT COCKPIT SHELL...

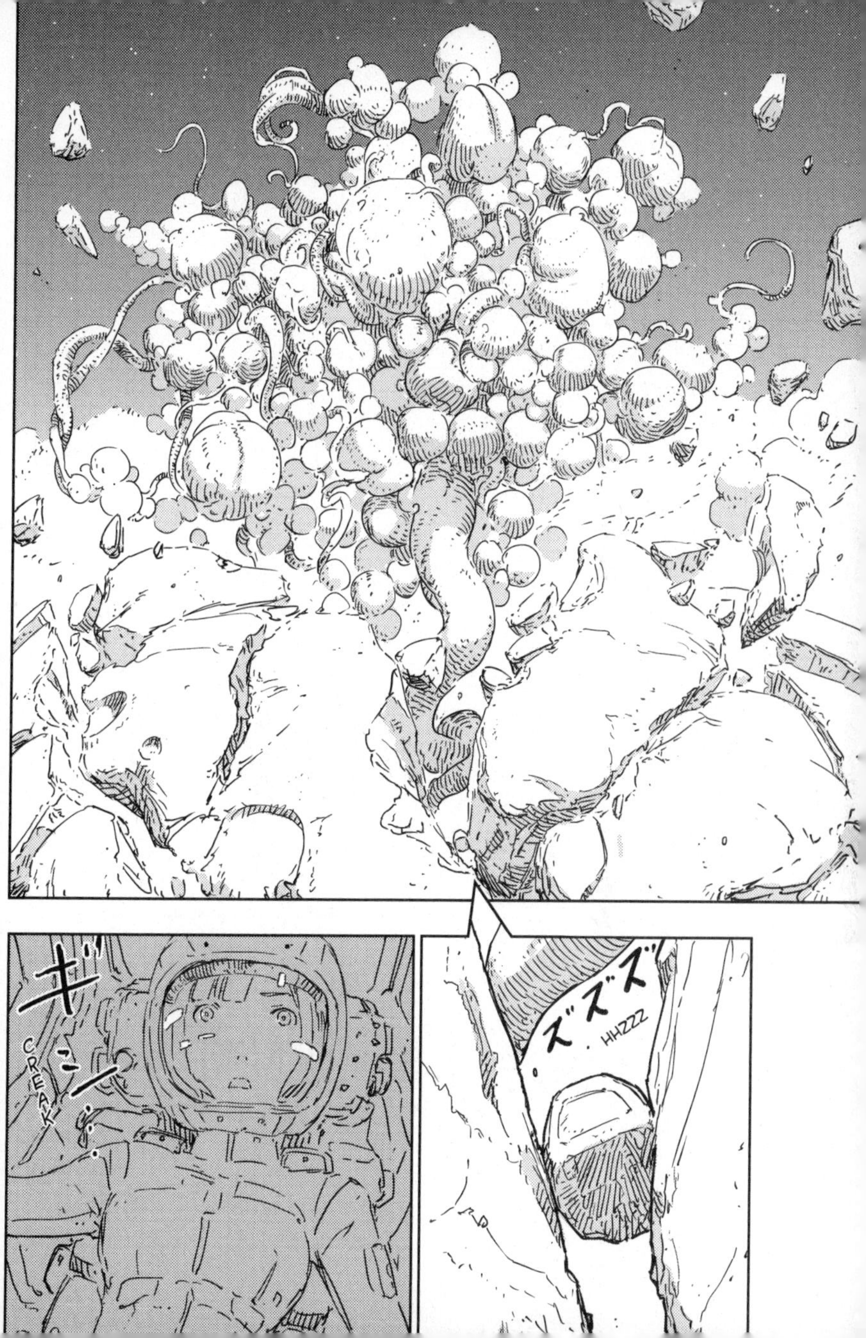
ズズズ
HHZZZ
ギ
CREAK

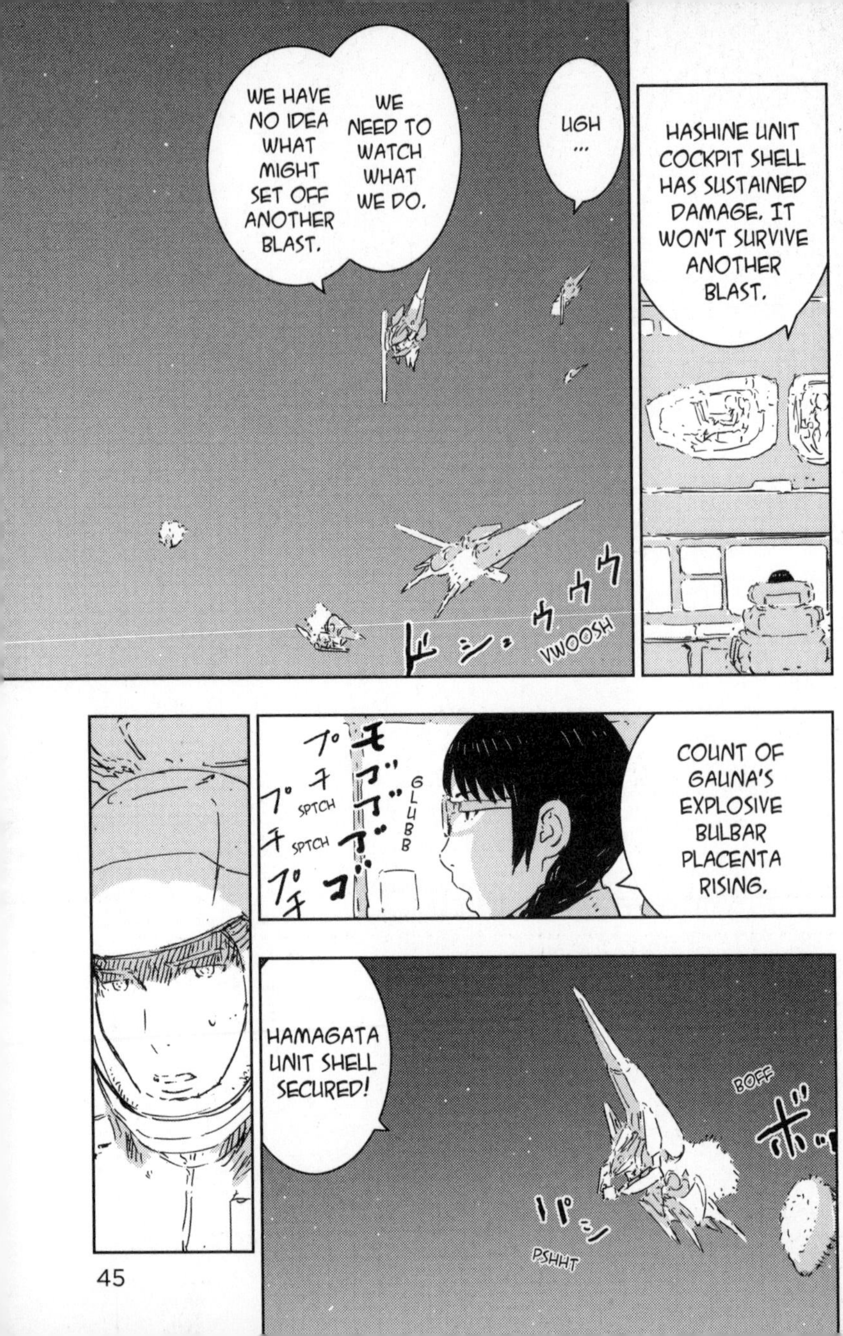

HASHINE UNIT COCKPIT SHELL HAS SUSTAINED DAMAGE. IT WON'T SURVIVE ANOTHER BLAST.
UGH ...
WE NEED TO WATCH WHAT WE DO.
WE HAVE NO IDEA WHAT MIGHT SET OFF ANOTHER BLAST.
VWOOSH
COUNT OF GAUNA'S EXPLOSIVE BULBAR PLACENTA RISING.
GLUBB
SPTCH
SPTCH
HAMAGATA UNIT SHELL SECURED!
BOFF
PSHHT

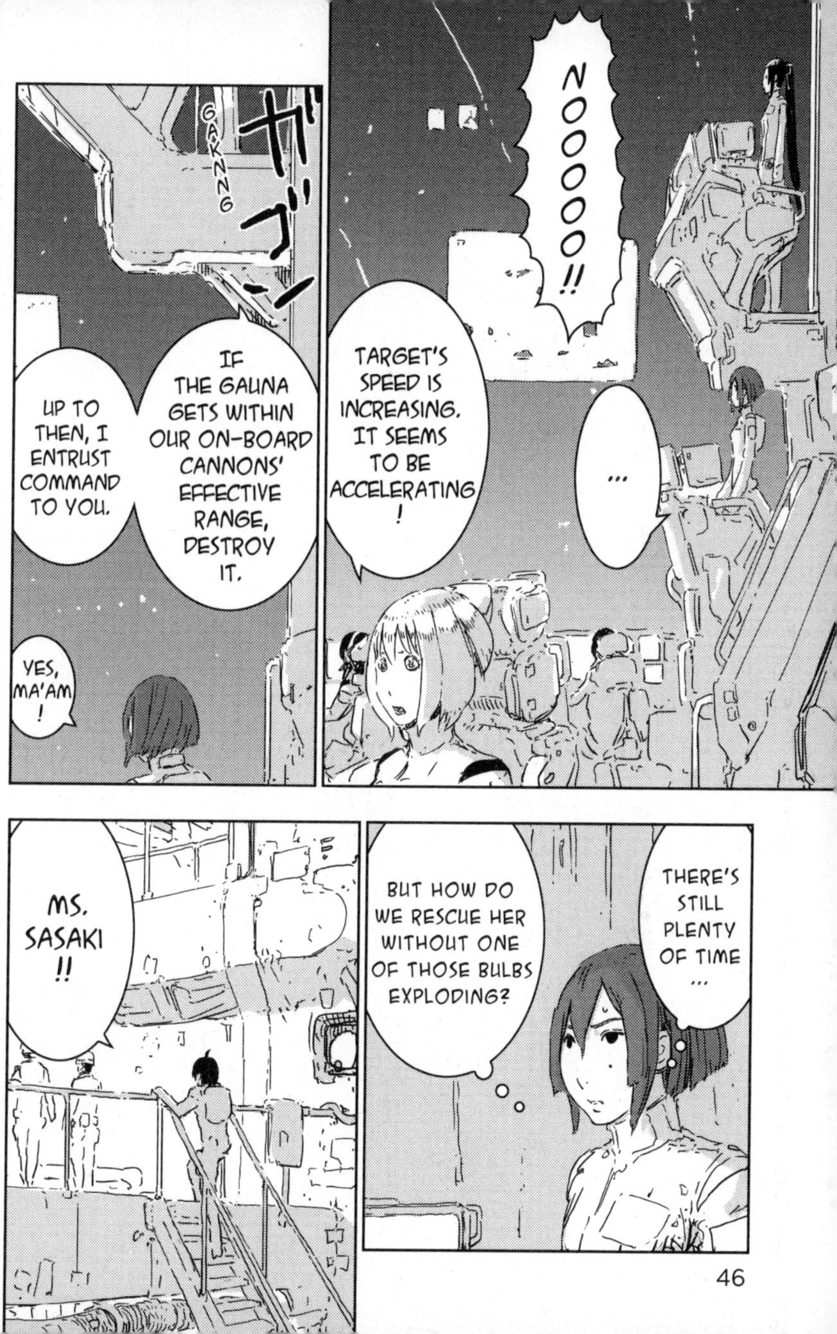
NOOOOOO!!
...
TARGET'S SPEED IS INCREASING. IT SEEMS TO BE ACCELERATING!
GAKNNG
IF THE GAUNA GETS WITHIN OUR ON-BOARD CANNONS' EFFECTIVE RANGE, DESTROY IT.
UP TO THEN, I ENTRUST COMMAND TO YOU.
YES, MA'AM!
THERE'S STILL PLENTY OF TIME...
BUT HOW DO WE RESCUE HER WITHOUT ONE OF THOSE BULBS EXPLODING?
MS. SASAKI!!

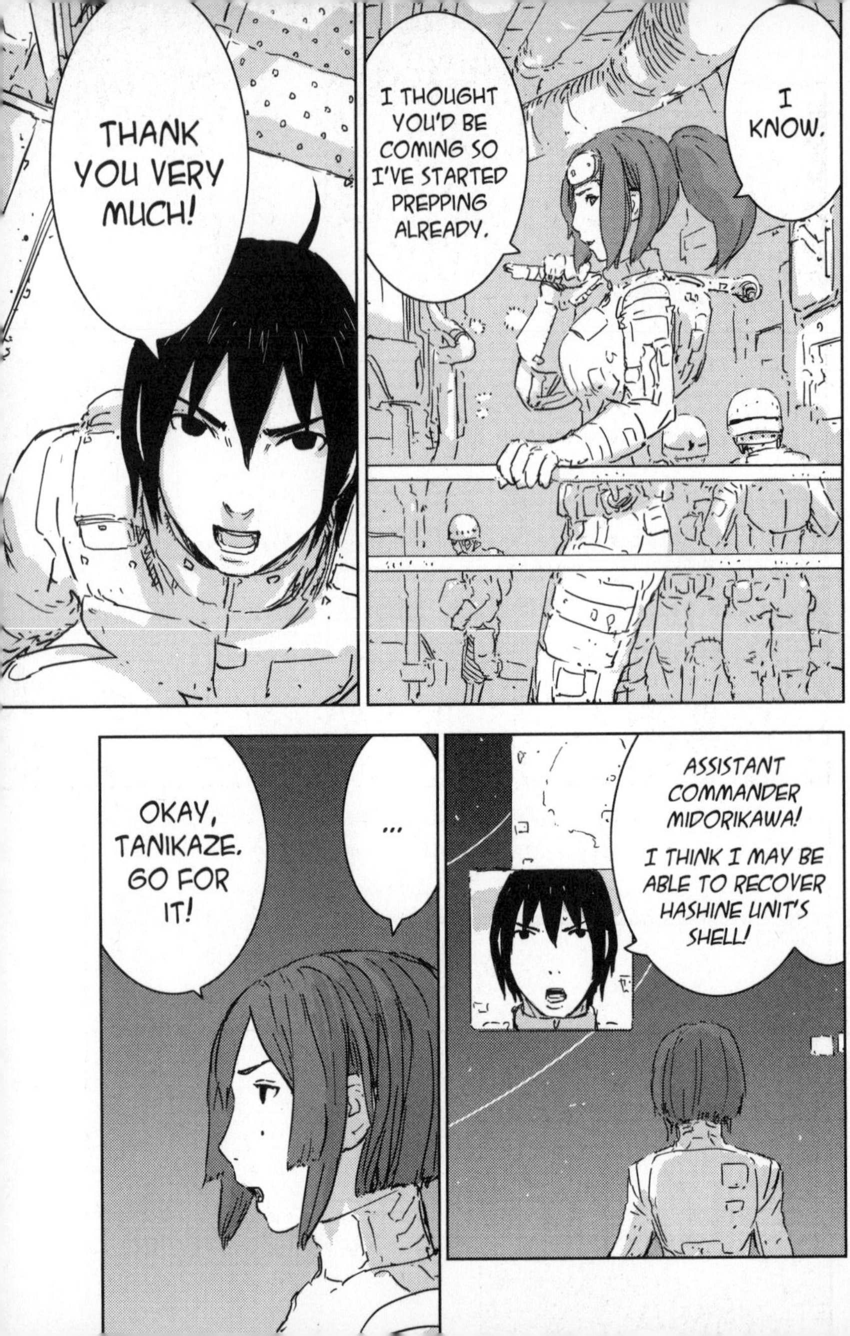
I KNOW.
I THOUGHT YOU'D BE COMING SO I'VE STARTED PREPPING ALREADY.
THANK YOU VERY MUCH!
ASSISTANT COMMANDER MIDORIKAWA!
I THINK I MAY BE ABLE TO RECOVER HASHINE UNIT'S SHELL!
...
OKAY, TANIKAZE. GO FOR IT!

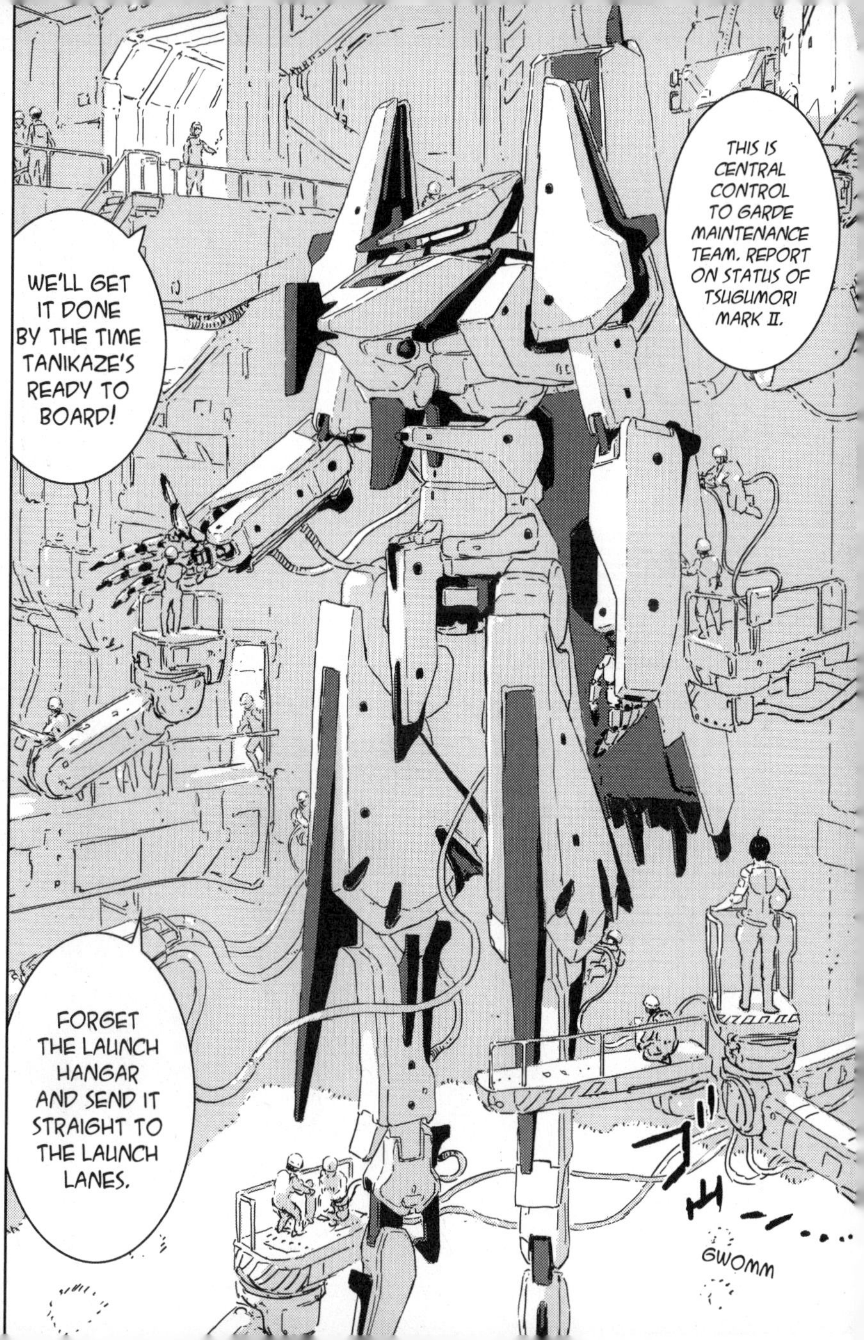
THIS IS CENTRAL CONTROL TO GARDE MAINTENANCE TEAM. REPORT ON STATUS OF TSUGUMORI MARK II.
WE'LL GET IT DONE BY THE TIME TANIKAZE'S READY TO BOARD!
FORGET THE LAUNCH HANGAR AND SEND IT STRAIGHT TO THE LAUNCH LANES.
GWOMM

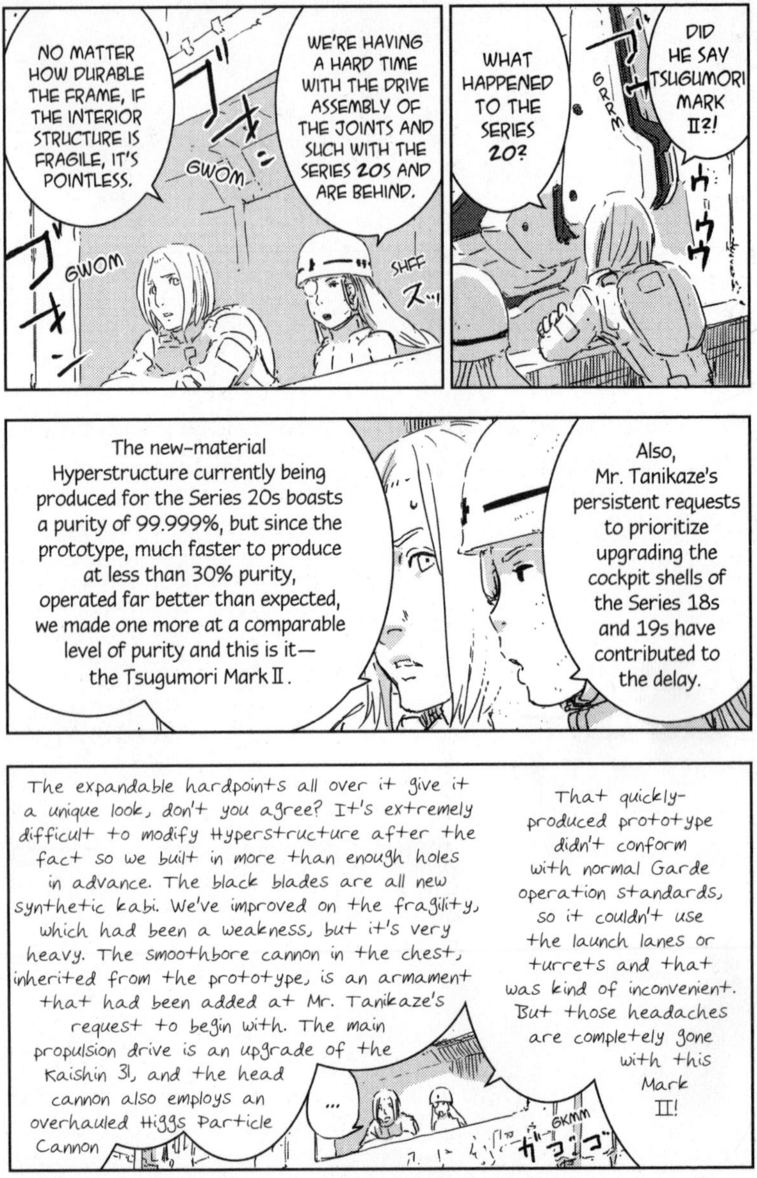
DID HE SAY TSUGUMORI MARK II?!
GRRM
WHAT HAPPENED TO THE SERIES 20?
WE'RE HAVING A HARD TIME WITH THE DRIVE ASSEMBLY OF THE JOINTS AND SUCH WITH THE SERIES 20S AND ARE BEHIND.
SHFF
NO MATTER HOW DURABLE THE FRAME, IF THE INTERIOR STRUCTURE IS FRAGILE, IT'S POINTLESS.
GWOM
GWOM
Also, Mr. Tanikaze's persistent requests to prioritize upgrading the cockpit shells of the Series 18s and 19s have contributed to the delay.
The new-material Hyperstructure currently being produced for the Series 20s boasts a purity of 99.999%, but since the prototype, much faster to produce at less than 30% purity, operated far better than expected, we made one more at a comparable level of purity and this is it—the Tsugumori Mark II.
That quickly-produced prototype didn't conform with normal Garde operation standards, so it couldn't use the launch lanes or turrets and that was kind of inconvenient. But those headaches are completely gone with this Mark II!
GKMM
...
The expandable hardpoints all over it give it a unique look, don't you agree? It's extremely difficult to modify Hyperstructure after the fact so we built in more than enough holes in advance. The black blades are all new synthetic kabi. We've improved on the fragility, which had been a weakness, but it's very heavy. The smoothbore cannon in the chest, inherited from the prototype, is an armament that had been added at Mr. Tanikaze's request to begin with. The main propulsion drive is an upgrade of the Kaishin 31, and the head cannon also employs an overhauled Higgs Particle Cannon

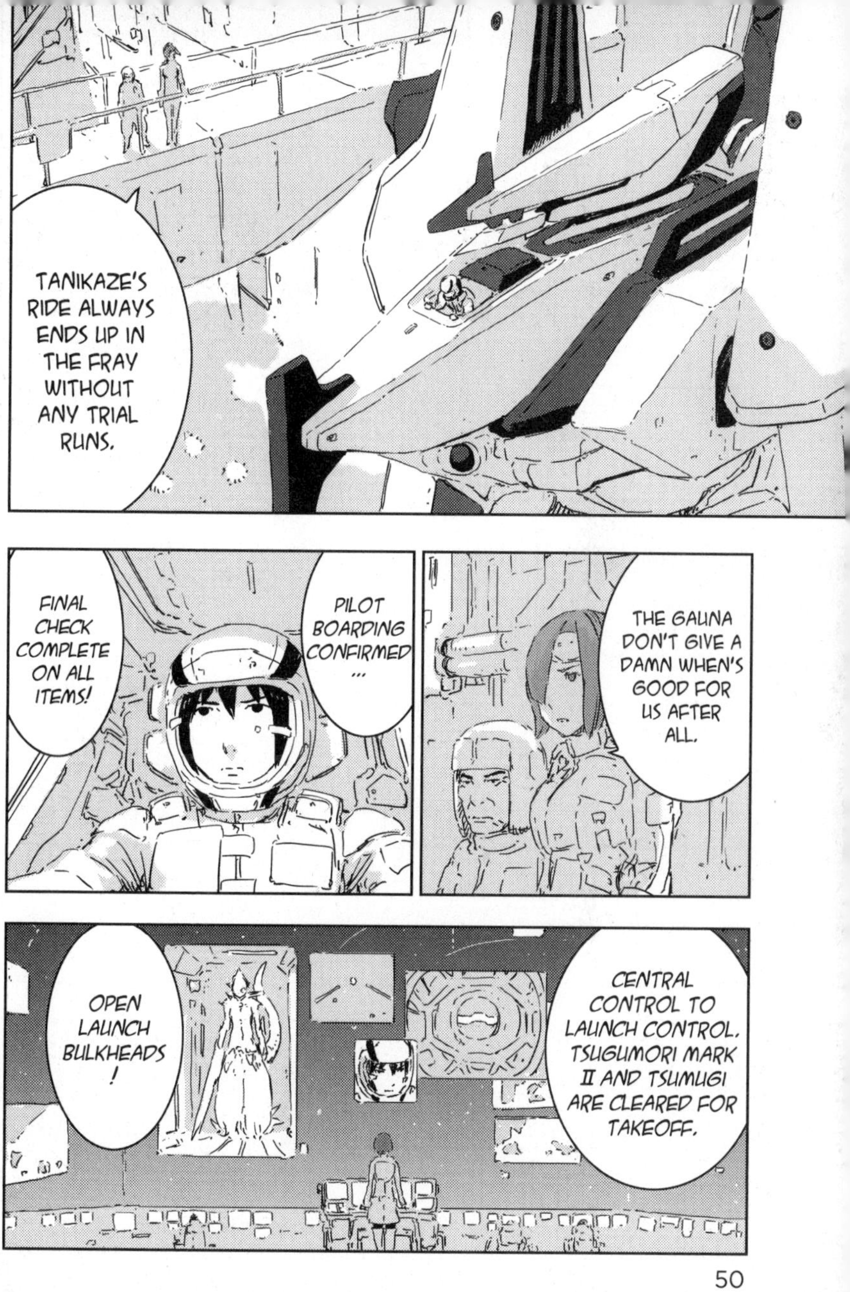
TANIKAZE'S RIDE ALWAYS ENDS UP IN THE FRAY WITHOUT ANY TRIAL RUNS.
THE GAUNA DON'T GIVE A DAMN WHEN'S GOOD FOR US AFTER ALL.
PILOT BOARDING CONFIRMED ...
FINAL CHECK COMPLETE ON ALL ITEMS!
CENTRAL CONTROL TO LAUNCH CONTROL, TSUGUMORI MARK II AND TSUMUGI ARE CLEARED FOR TAKEOFF.
OPEN LAUNCH BULKHEADS!

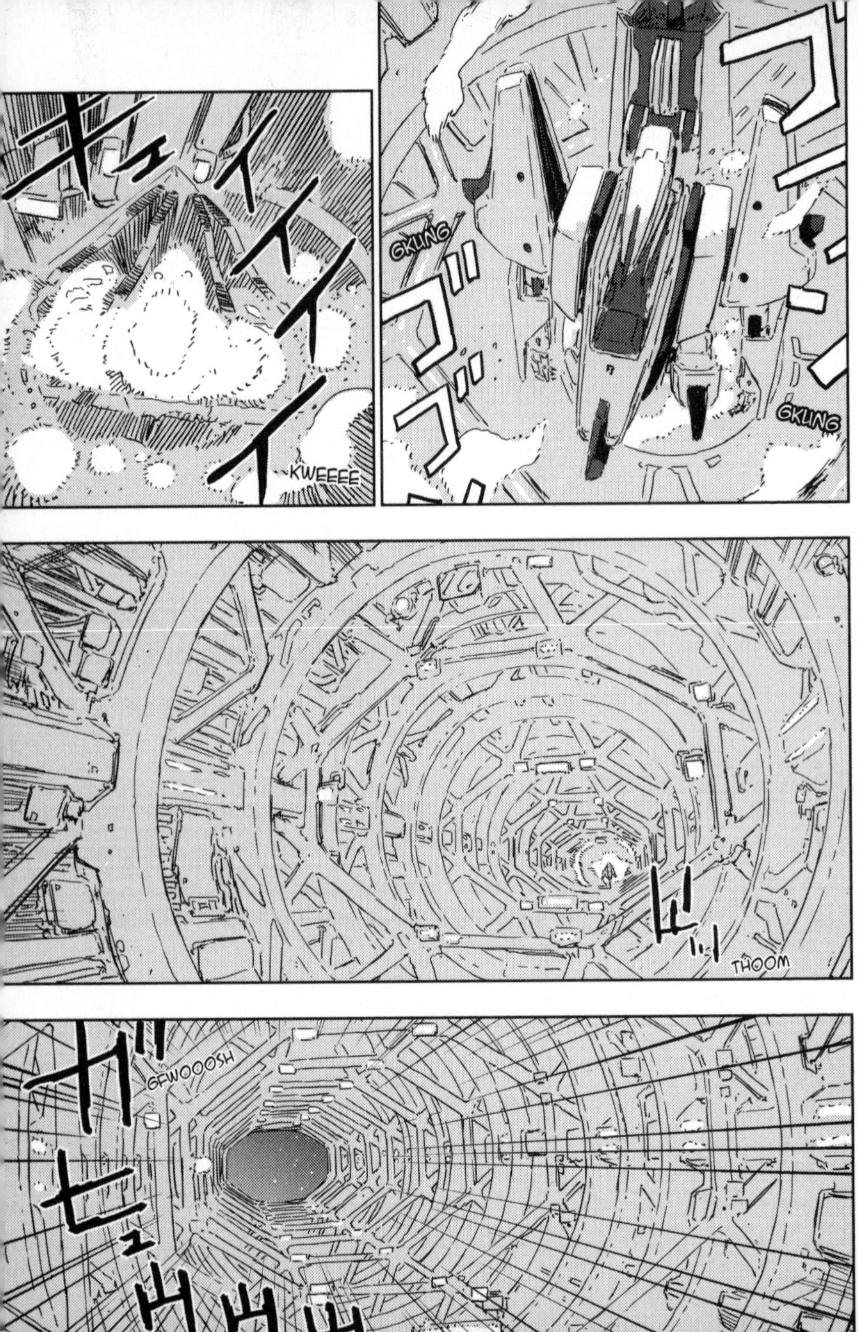
GKUNG
GKUNG
KWEEEE
THOOM
GFWOOOSH

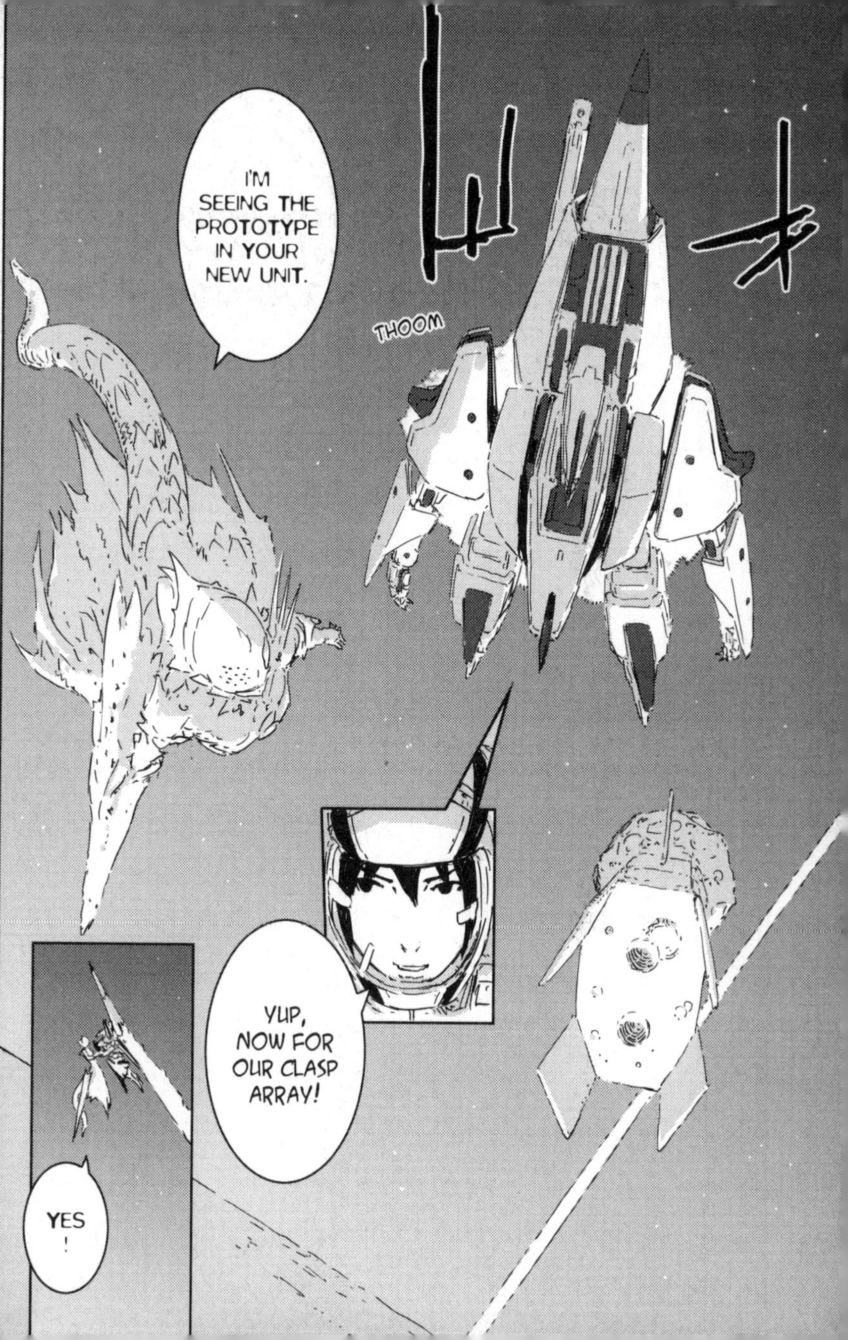
I'M SEEING THE PROTOTYPE IN YOUR NEW UNIT.
THOOM
YUP, NOW FOR OUR CLASP ARRAY!
YES!

シドニアの騎士
KNIGHTS OF SIDONIA

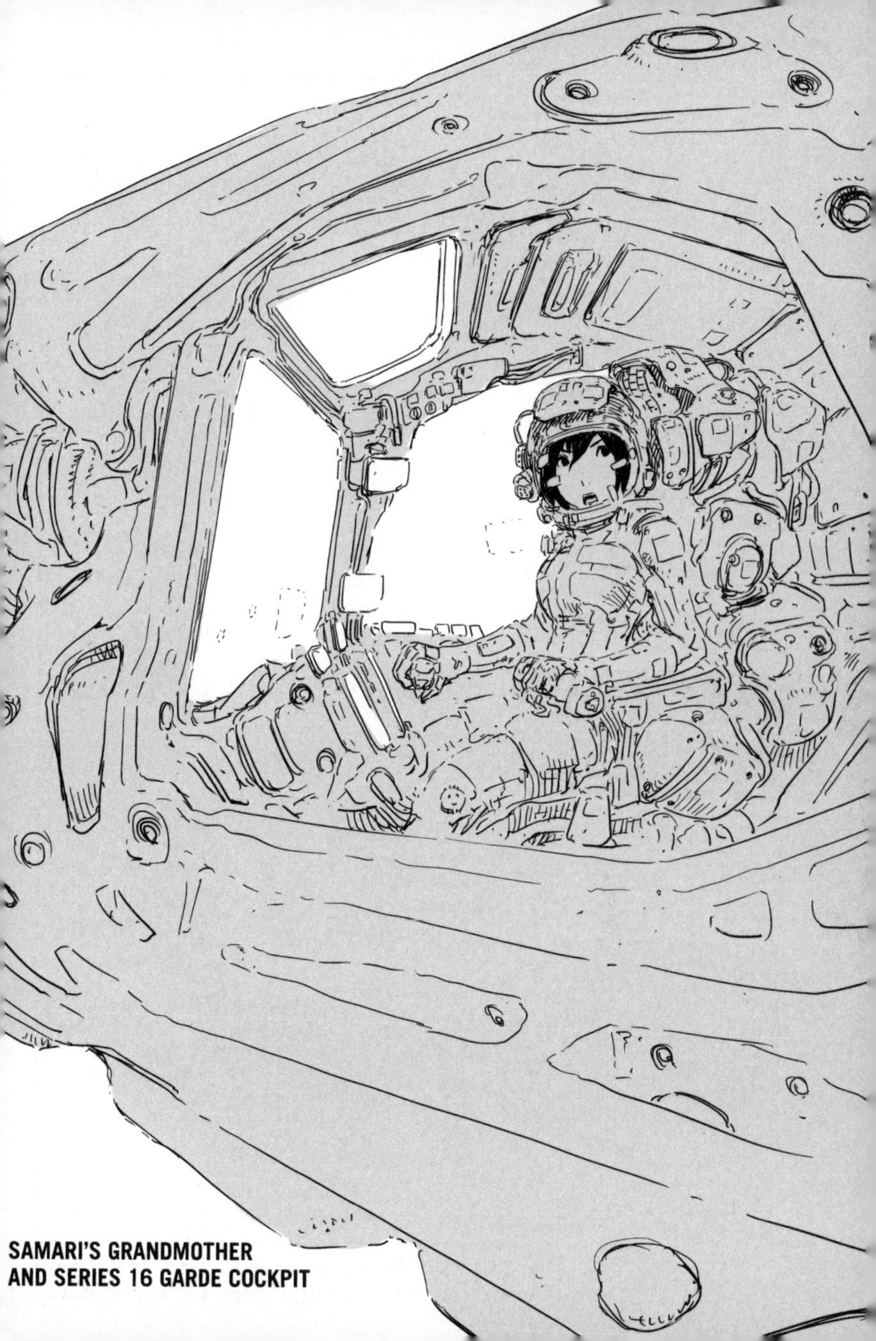

SAMARI'S GRANDMOTHER
AND SERIES 16 GARDE COCKPIT

Chapter 62: The New Pilots' Maiden Battle—Part Two

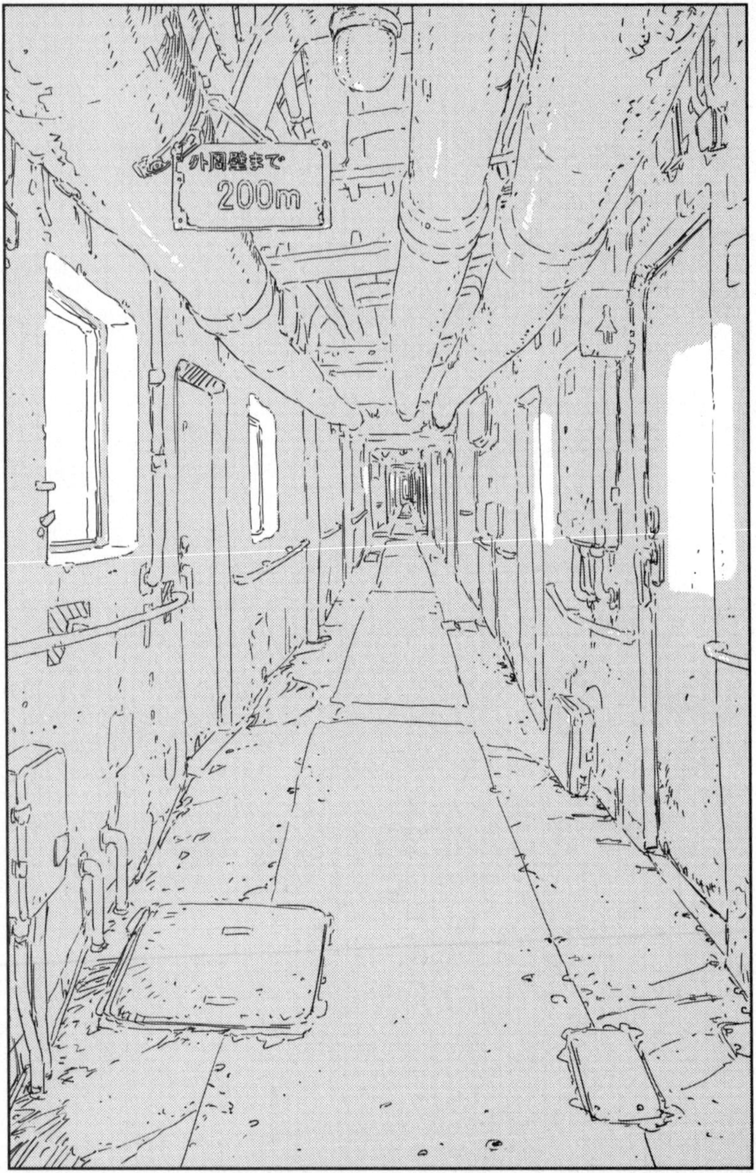
外周壁まで
200m

One Hundred Sights of Sidonia Part Forty-Seven:
Outer Circumference Wall Connecting Bridge Interior Hallway

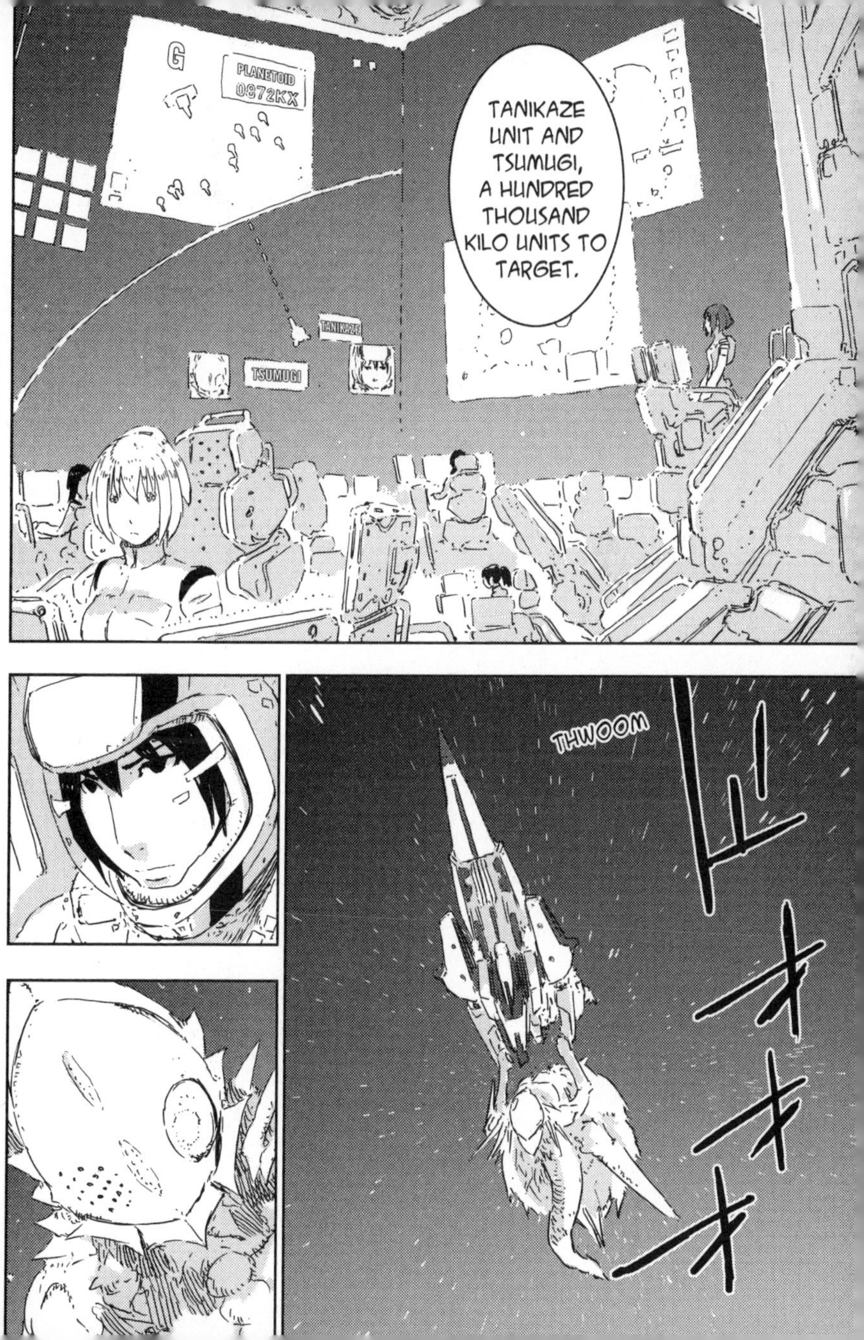
G
PLANETOID
0872KX
TANIKAZE
TSUMUGI
TANIKAZE UNIT AND TSUMUGI, A HUNDRED THOUSAND KILO UNITS TO TARGET.
THWOOM

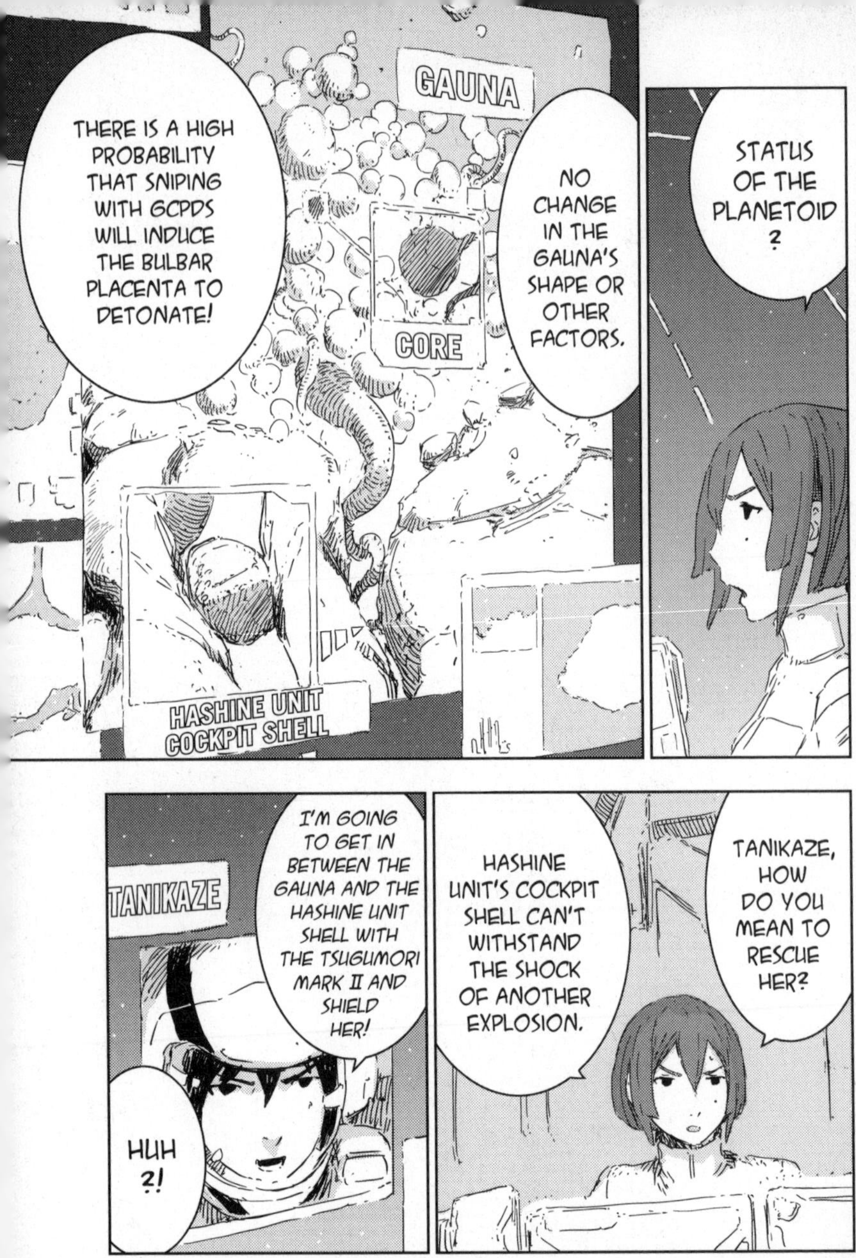
STATUS OF THE PLANETOID ?
NO CHANGE IN THE GAUNA'S SHAPE OR OTHER FACTORS.
GAUNA
THERE IS A HIGH PROBABILITY THAT SNIPING WITH GCPDS WILL INDUCE THE BULBAR PLACENTA TO DETONATE!
CORE
HASHINE UNIT COCKPIT SHELL
TANIKAZE, HOW DO YOU MEAN TO RESCUE HER?
HASHINE UNIT'S COCKPIT SHELL CAN'T WITHSTAND THE SHOCK OF ANOTHER EXPLOSION.
I'M GOING TO GET IN BETWEEN THE GAUNA AND THE HASHINE UNIT SHELL WITH THE TSUGUMORI MARK II AND SHIELD HER!
TANIKAZE
HUH ?!

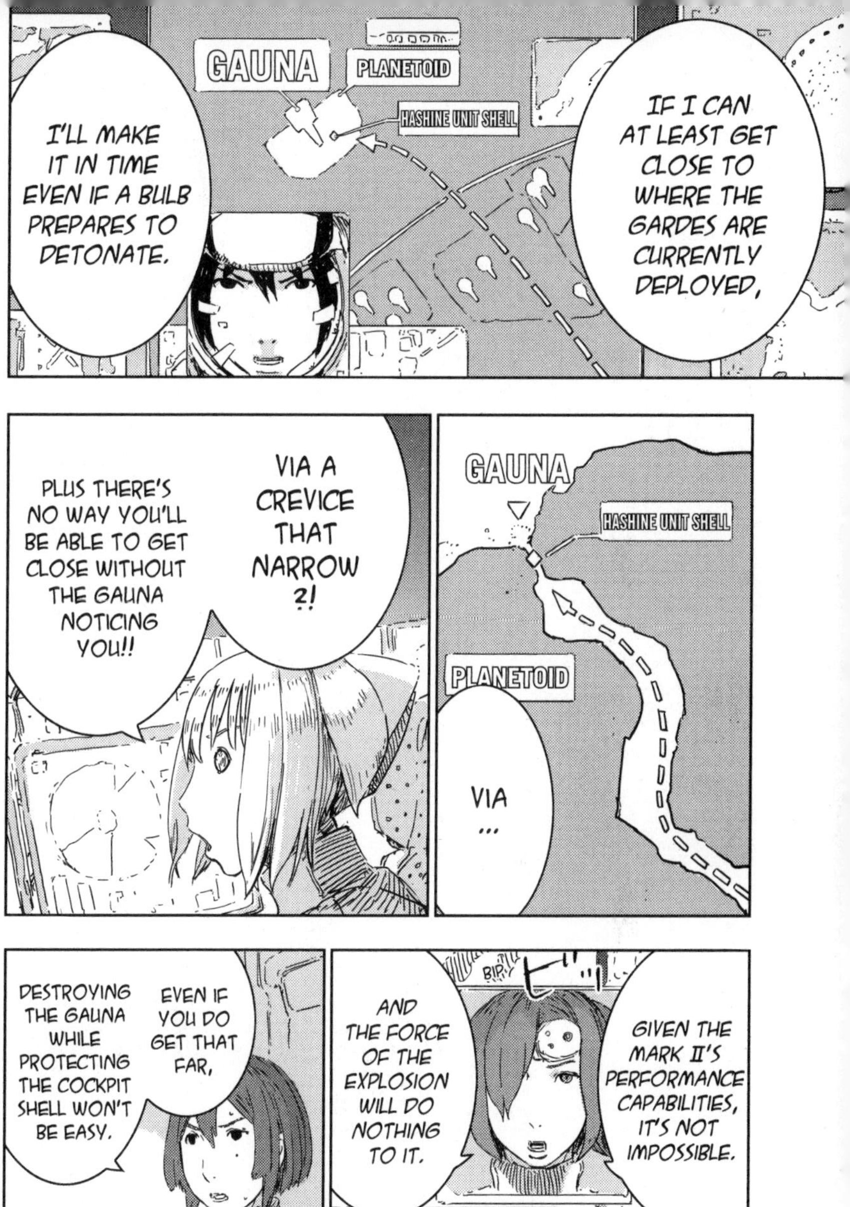
GAUNA
PLANETOID
HASHINE UNIT SHELL
IF I CAN AT LEAST GET CLOSE TO WHERE THE GARDES ARE CURRENTLY DEPLOYED,
I'LL MAKE IT IN TIME EVEN IF A BULB PREPARES TO DETONATE.
GAUNA
HASHINE UNIT SHELL
PLANETOID
VIA ...
VIA A CREVICE THAT NARROW ?!
PLUS THERE'S NO WAY YOU'LL BE ABLE TO GET CLOSE WITHOUT THE GAUNA NOTICING YOU!!
BIP
GIVEN THE MARK II'S PERFORMANCE CAPABILITIES, IT'S NOT IMPOSSIBLE.
AND THE FORCE OF THE EXPLOSION WILL DO NOTHING TO IT.
EVEN IF YOU DO GET THAT FAR,
DESTROYING THE GAUNA WHILE PROTECTING THE COCKPIT SHELL WON'T BE EASY.

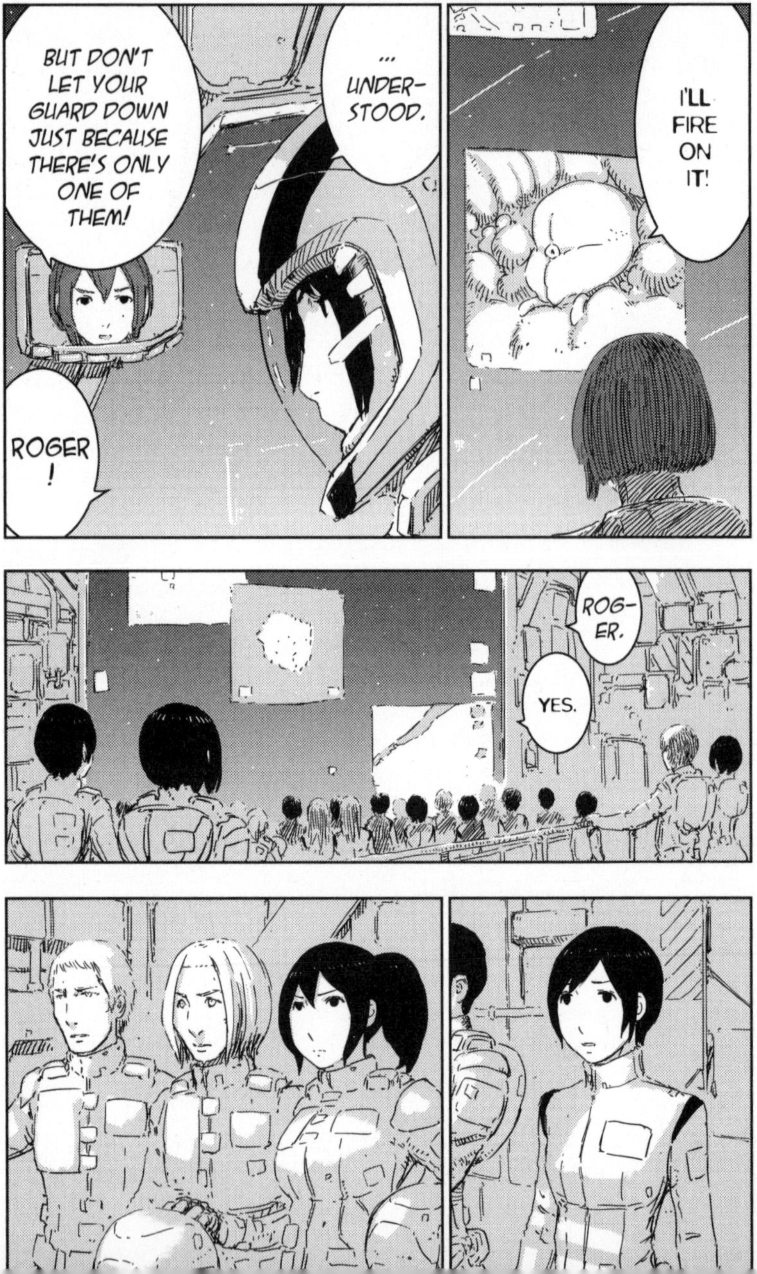
I'LL FIRE ON IT!
... UNDER-STOOD.
BUT DON'T LET YOUR GUARD DOWN JUST BECAUSE THERE'S ONLY ONE OF THEM!
ROGER!
ROG-ER.
YES.

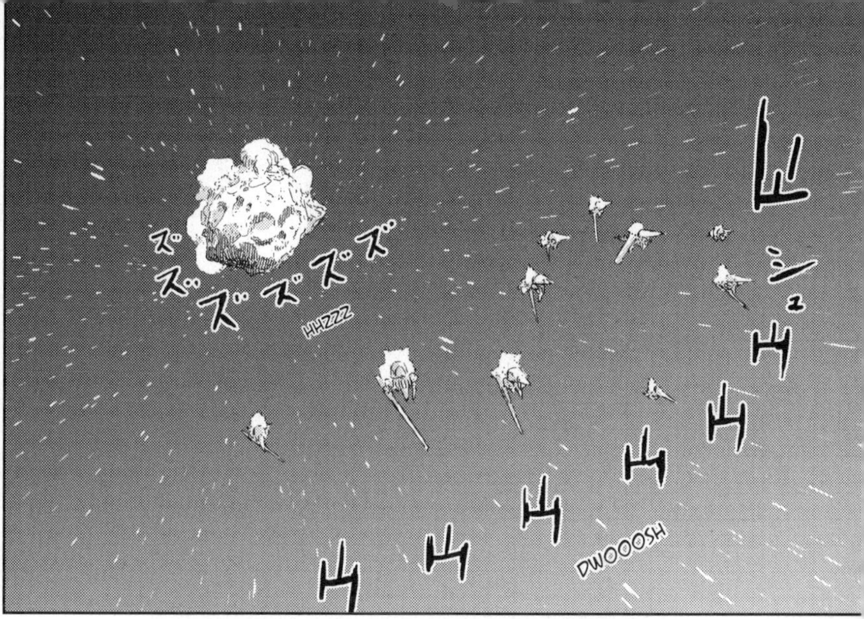
ズズズズズ
HHZZZ
ドシュ
DWOOOSH
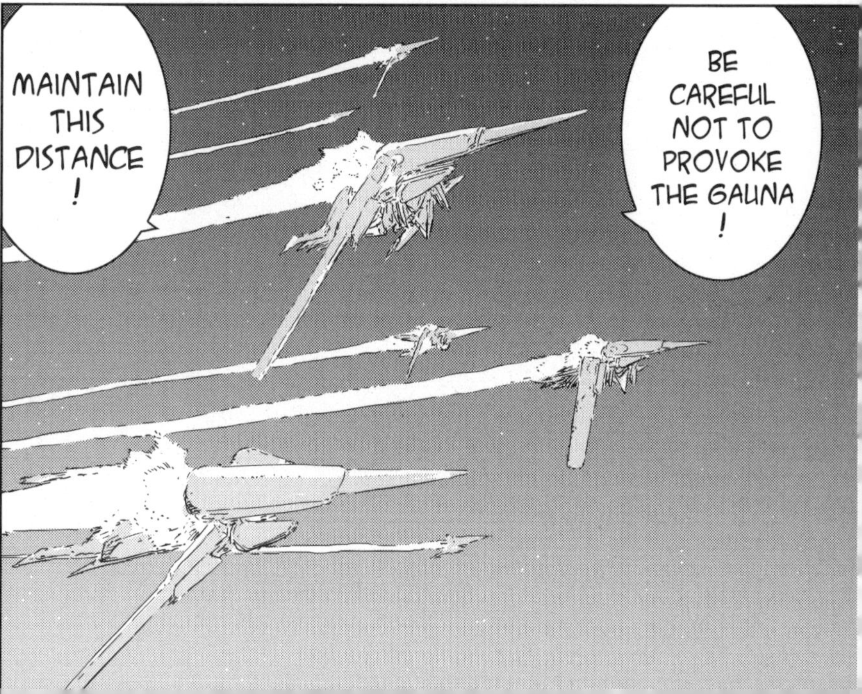
BE CAREFUL NOT TO PROVOKE THE GAUNA!
MAINTAIN THIS DISTANCE!

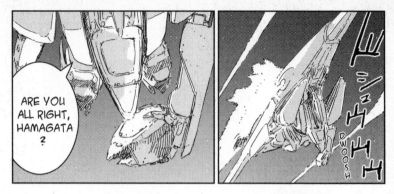

ARE YOU ALL RIGHT, HAMAGATA?

BECAUSE I TOOK OFF LIKE THAT, HASHINE...

Y-YES...

WHAT WAS I THINKING...

...DAMN IT.

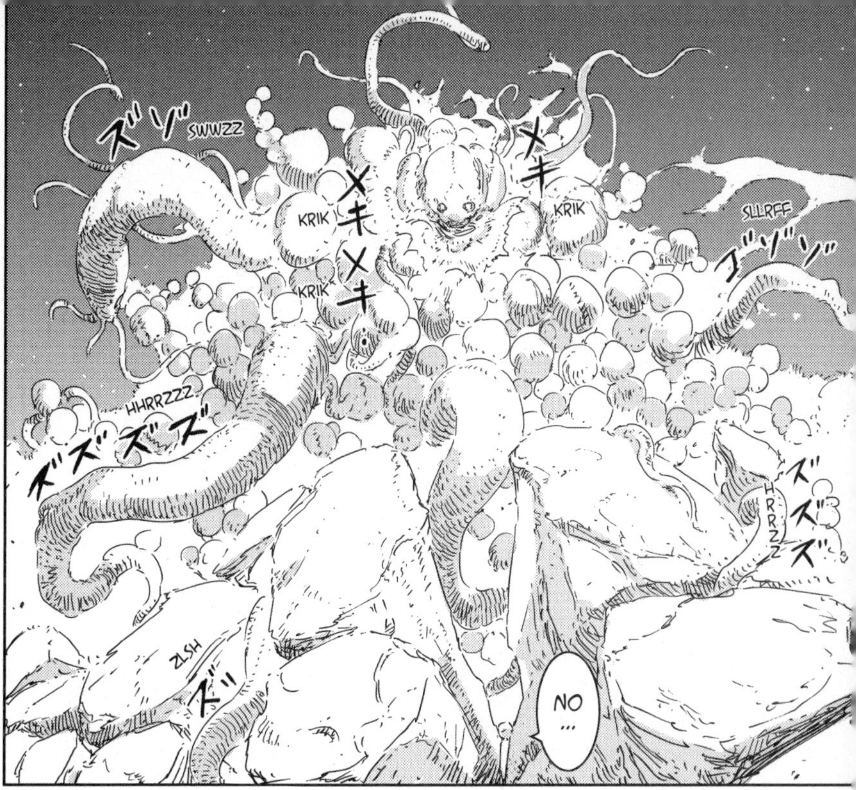
メキ
SLLRFF
ゴゾゾ
KRIK
メキメキ
KRIK
KRIK
ズゾ
SWWZZ
HRRZZZ
ズズズ
HHRRZZZ
ズズズズ
ZLSH
ズ
NO ...

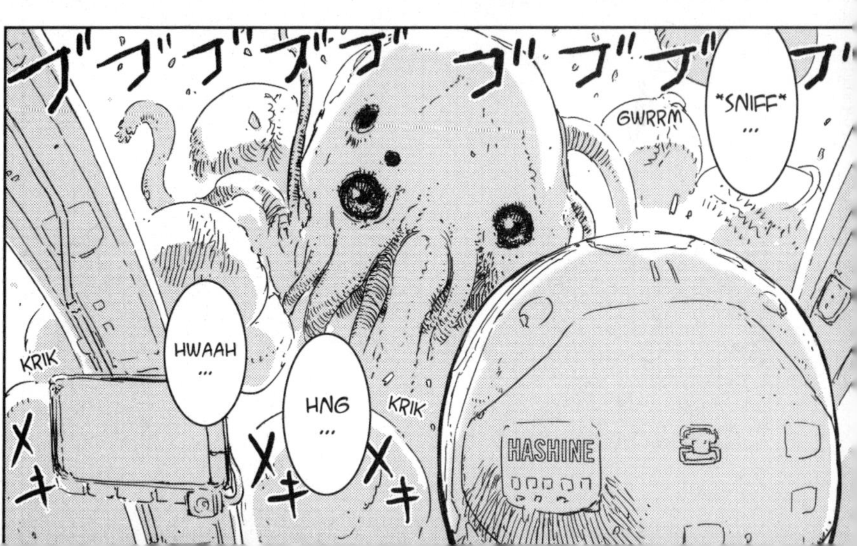
SNIFF ...
GWRRM
HASHINE
KRIK
HNG ...
メキ
HWAAH ...
KRIK
メキ
メキ

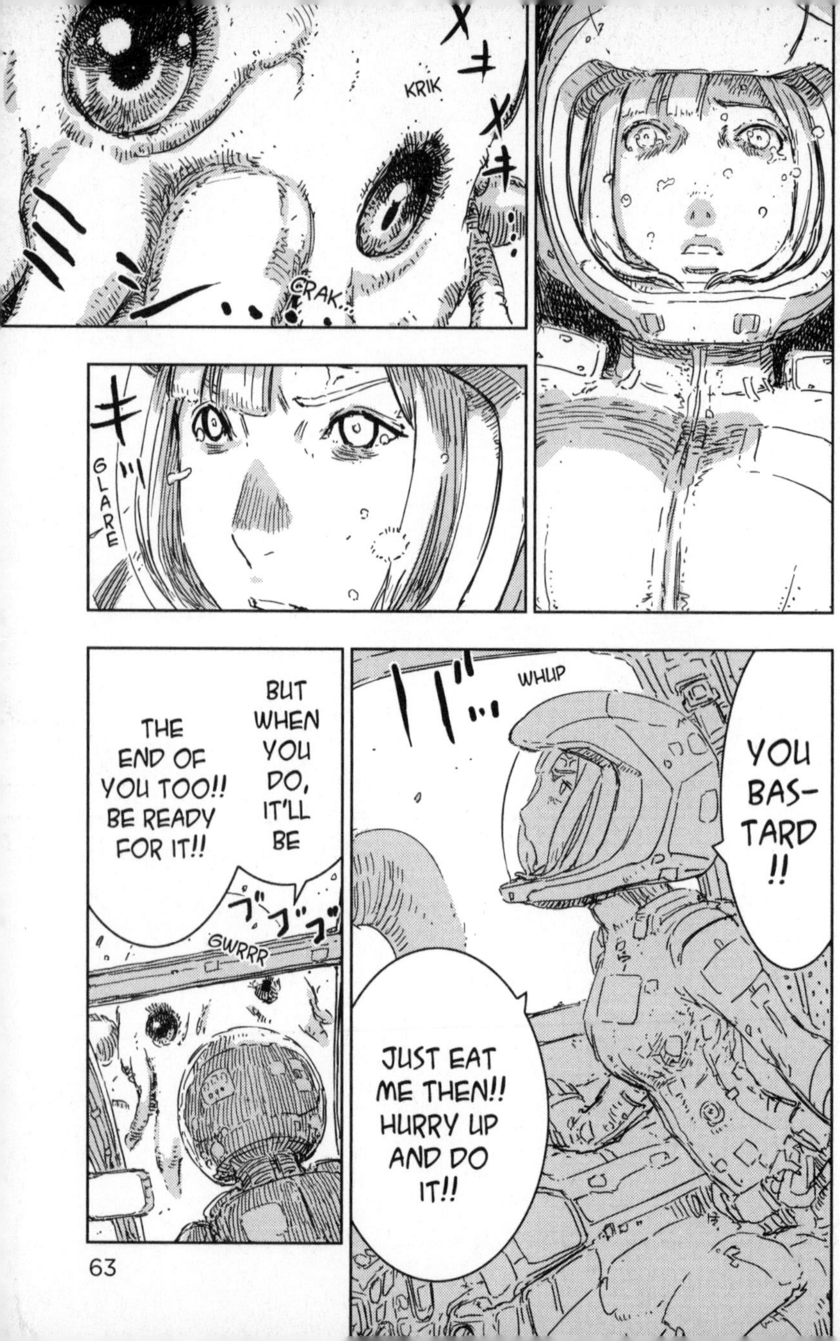
KRIK
CRAK
GLARE
WHUP
YOU BAS-TARD!!
JUST EAT ME THEN!! HURRY UP AND DO IT!!
BUT WHEN YOU DO, IT'LL BE
THE END OF YOU TOO!! BE READY FOR IT!!
GWRRR

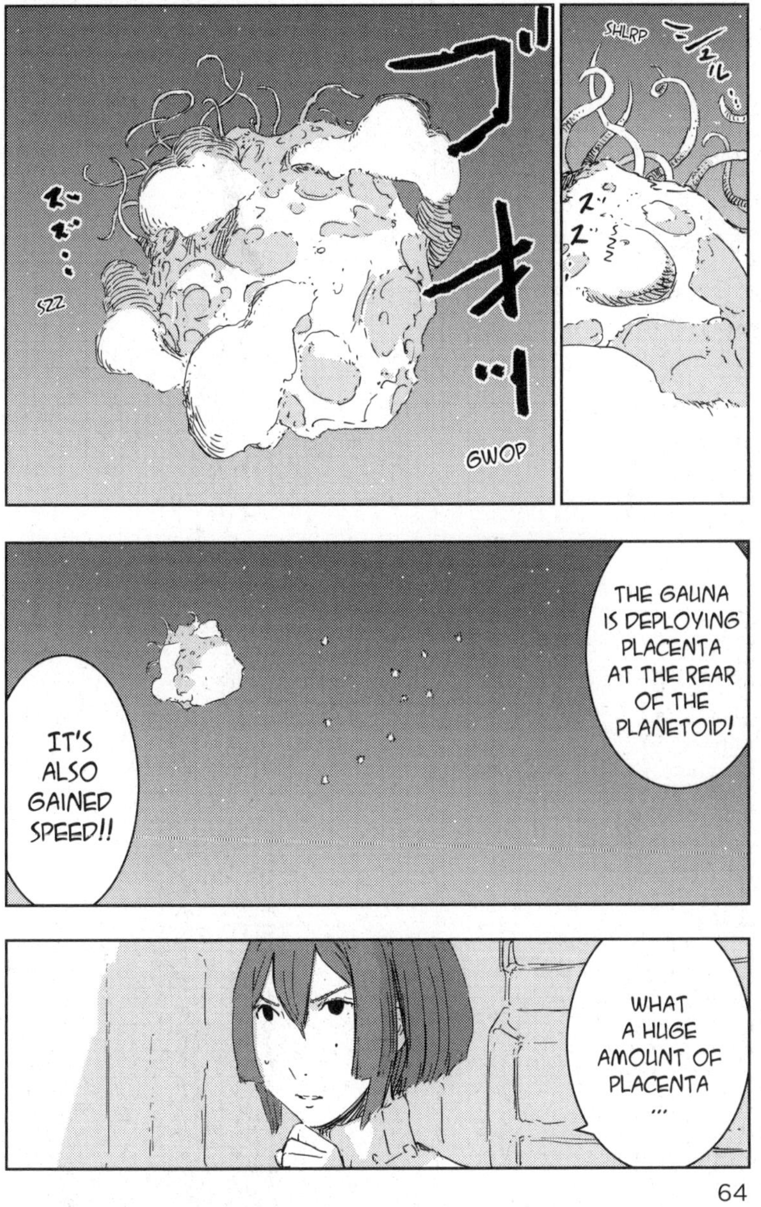
SHLRP
SZZ
GWOP
SZZ
THE GAUNA IS DEPLOYING PLACENTA AT THE REAR OF THE PLANETOID!
IT'S ALSO GAINED SPEED!!
WHAT A HUGE AMOUNT OF PLACENTA ...

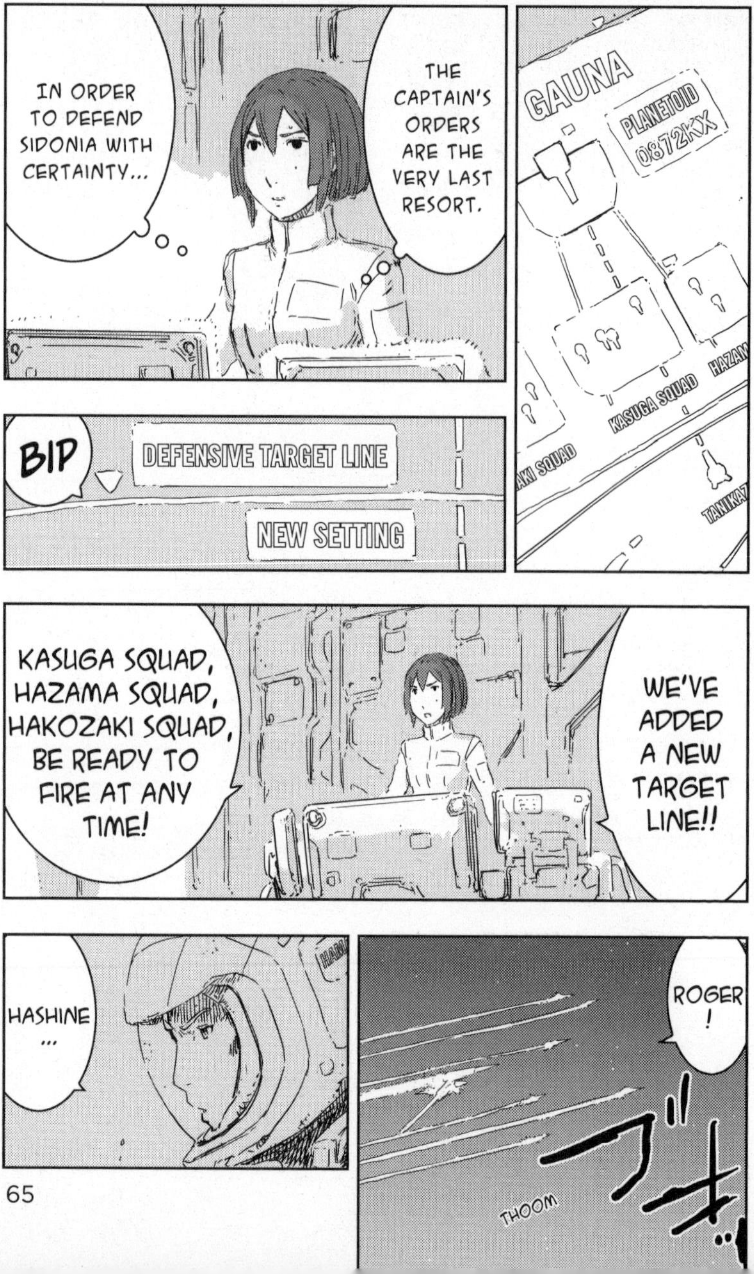
GAUNA
PLANETOID 0872KX
HAZAM
KASUGA SQUAD
AKI SQUAD
TANIKAZ
THE CAPTAIN'S ORDERS ARE THE VERY LAST RESORT.
IN ORDER TO DEFEND SIDONIA WITH CERTAINTY...
DEFENSIVE TARGET LINE
NEW SETTING
BIP
WE'VE ADDED A NEW TARGET LINE!!
KASUGA SQUAD, HAZAMA SQUAD, HAKOZAKI SQUAD, BE READY TO FIRE AT ANY TIME!
ROGER!
THOOM
HASHINE...

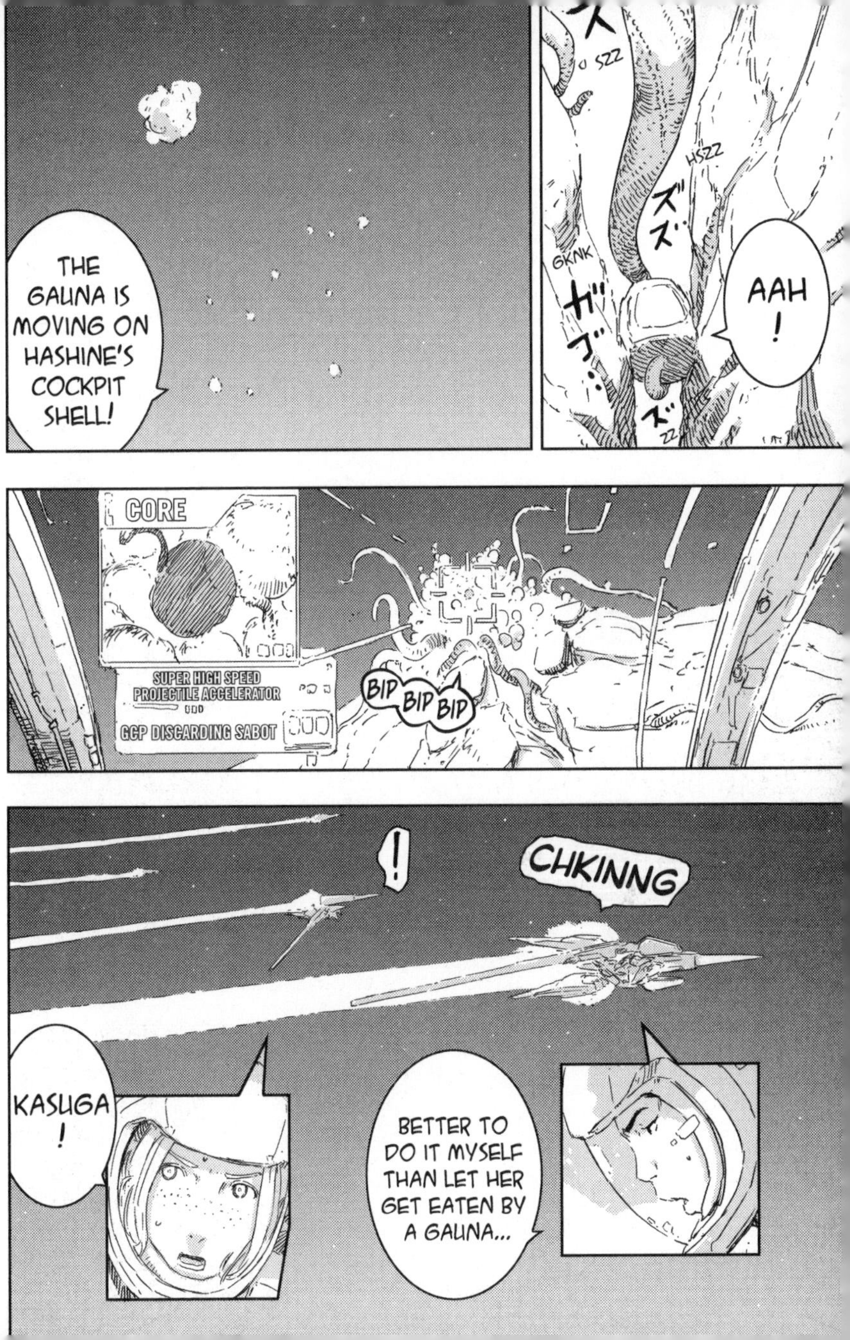

SZZ
HSZZ
ズズ
GKNK
ガゴ…
ズ
ZZ
AAH!
THE GAUNA IS MOVING ON HASHINE'S COCKPIT SHELL!
CORE
SUPER HIGH SPEED PROJECTILE ACCELERATOR
GCP DISCARDING SABOT
BIP BIP BIP
CHKINNG
!
BETTER TO DO IT MYSELF THAN LET HER GET EATEN BY A GAUNA...
KASUGA!

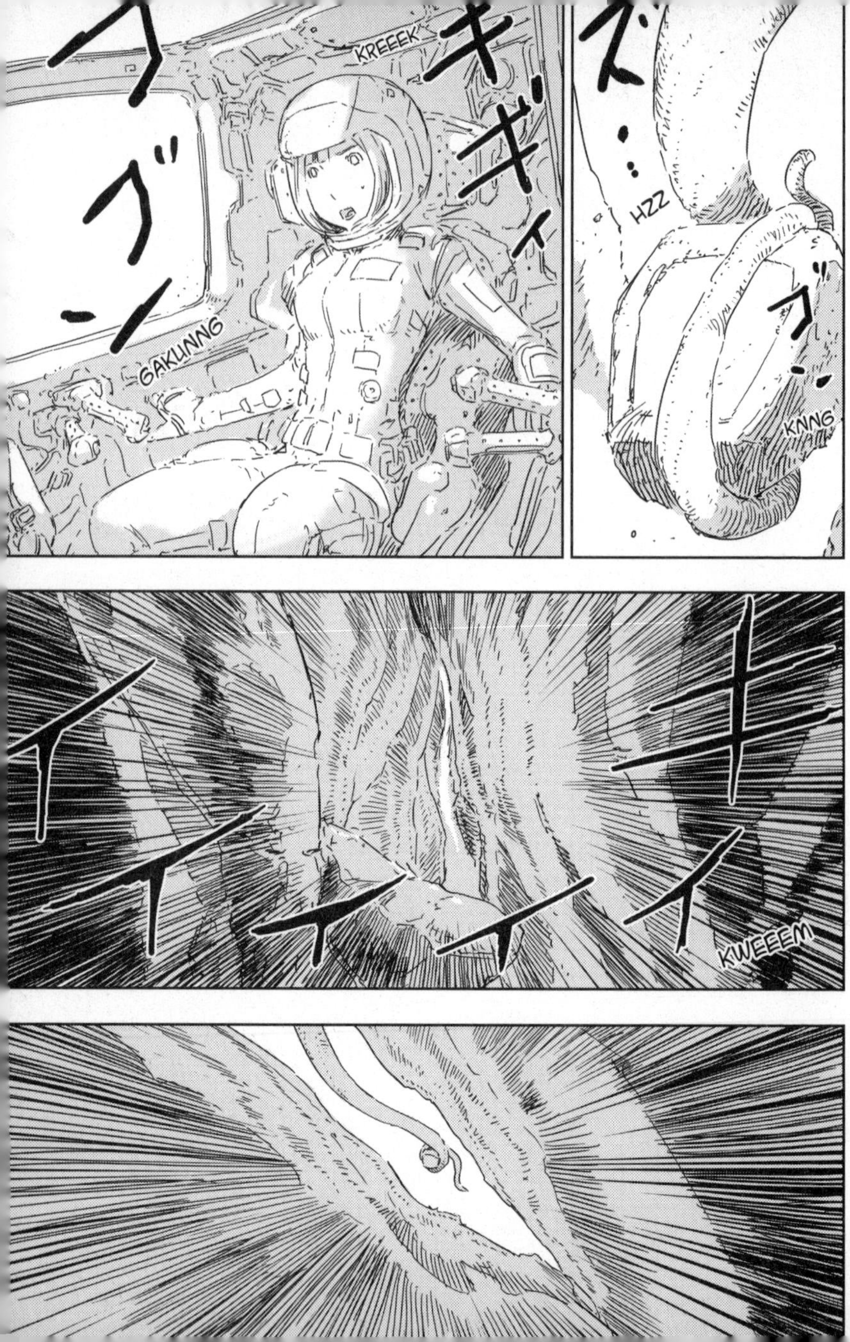
ズ…
HZZ
ゴ…
KNNG
ギギィ
KREEEK
ガグン
GAKUNNG
キイイイイ
KWEEEM

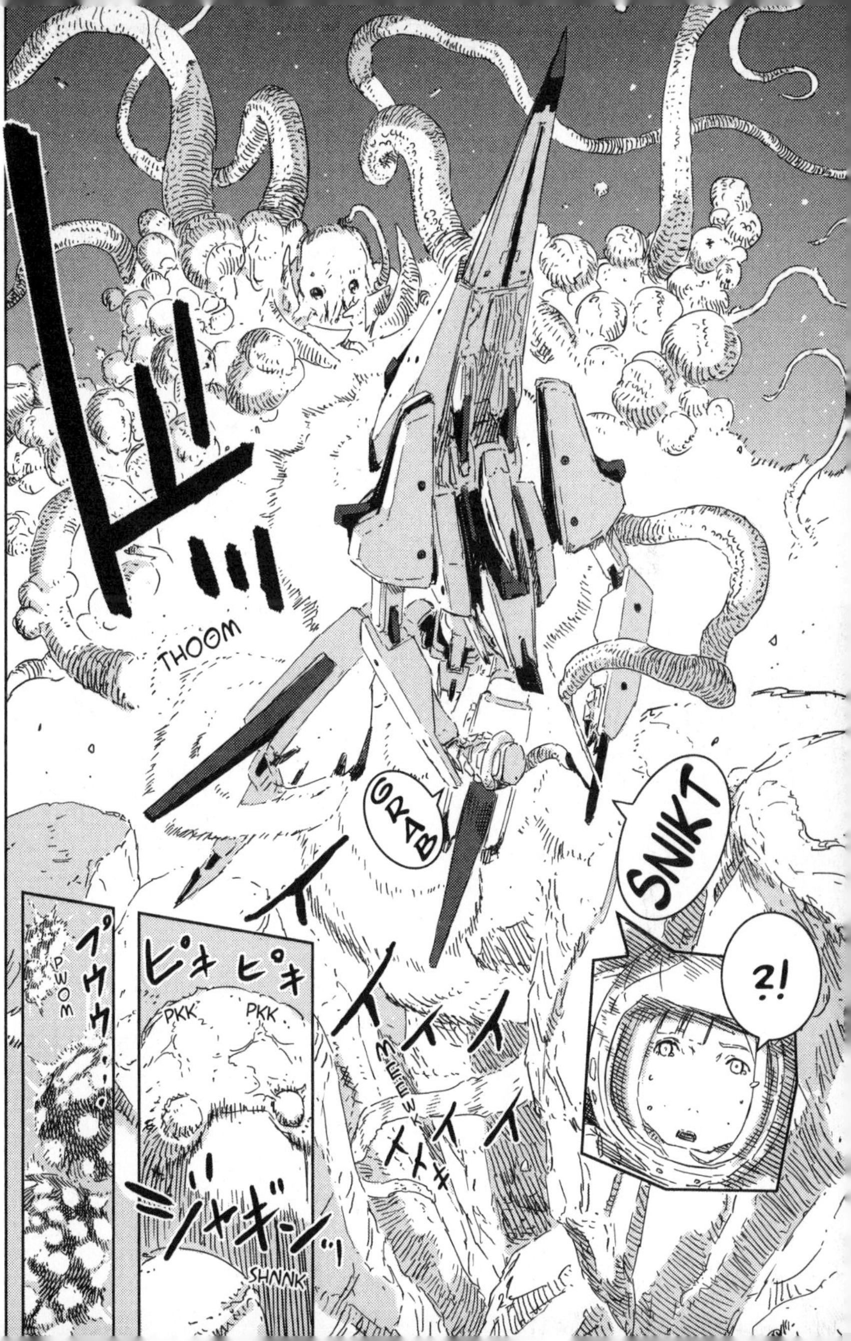

ドッ
THOOM
GRAB
SNIKT
?!
ピキ ピキ
PKK PKK
ジャギーンッ
SHNNK
プウゥ
PWOM

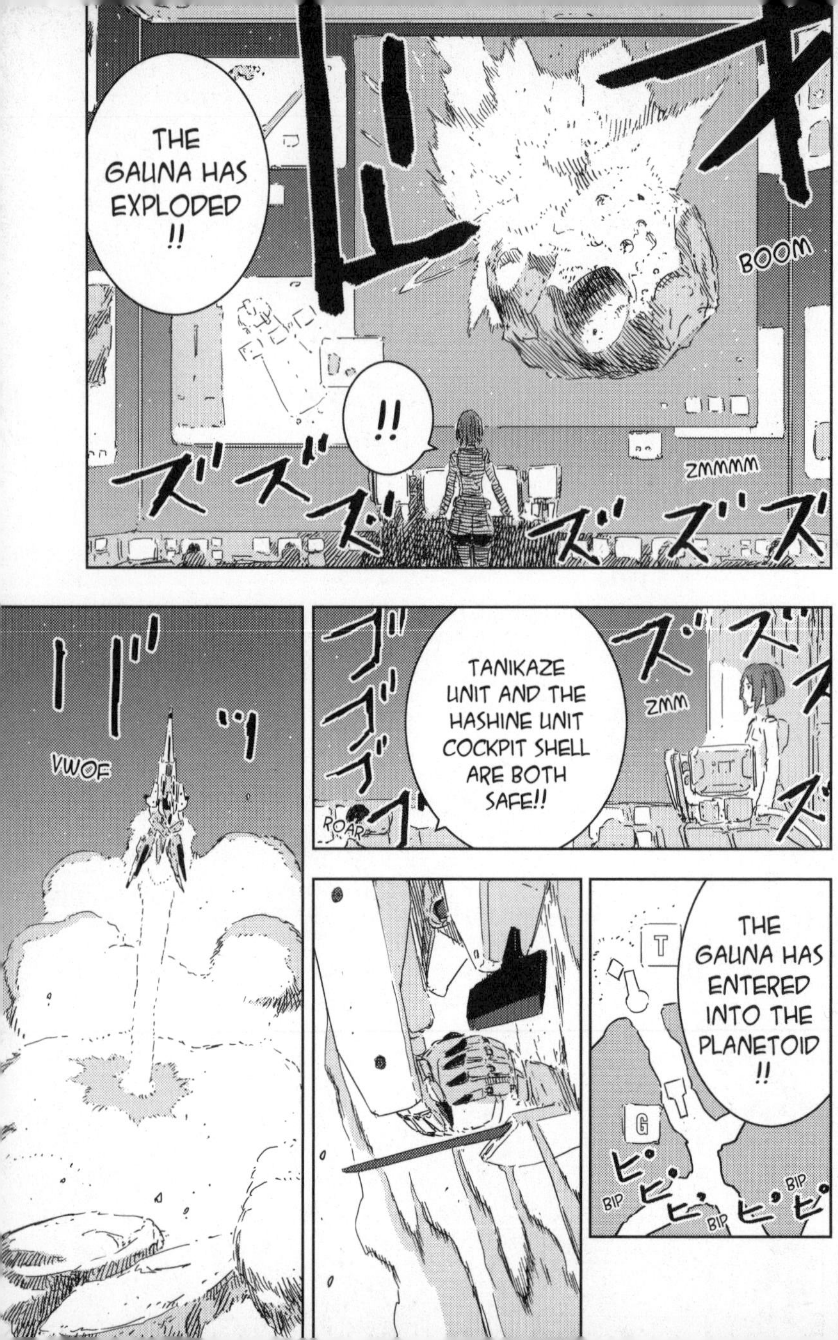
THE GAUNA HAS EXPLODED !!
BOOM
!!
ZMMMM
TANIKAZE UNIT AND THE HASHINE UNIT COCKPIT SHELL ARE BOTH SAFE!!
ZMM
ROAR
THE GAUNA HAS ENTERED INTO THE PLANETOID !!
T
G
BIP
BIP
BIP
VWOF

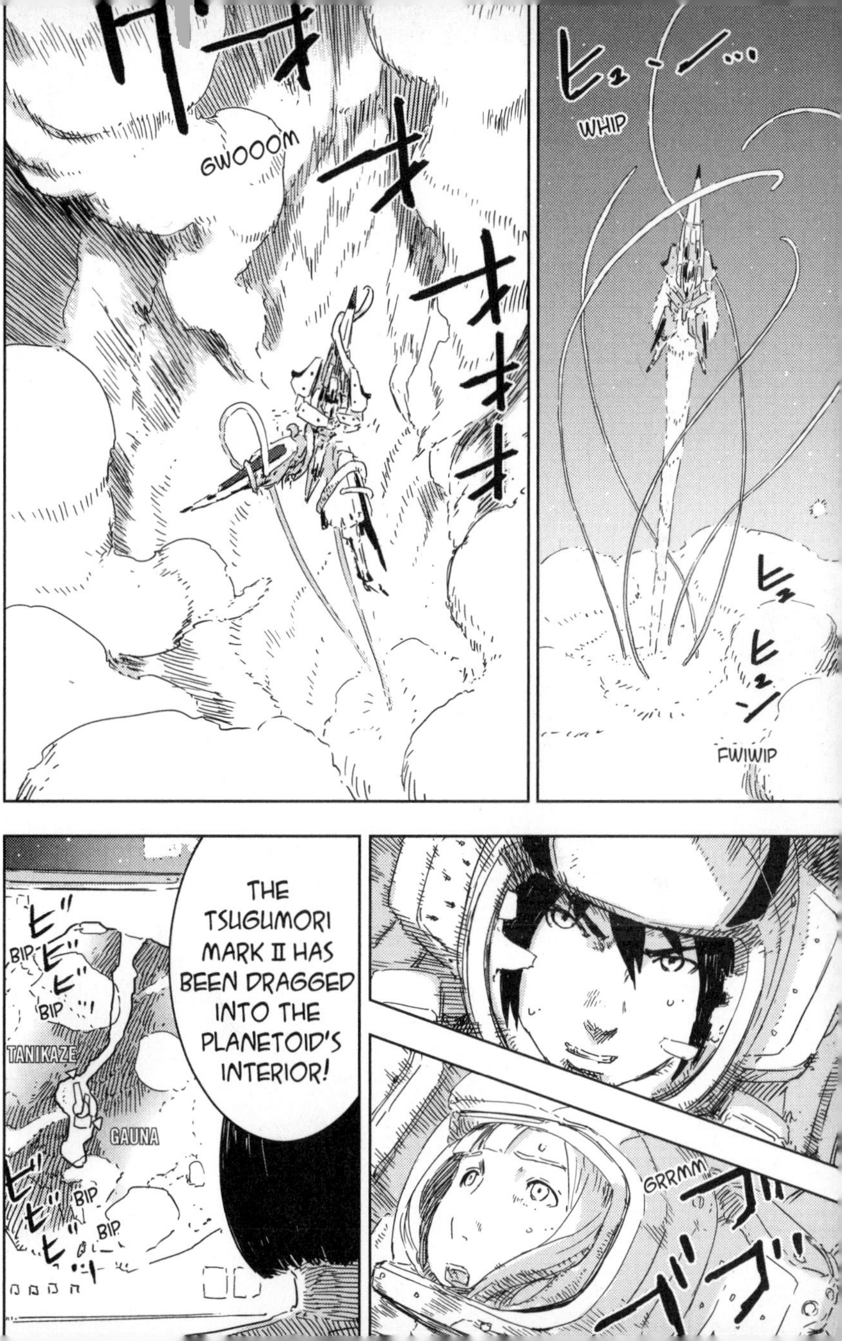
WHIP
FWIWIP
GWOOOM
GRRMM
THE TSUGUMORI MARK II HAS BEEN DRAGGED INTO THE PLANETOID'S INTERIOR!
BIP
BIP
TANIKAZE
GAUNA
BIP
BIP

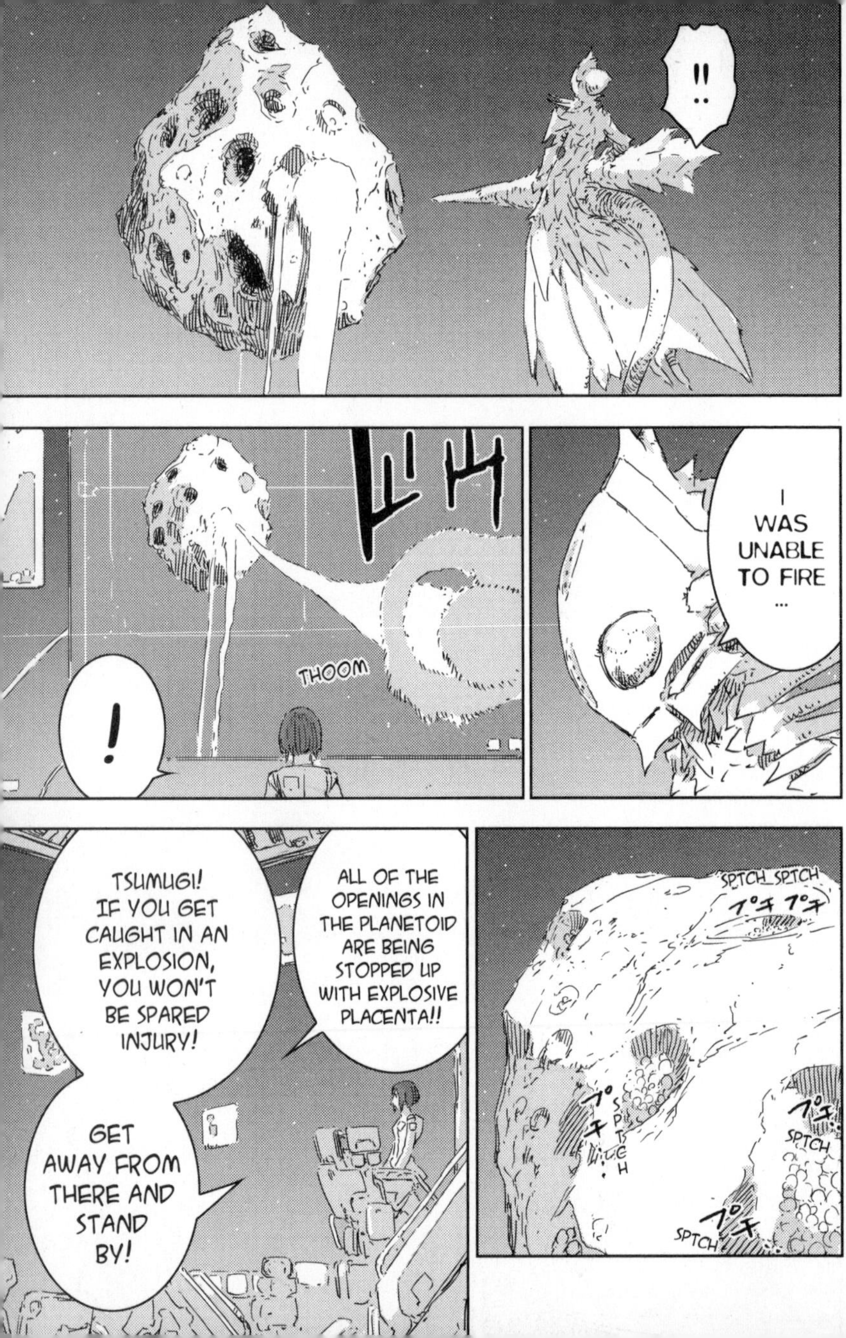
!!
I WAS UNABLE TO FIRE ...
THOOM
!
SPTCH SPTCH
プチ プチ
プチ
SPTCH
プチ
SPTCH
プチ
SPTCH
ALL OF THE OPENINGS IN THE PLANETOID ARE BEING STOPPED UP WITH EXPLOSIVE PLACENTA!!
TSUMUGI! IF YOU GET CAUGHT IN AN EXPLOSION, YOU WON'T BE SPARED INJURY!
GET AWAY FROM THERE AND STAND BY!

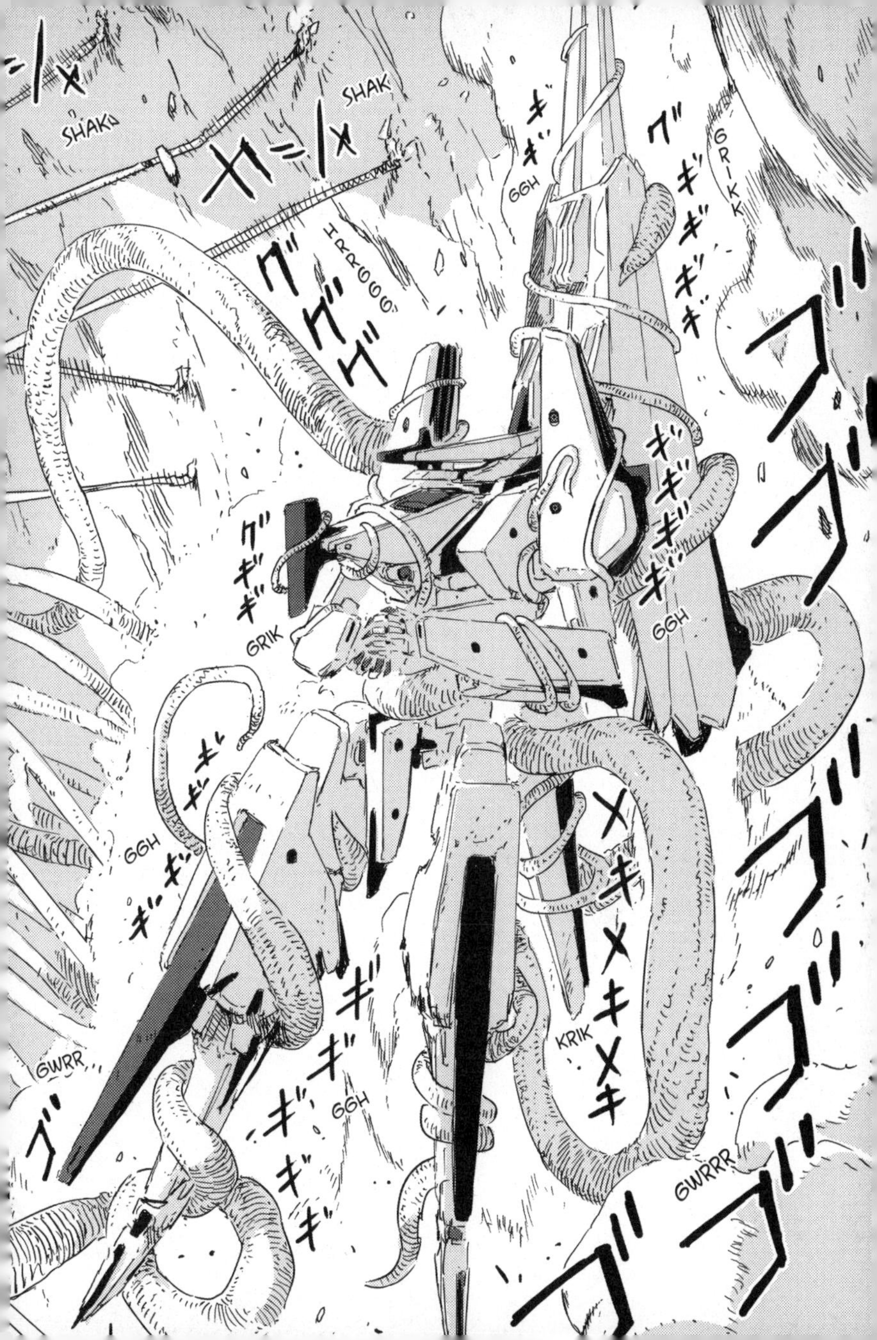
GRIKK
GGH
SHAK
SHAK
IRRRGGG
GGH
GRIK
GGH
KRIK
GWRRR
GGH
GWRR

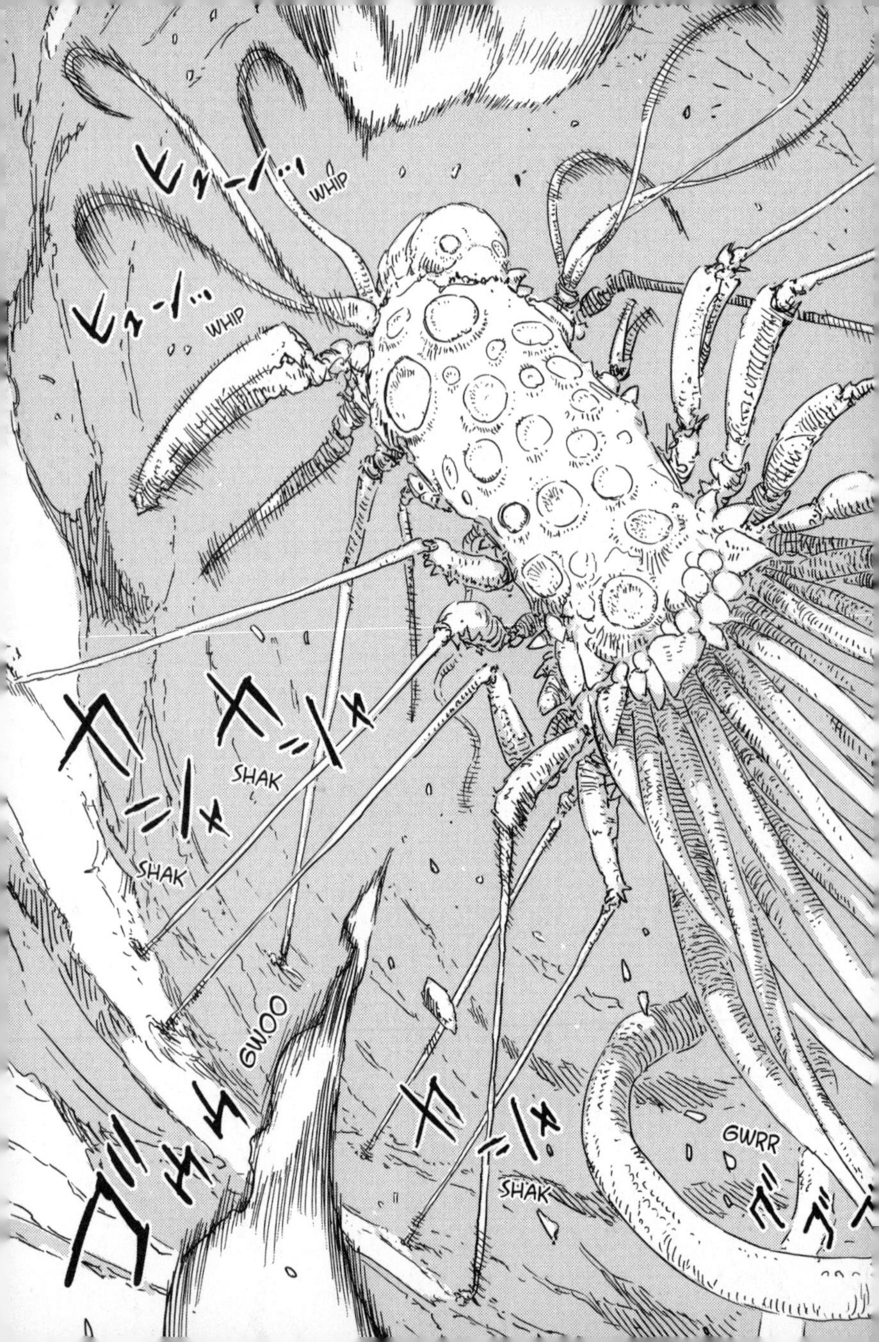
WHIP
WHIP
SHAK
SHAK
GWOO
GWRR
SHAK

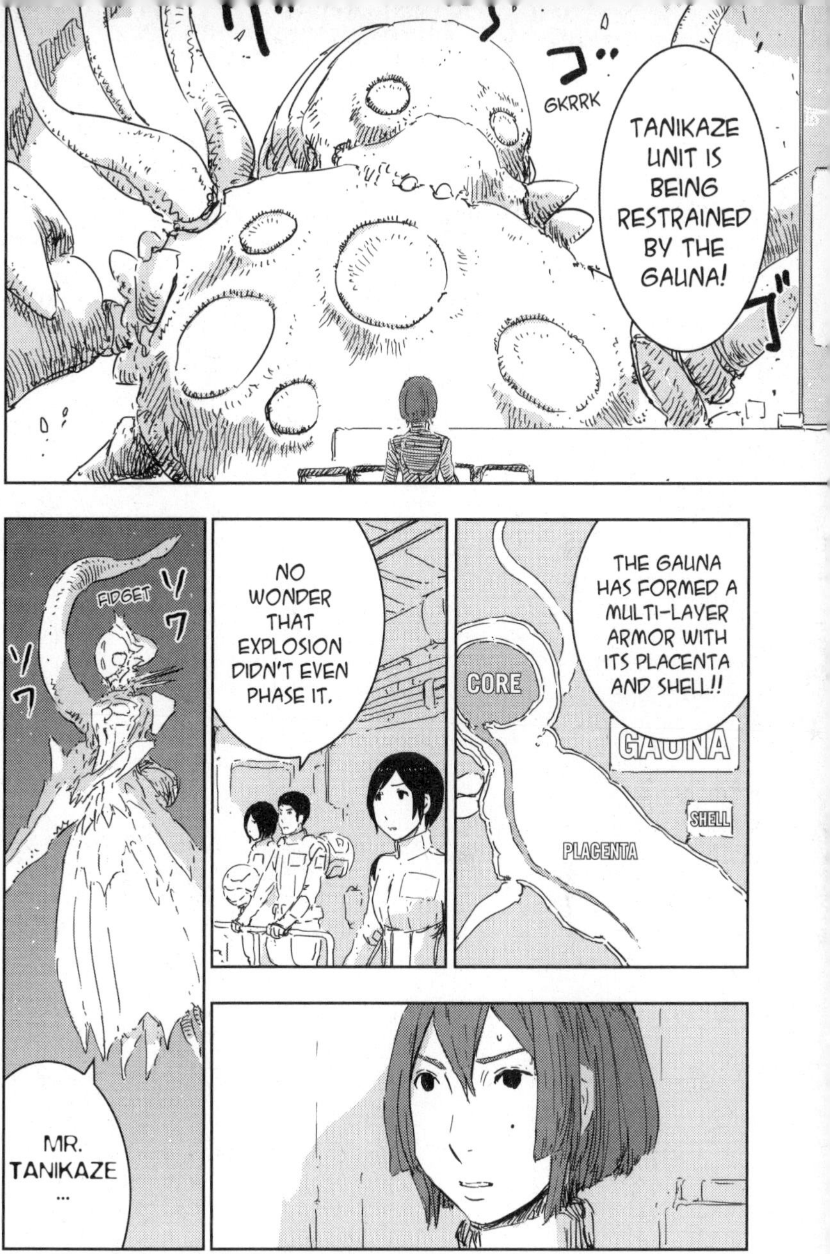
GKRRK
TANIKAZE UNIT IS BEING RESTRAINED BY THE GAUNA!
THE GAUNA HAS FORMED A MULTI-LAYER ARMOR WITH ITS PLACENTA AND SHELL!!
CORE
GAUNA
SHELL
PLACENTA
NO WONDER THAT EXPLOSION DIDN'T EVEN PHASE IT.
FIDGET
MR. TANIKAZE ...

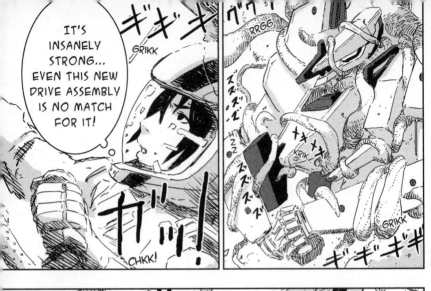

RRGG
HZZ
KRIK
GRIKK
IT'S INSANELY STRONG... EVEN THIS NEW DRIVE ASSEMBLY IS NO MATCH FOR IT!
GRIKK
CHKK!
GWEEM
EEGW
GGT
GWRR
GGT
GKREE
VREE
LEFT ARM MOTIVE POWER LIMIT
VREE
VRE
FWHUPP

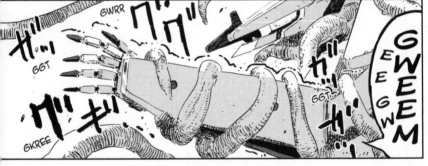

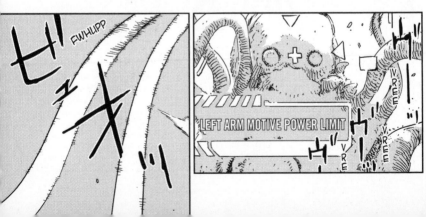

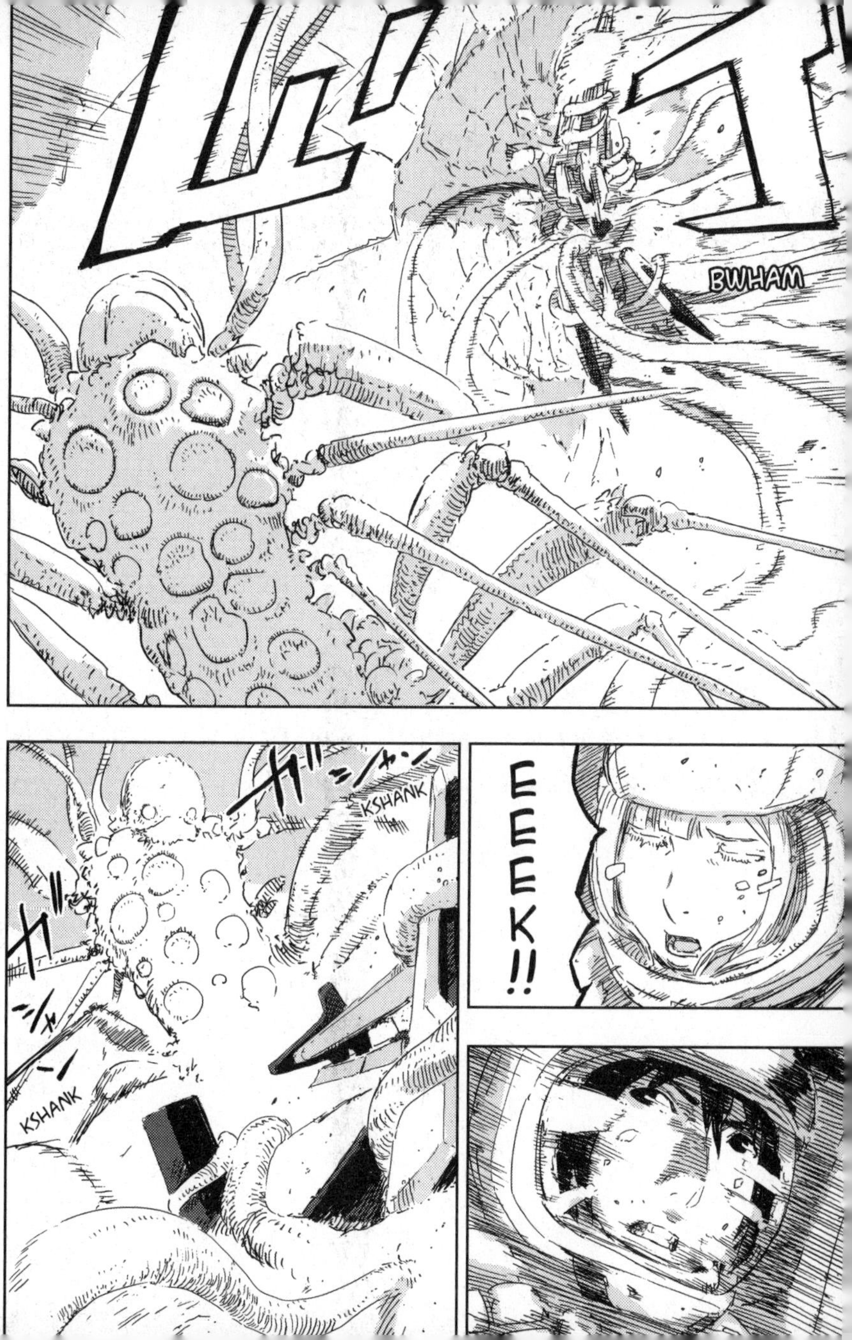
BWHAM
EEEK!!
KSHANK
KSHANK

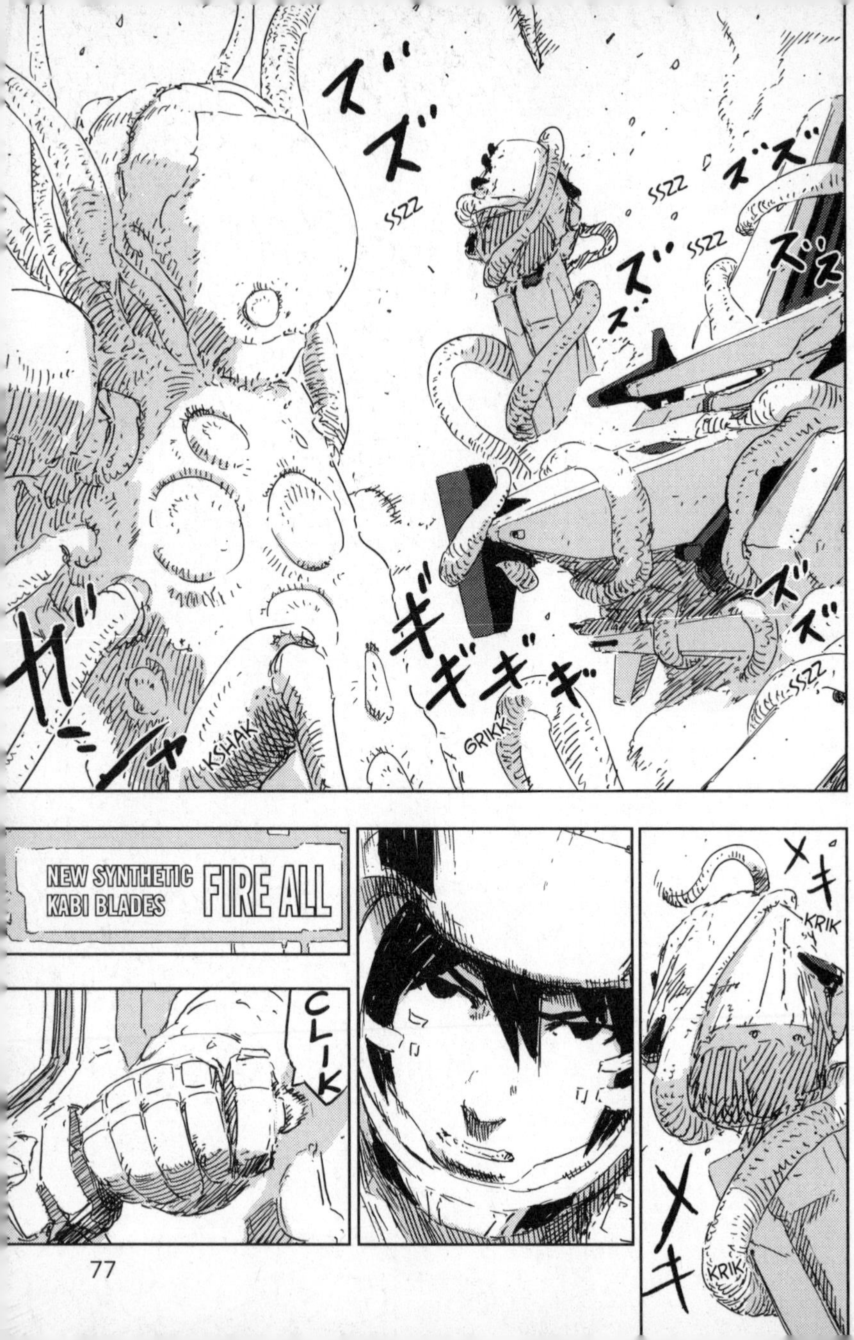
SSZZ
SSZZ
SSZZ
SSZZ
GRIKK
KSHAK
KRIK
KRIK
NEW SYNTHETIC KABI BLADES
FIRE ALL
CLIK

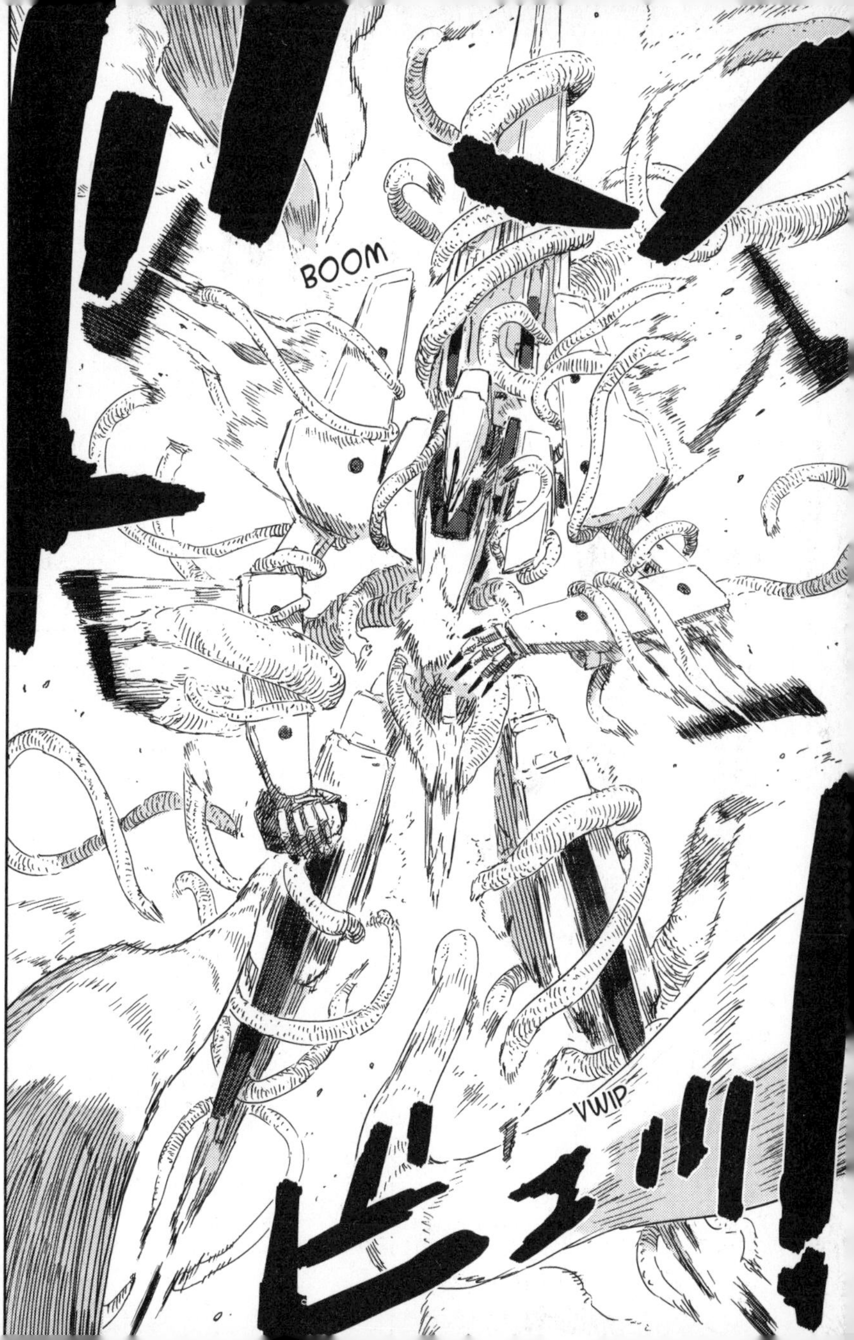
BOOM
VWIP
ビュッ!!

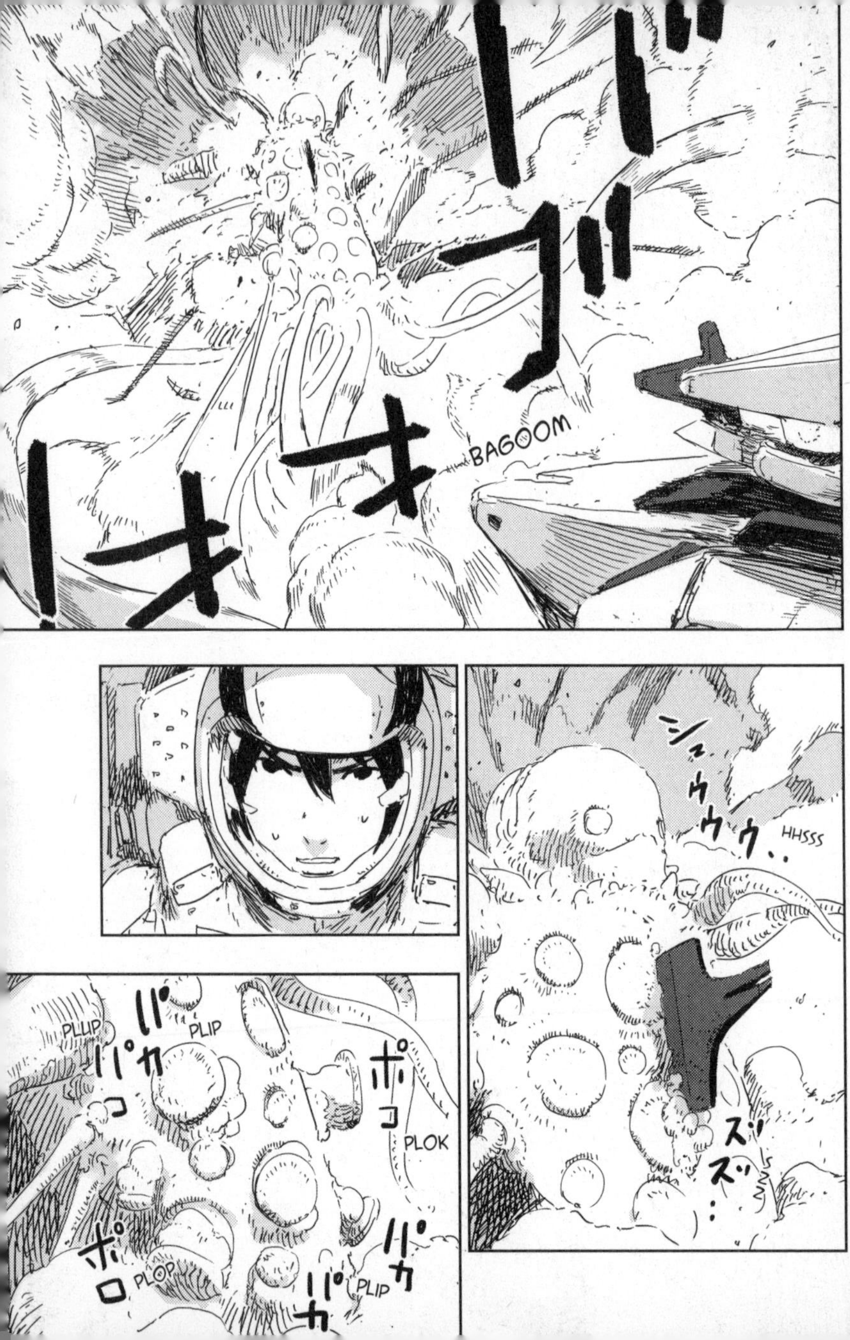
ドブオオ!!
BAGOOM
シュウウウ..
HHSSS
ズズッ..
ポコ
PLOK
パ
PLIP
パカッ
PLUP
パカ
PLIP
パカ
ポロ
PLOP

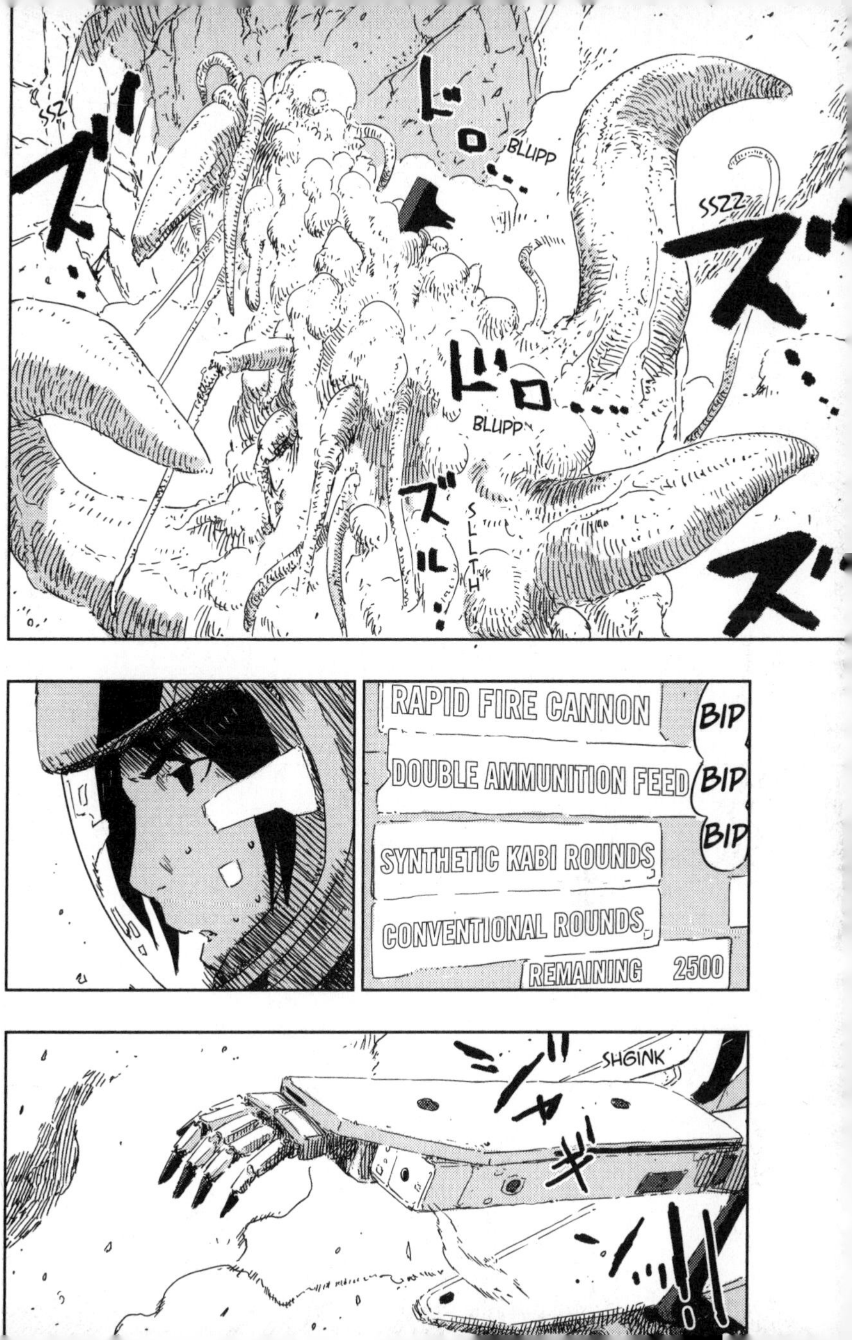
ズ…
SSZZ
ズ
ドロ….
BLUPP
ドロ…
BLUPP
ズル…
SLLTH
ズ…
SSZZ
RAPID FIRE CANNON
BIP
DOUBLE AMMUNITION FEED
BIP
BIP
SYNTHETIC KABI ROUNDS
CONVENTIONAL ROUNDS
REMAINING 2500
ジャギ
SHGINK

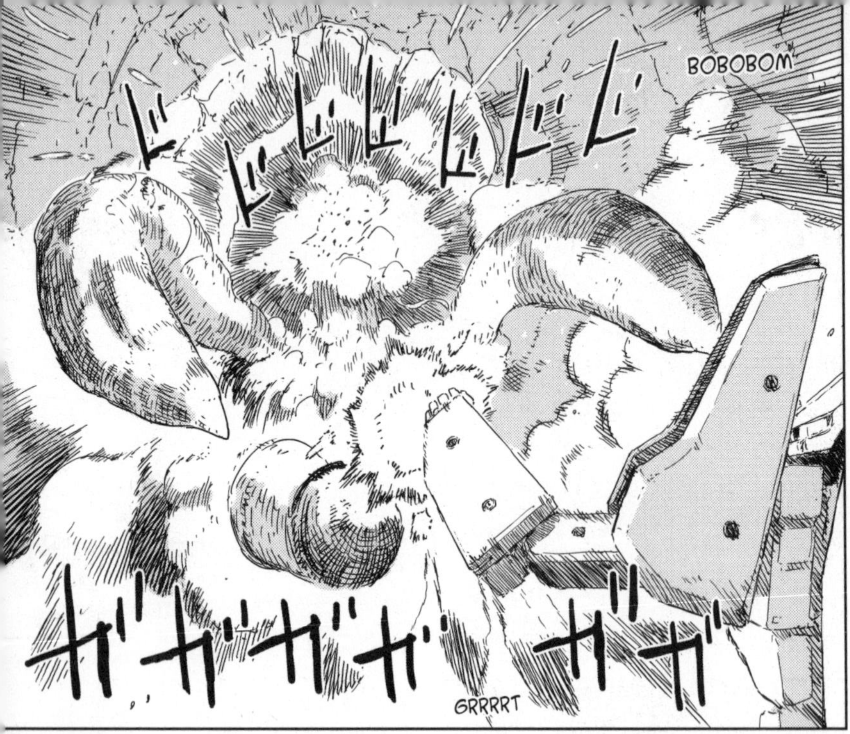
BOBOBOM
GRRRRT

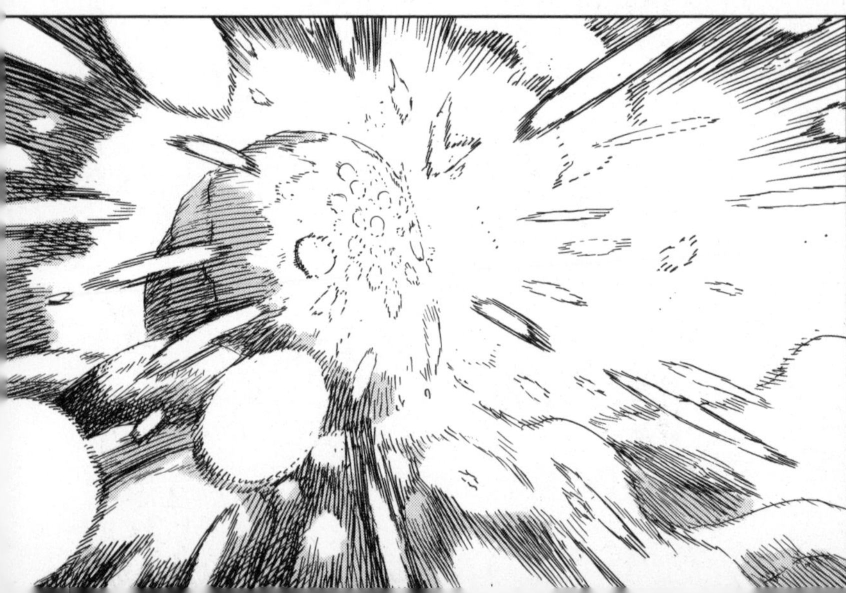

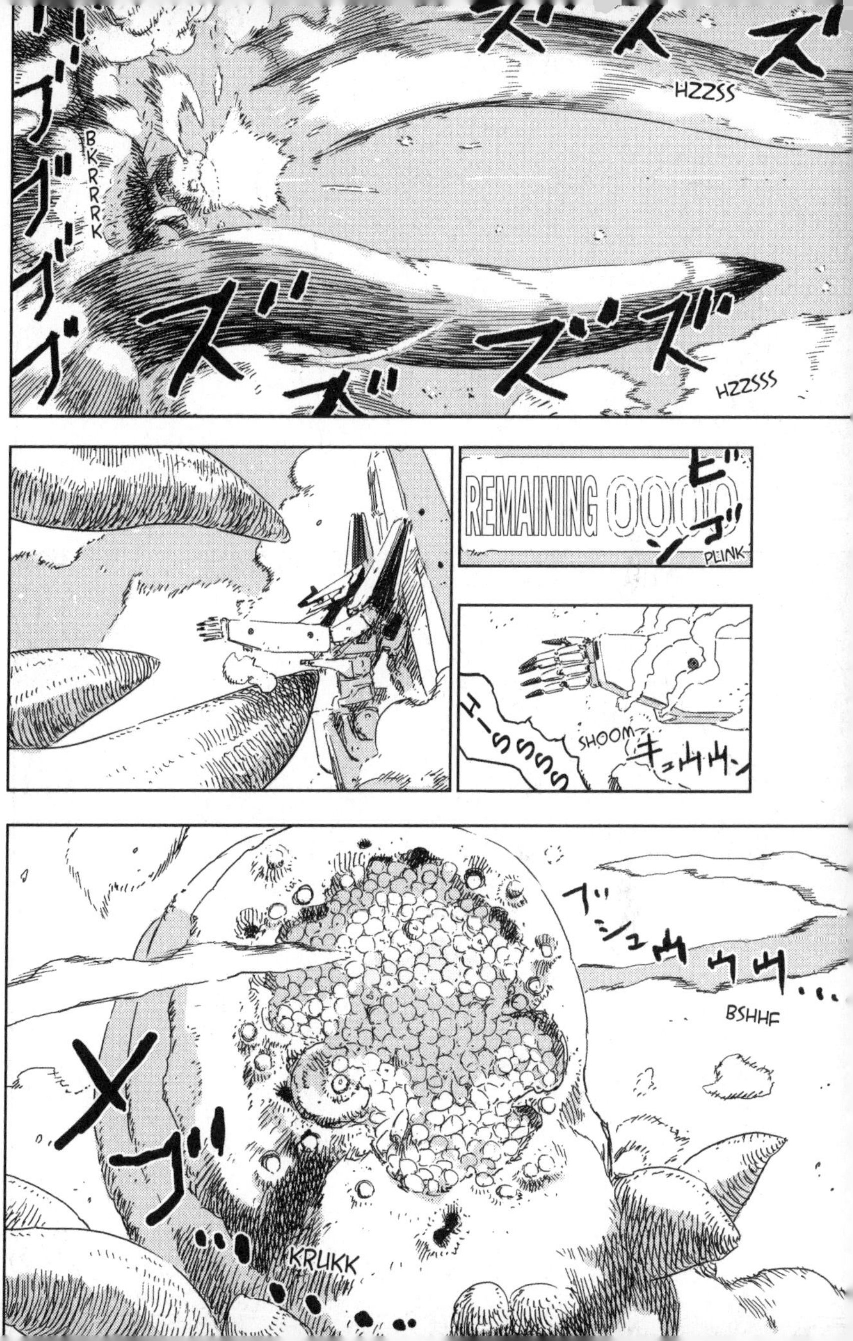
HZZSS
BKRRRK
HZZSSS
REMAINING 0000
PLINK
SHOOM
BSHHF
KRUKK

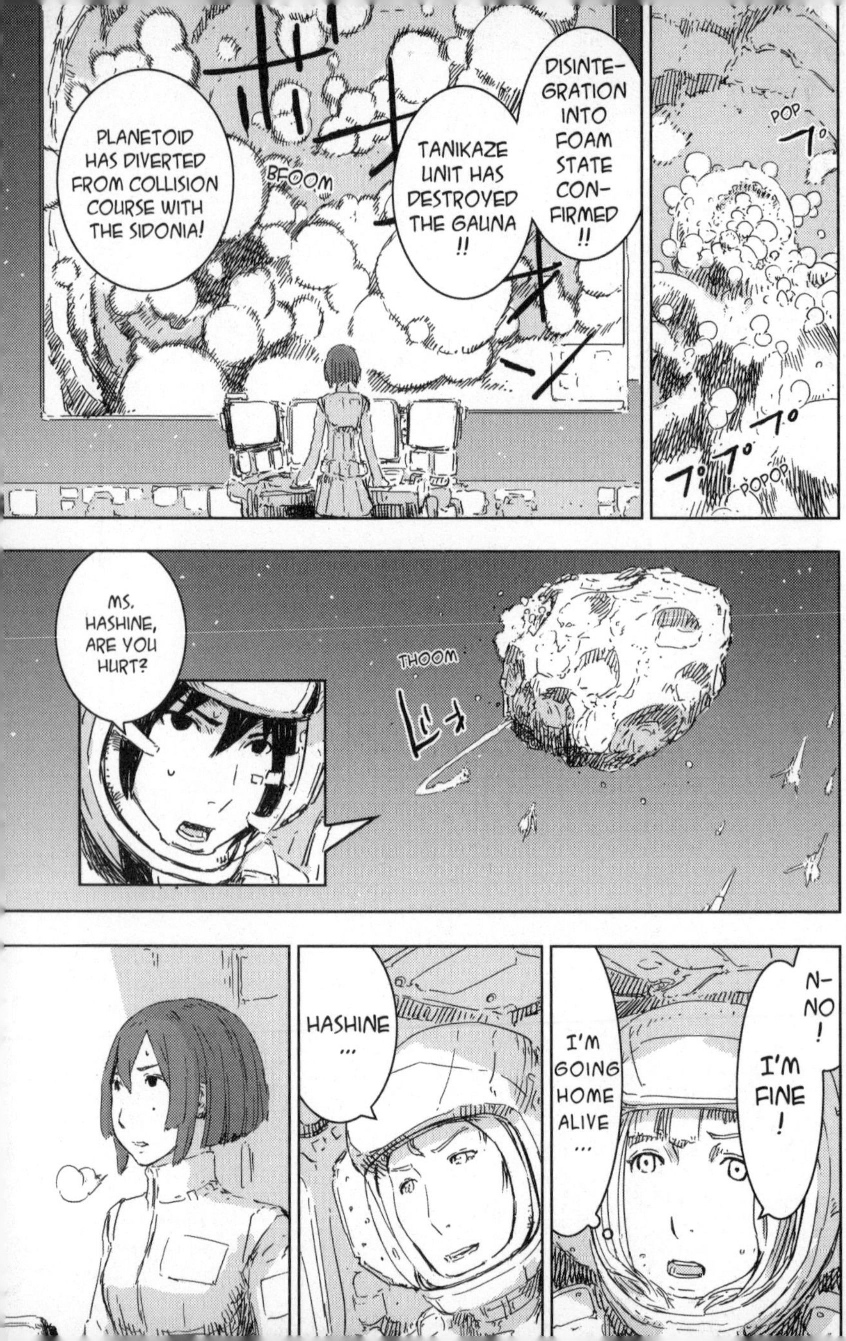
POP
POPOP
DISINTE-GRATION INTO FOAM STATE CON-FIRMED !!
TANIKAZE UNIT HAS DESTROYED THE GAUNA !!
BFOOM
PLANETOID HAS DIVERTED FROM COLLISION COURSE WITH THE SIDONIA!
THOOM
MS. HASHINE, ARE YOU HURT?
N-NO! I'M FINE!
I'M GOING HOME ALIVE...
HASHINE...

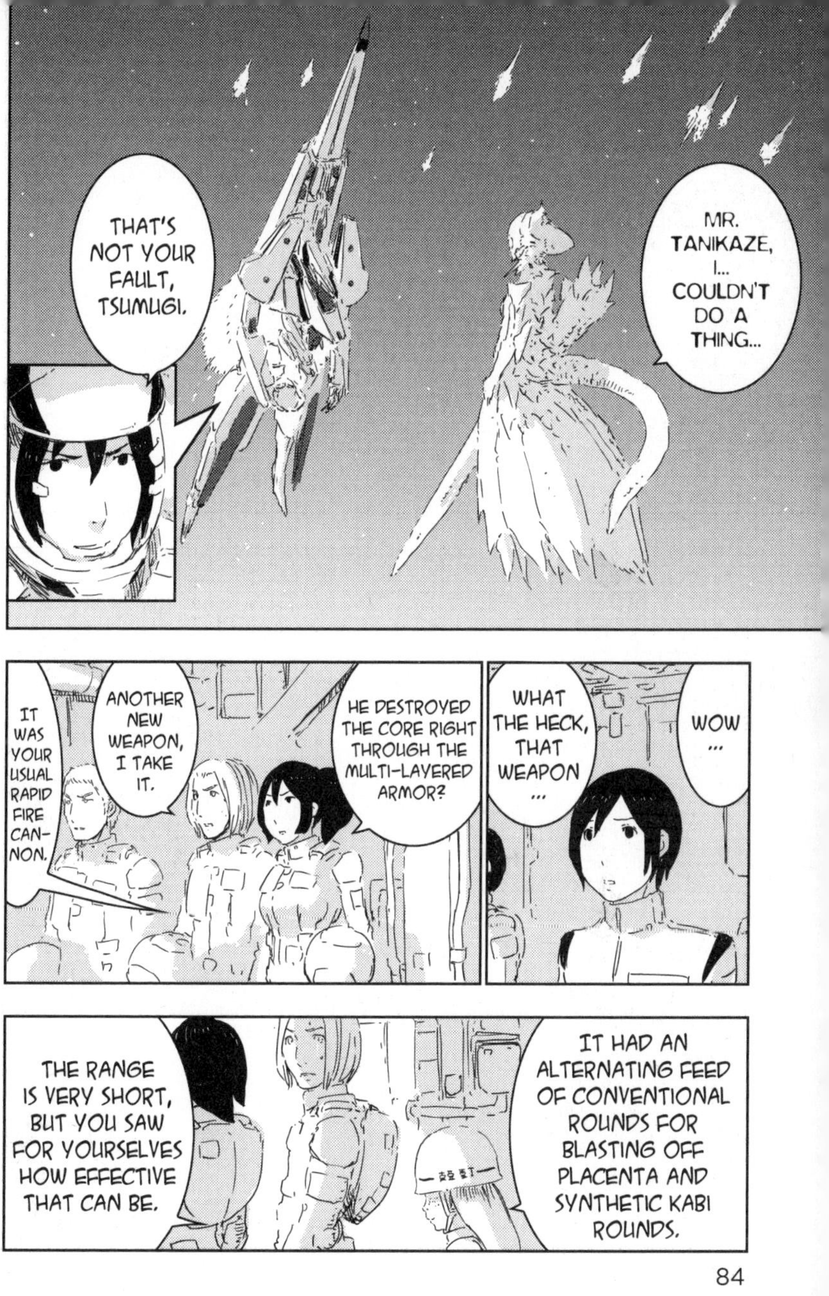
MR. TANIKAZE, I... COULDN'T DO A THING...
THAT'S NOT YOUR FAULT, TSUMUGI.
WOW ...
WHAT THE HECK, THAT WEAPON ...
HE DESTROYED THE CORE RIGHT THROUGH THE MULTI-LAYERED ARMOR?
ANOTHER NEW WEAPON, I TAKE IT.
IT WAS YOUR USUAL RAPID FIRE CAN-NON.
IT HAD AN ALTERNATING FEED OF CONVENTIONAL ROUNDS FOR BLASTING OFF PLACENTA AND SYNTHETIC KABI ROUNDS.
THE RANGE IS VERY SHORT, BUT YOU SAW FOR YOURSELVES HOW EFFECTIVE THAT CAN BE.

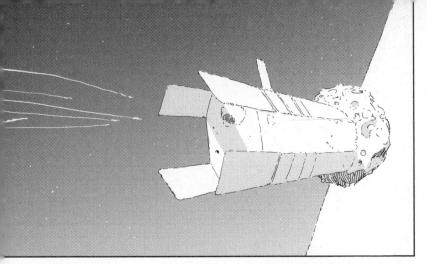

そ〜〜……

SLINK

ゴ'ゴ'ゞゞゞゞ

GRMM

SERIOUSLY?!

ALMOST ALL THE ANTI-GAUNA BLADES ARE GONE...

WHOLE HOG?! TANI-KAZE!!

ACK!

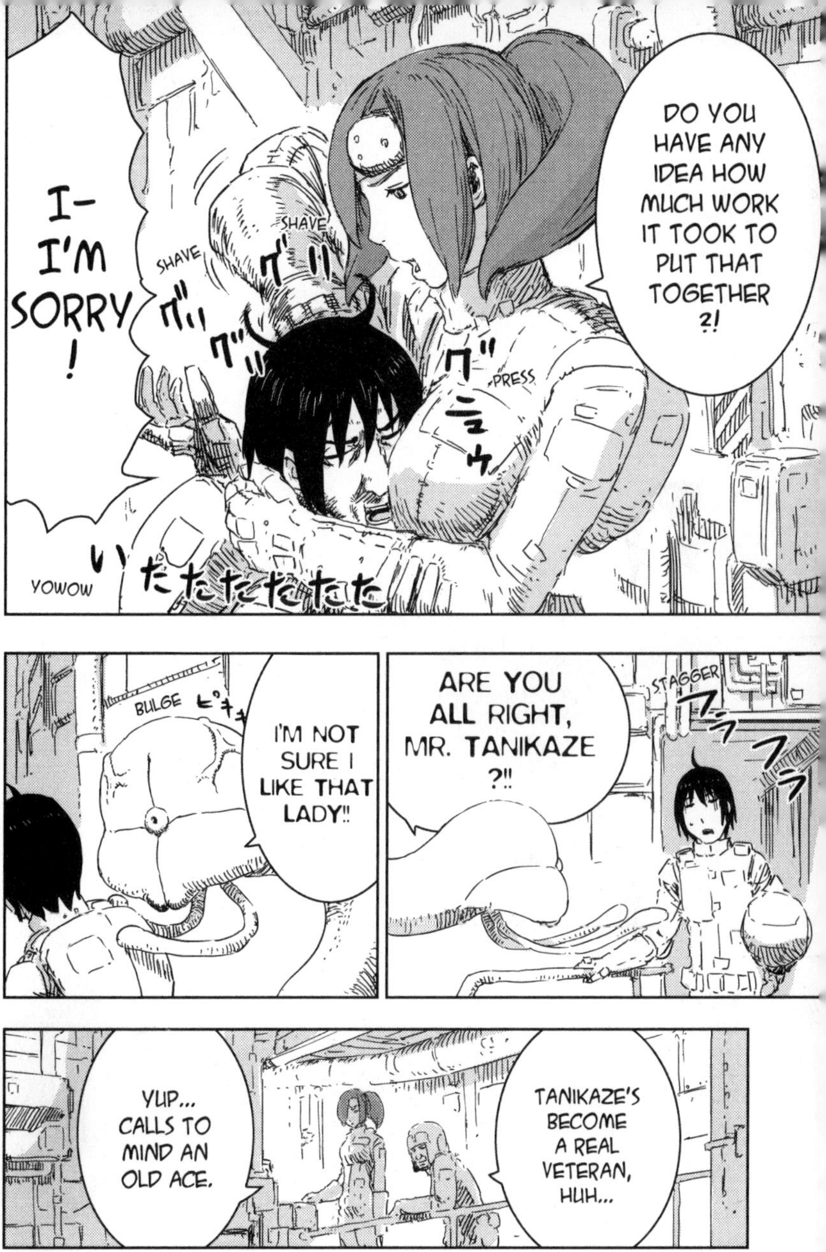

DO YOU HAVE ANY IDEA HOW MUCH WORK IT TOOK TO PUT THAT TOGETHER ?!
PRESS
SHAVE
SHAVE
I– I'M SORRY !
YOWOW
いだたたたたた
STAGGER
ARE YOU ALL RIGHT, MR. TANIKAZE ?!!
I'M NOT SURE I LIKE THAT LADY!!
BULGE
TANIKAZE'S BECOME A REAL VETERAN, HUH...
YUP... CALLS TO MIND AN OLD ACE.

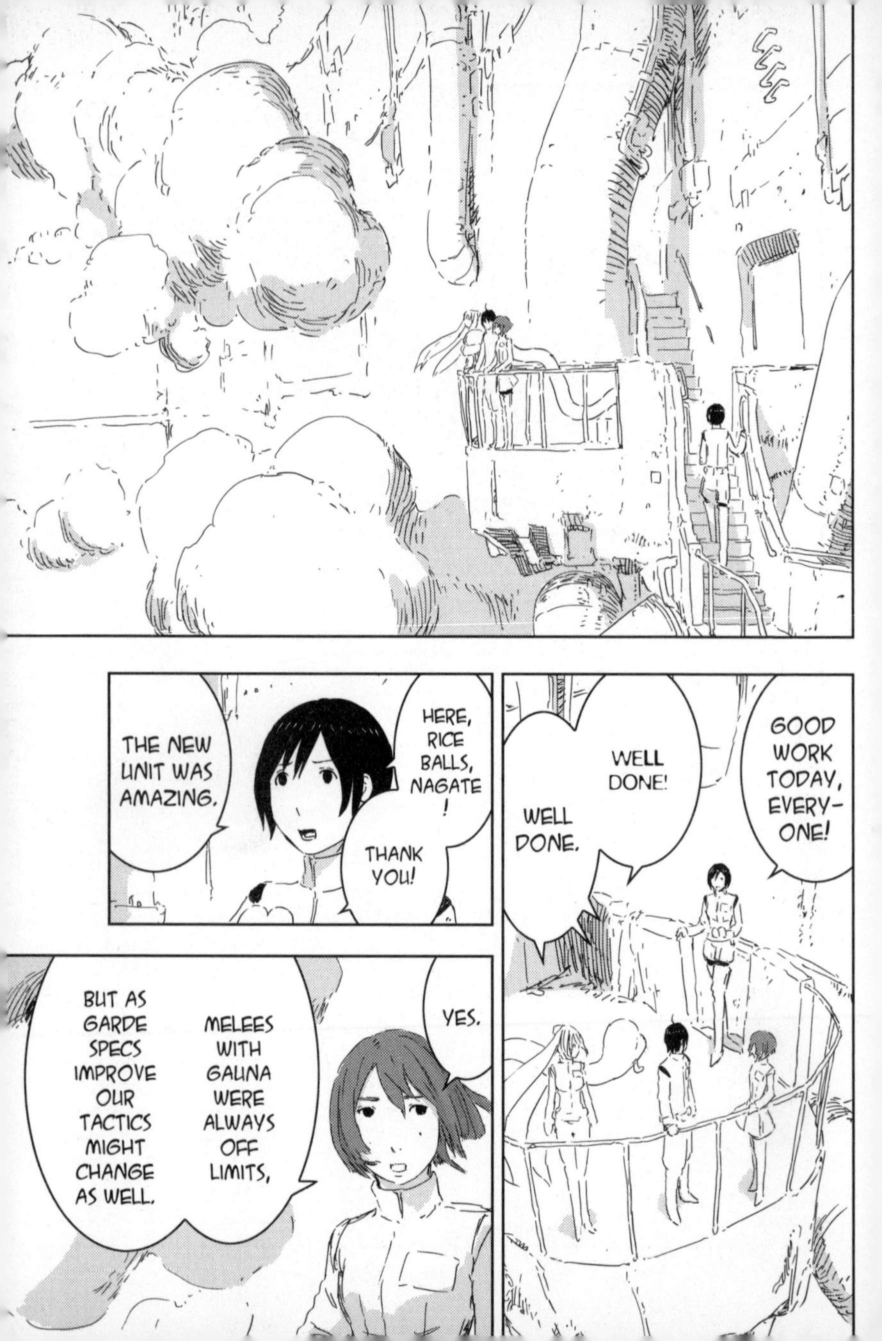
GOOD WORK TODAY, EVERY-ONE!
WELL DONE!
WELL DONE.
HERE, RICE BALLS, NAGATE!
THANK YOU!
THE NEW UNIT WAS AMAZING.
YES.
MELEES WITH GAUNA WERE ALWAYS OFF LIMITS,
BUT AS GARDE SPECS IMPROVE OUR TACTICS MIGHT CHANGE AS WELL.

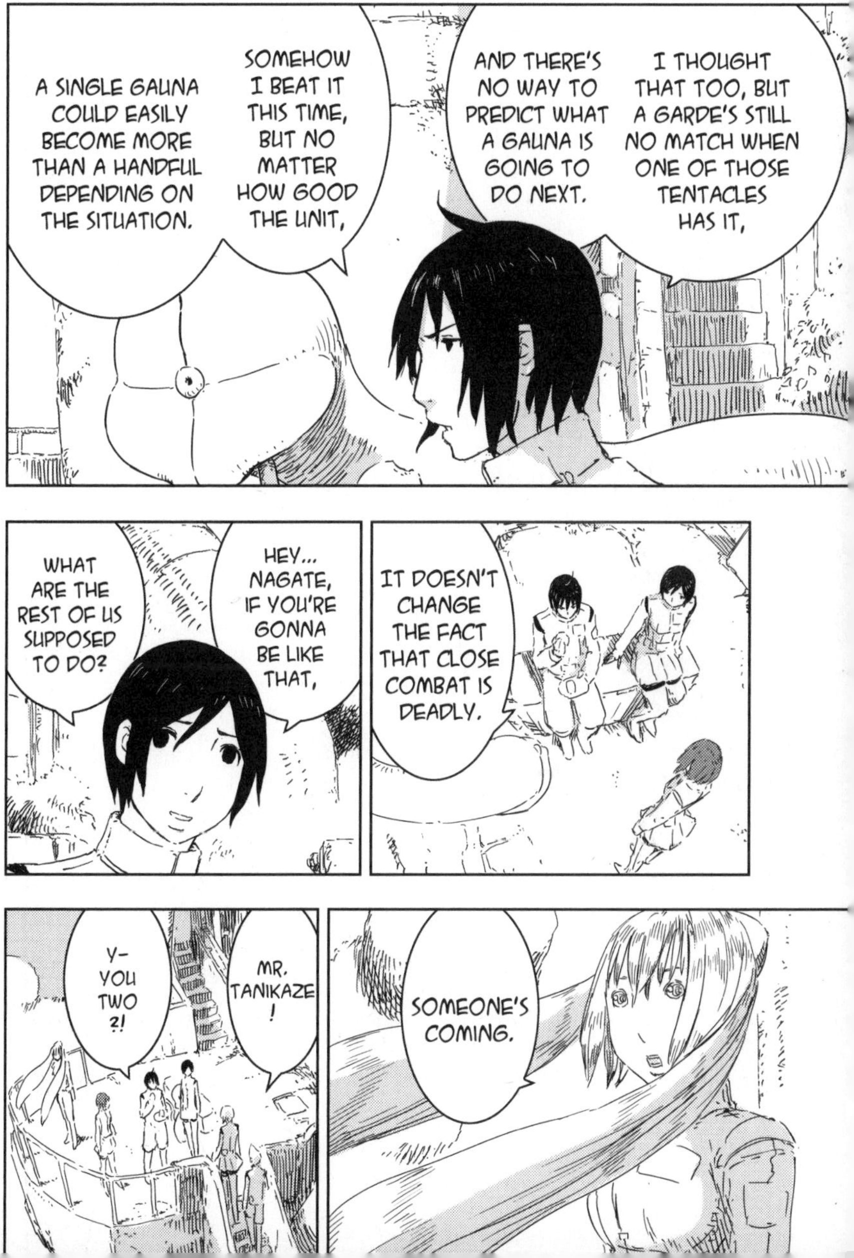
I THOUGHT THAT TOO, BUT A GARDE'S STILL NO MATCH WHEN ONE OF THOSE TENTACLES HAS IT,
AND THERE'S NO WAY TO PREDICT WHAT A GAUNA IS GOING TO DO NEXT.
SOMEHOW I BEAT IT THIS TIME, BUT NO MATTER HOW GOOD THE UNIT,
A SINGLE GAUNA COULD EASILY BECOME MORE THAN A HANDFUL DEPENDING ON THE SITUATION.
IT DOESN'T CHANGE THE FACT THAT CLOSE COMBAT IS DEADLY.
HEY... NAGATE, IF YOU'RE GONNA BE LIKE THAT,
WHAT ARE THE REST OF US SUPPOSED TO DO?
SOMEONE'S COMING.
MR. TANIKAZE!
Y-YOU TWO?!

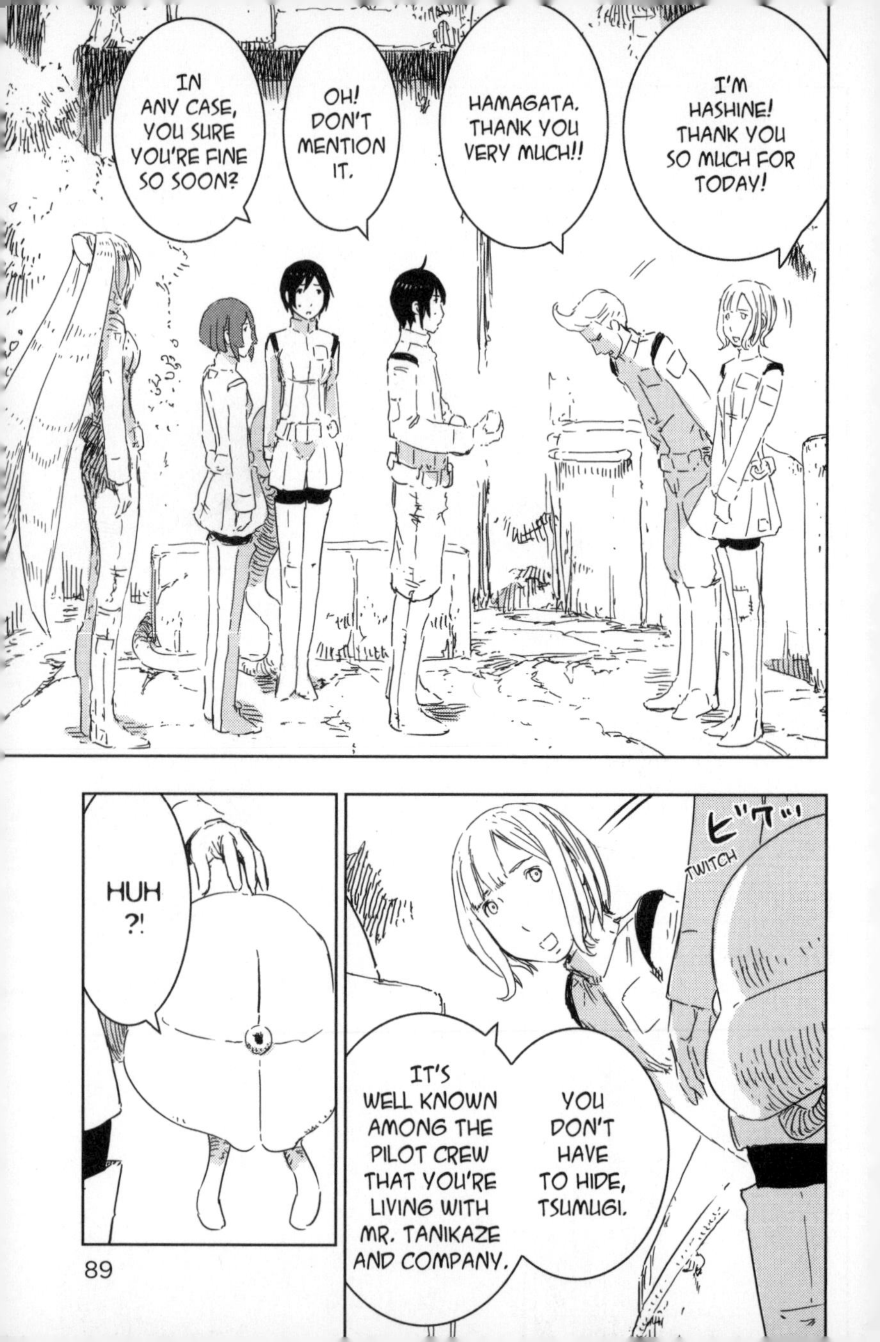
I'M HASHINE! THANK YOU SO MUCH FOR TODAY!
HAMAGATA. THANK YOU VERY MUCH!!
OH! DON'T MENTION IT.
IN ANY CASE, YOU SURE YOU'RE FINE SO SOON?
ビクッ
TWITCH
YOU DON'T HAVE TO HIDE, TSUMUGI.
IT'S WELL KNOWN AMONG THE PILOT CREW THAT YOU'RE LIVING WITH MR. TANIKAZE AND COMPANY.
HUH ?!

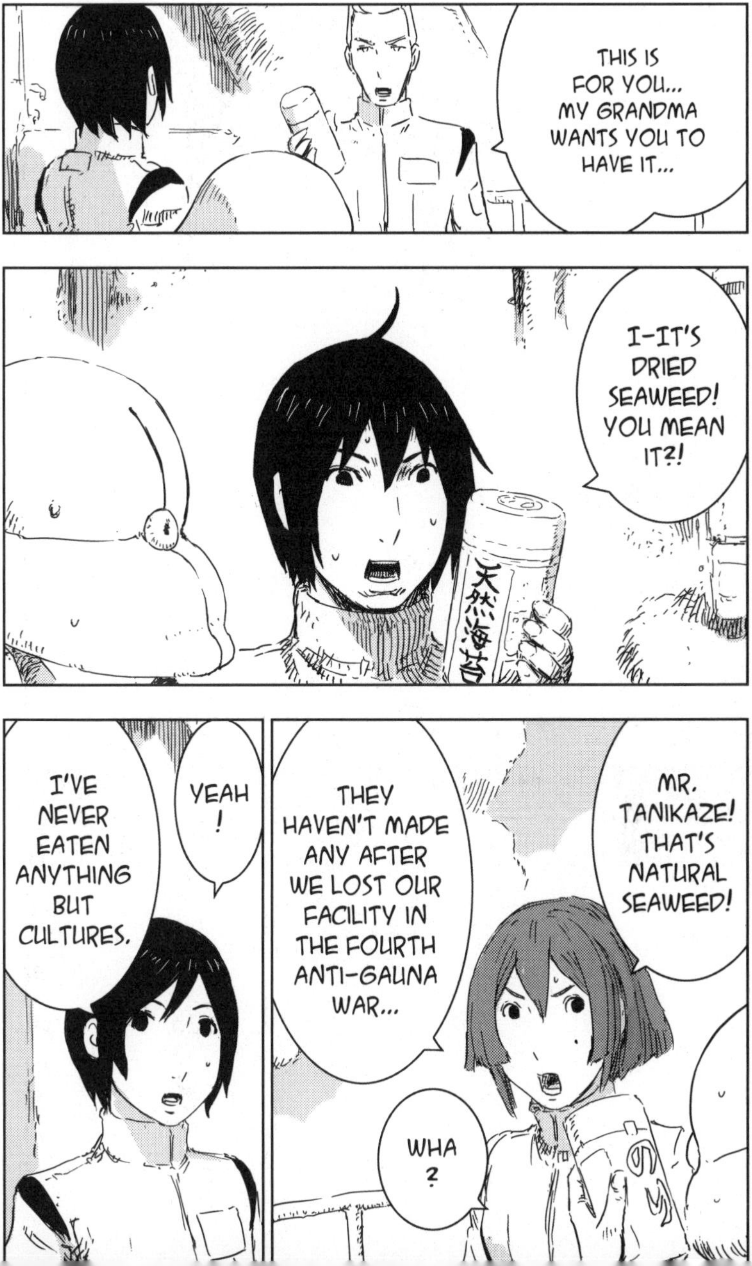
THIS IS FOR YOU... MY GRANDMA WANTS YOU TO HAVE IT...
I-IT'S DRIED SEAWEED! YOU MEAN IT?!
天然海苔
MR. TANIKAZE! THAT'S NATURAL SEAWEED!
THEY HAVEN'T MADE ANY AFTER WE LOST OUR FACILITY IN THE FOURTH ANTI-GAUNA WAR...
WHA?
のり
YEAH!
I'VE NEVER EATEN ANYTHING BUT CULTURES.

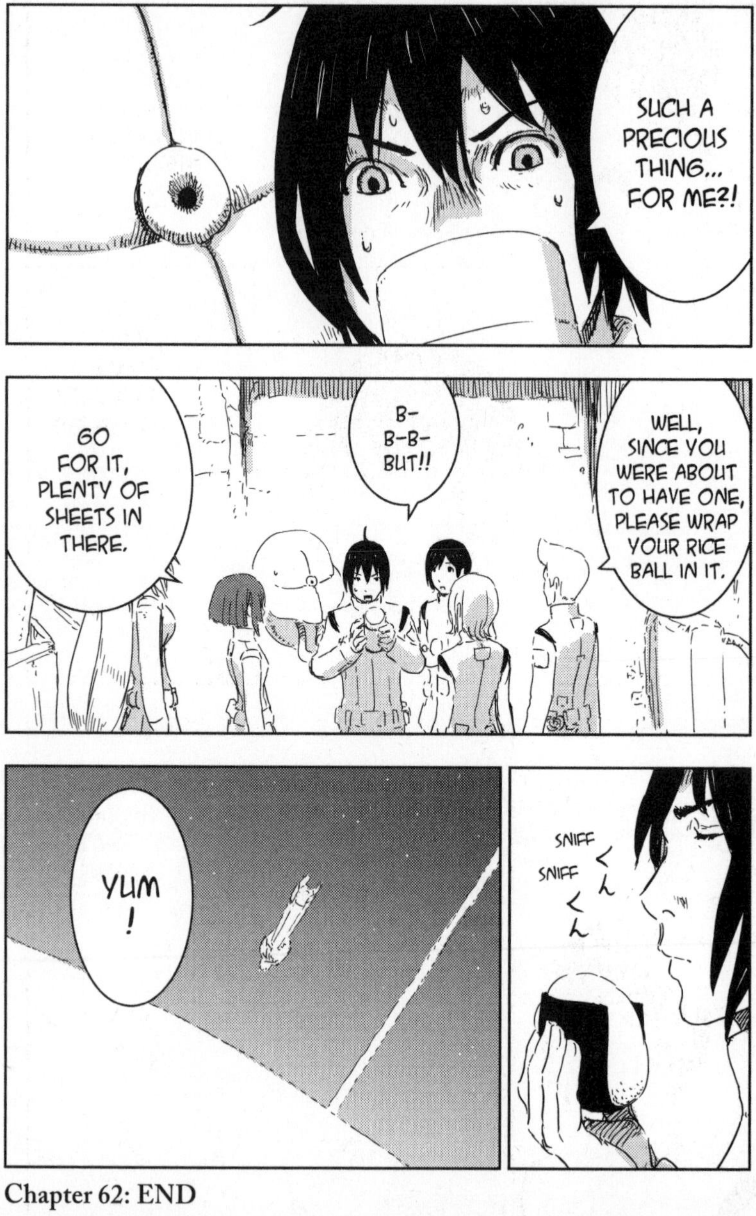
SUCH A PRECIOUS THING... FOR ME?!
WELL, SINCE YOU WERE ABOUT TO HAVE ONE, PLEASE WRAP YOUR RICE BALL IN IT.
B- B-B- BUT!!
GO FOR IT, PLENTY OF SHEETS IN THERE.
SNIFF くん
SNIFF くん
YUM !

Chapter 62: END

シドニアの騎士

KNIGHTS OF SIDONIA

Chapter 63: Tsumugi Shiraui's Dream

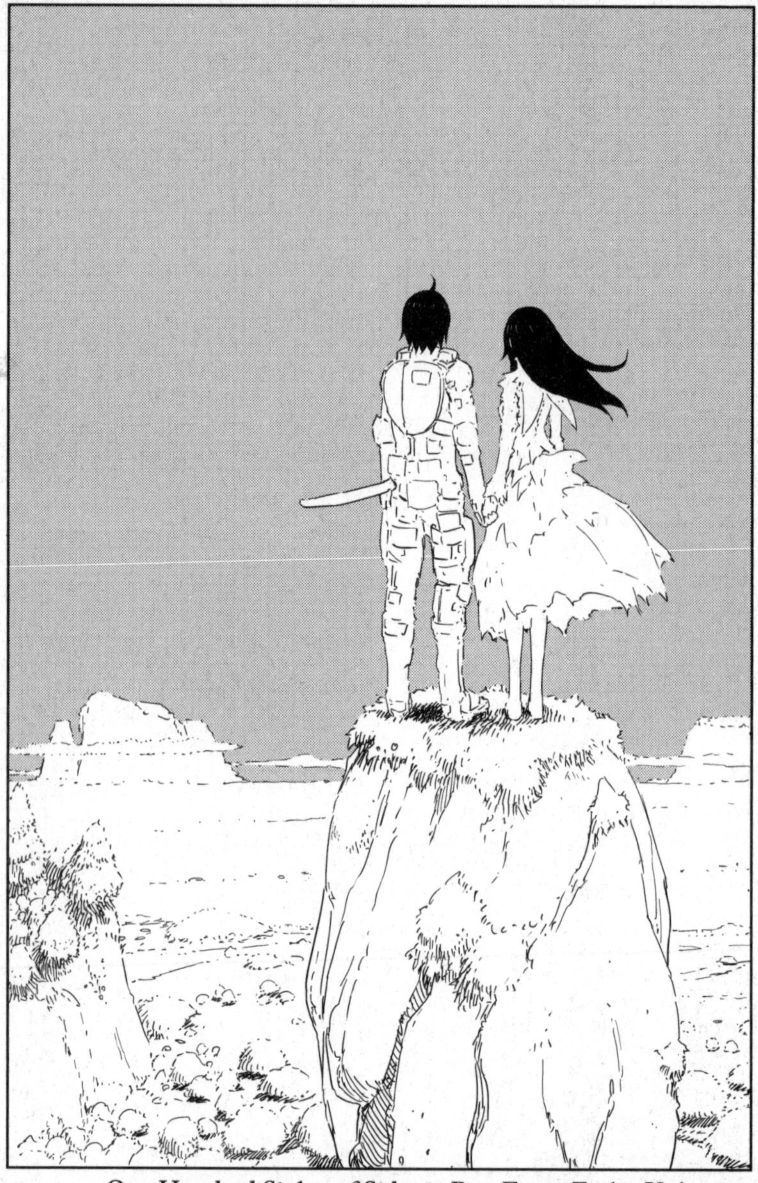

One Hundred Sights of Sidonia Part Forty-Eight: Unknown

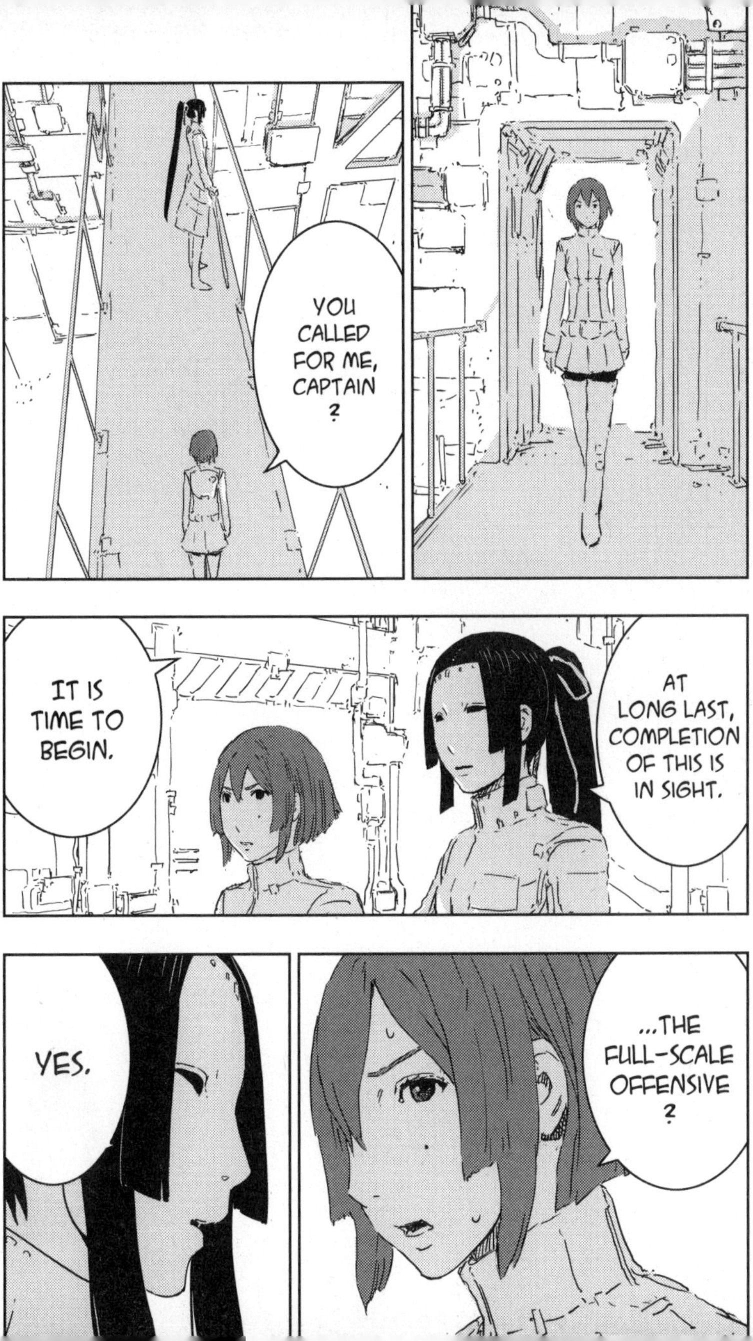
YOU CALLED FOR ME, CAPTAIN?
AT LONG LAST, COMPLETION OF THIS IS IN SIGHT.
IT IS TIME TO BEGIN.
...THE FULL-SCALE OFFENSIVE?
YES.

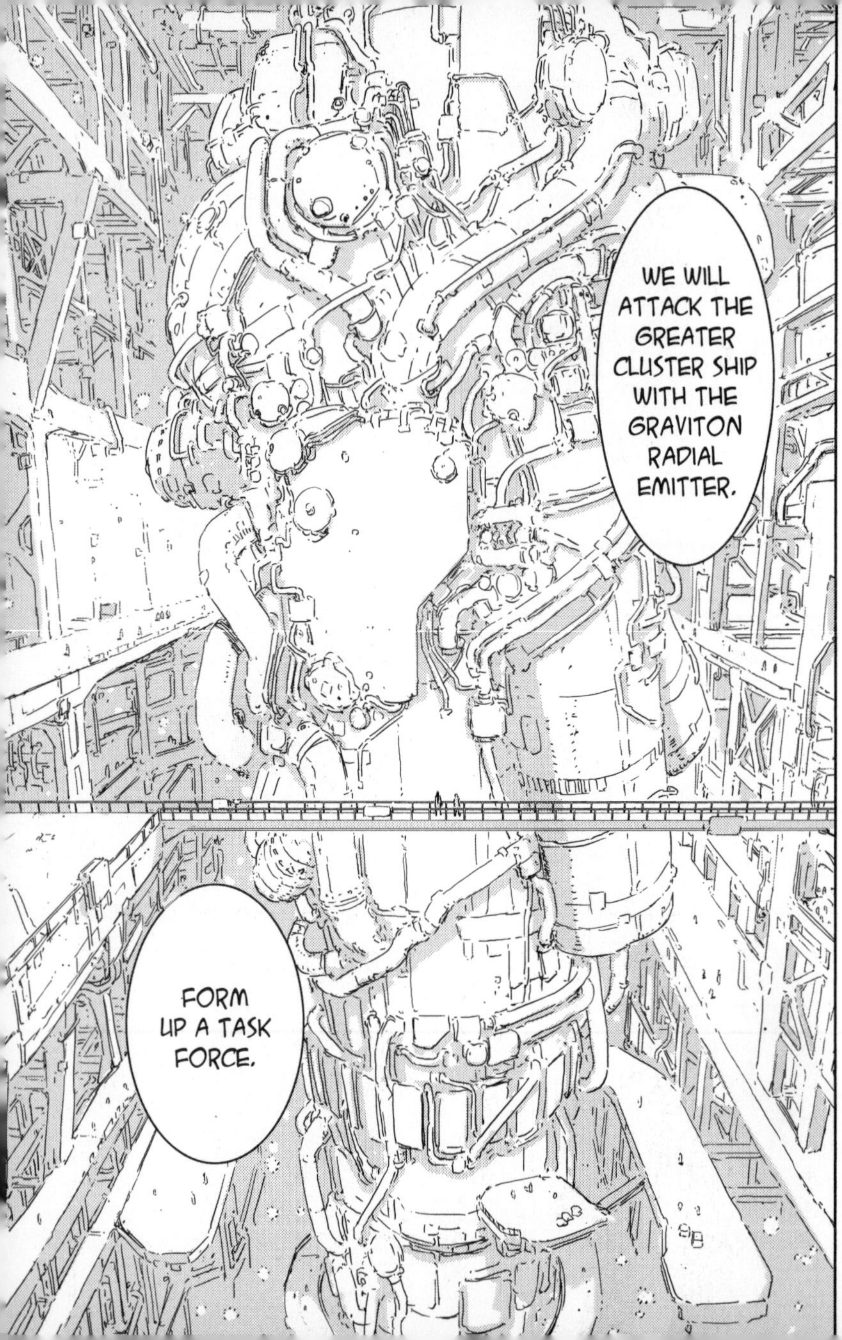
WE WILL ATTACK THE GREATER CLUSTER SHIP WITH THE GRAVITON RADIAL EMITTER.
FORM UP A TASK FORCE.

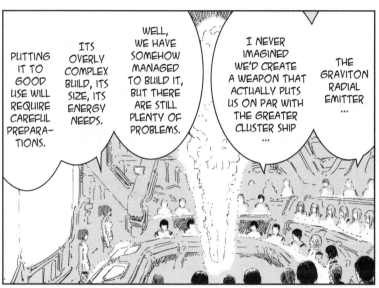

THE GRAVITON RADIAL EMITTER ...
I NEVER IMAGINED WE'D CREATE A WEAPON THAT ACTUALLY PUTS US ON PAR WITH THE GREATER CLUSTER SHIP ...
WELL, WE HAVE SOMEHOW MANAGED TO BUILD IT, BUT THERE ARE STILL PLENTY OF PROBLEMS.
ITS OVERLY COMPLEX BUILD, ITS SIZE, ITS ENERGY NEEDS.
PUTTING IT TO GOOD USE WILL REQUIRE CAREFUL PREPARA-TIONS.
THE ENERGY NEEDED FOR ONE SHOT IS...
...TEN, HUNDRED, THOUSAND, TEN THOU ...
WHA?! I-IS THIS A JOKE?!
THE FIGURES ARE NO MISTAKE... WE DID ALL WE COULD,
BUT THIS IS THE LIMIT OF TOHA HEAVY INDUSTRIES' CURRENT TECH...
SO THAT'S WHAT THE SEMI-AUTONOMOUS CONVERSION ORGAN WAS FOR.

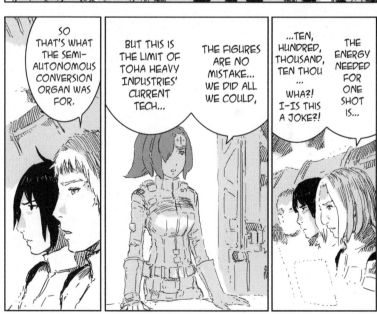

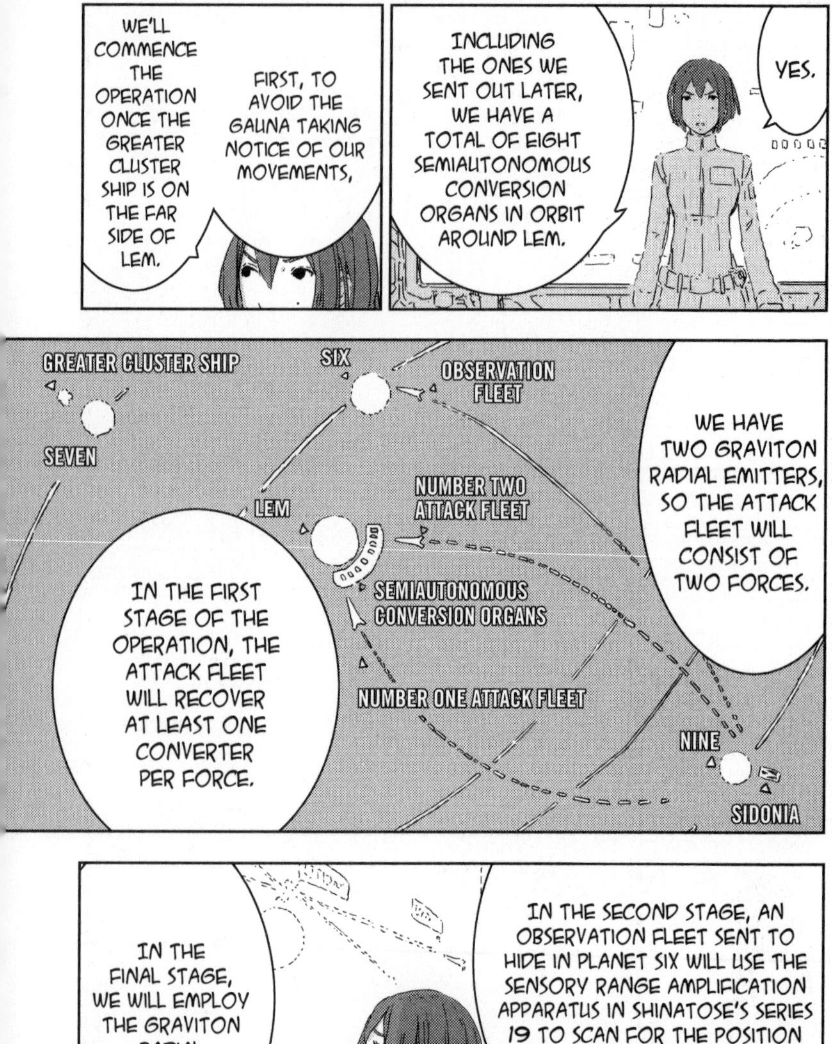
YES.
INCLUDING THE ONES WE SENT OUT LATER, WE HAVE A TOTAL OF EIGHT SEMIAUTONOMOUS CONVERSION ORGANS IN ORBIT AROUND LEM.
FIRST, TO AVOID THE GAUNA TAKING NOTICE OF OUR MOVEMENTS,
WE'LL COMMENCE THE OPERATION ONCE THE GREATER CLUSTER SHIP IS ON THE FAR SIDE OF LEM.
WE HAVE TWO GRAVITON RADIAL EMITTERS, SO THE ATTACK FLEET WILL CONSIST OF TWO FORCES.
OBSERVATION FLEET
SIX
GREATER CLUSTER SHIP
SEVEN
NUMBER TWO ATTACK FLEET
LEM
SEMIAUTONOMOUS CONVERSION ORGANS
NUMBER ONE ATTACK FLEET
NINE
SIDONIA
IN THE FIRST STAGE OF THE OPERATION, THE ATTACK FLEET WILL RECOVER AT LEAST ONE CONVERTER PER FORCE.
IN THE SECOND STAGE, AN OBSERVATION FLEET SENT TO HIDE IN PLANET SIX WILL USE THE SENSORY RANGE AMPLIFICATION APPARATUS IN SHINATOSE'S SERIES 19 TO SCAN FOR THE POSITION OF THE GREATER CLUSTER SHIP'S MAIN CORE.
IN THE FINAL STAGE, WE WILL EMPLOY THE GRAVITON RADIAL EMITTERS.

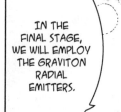

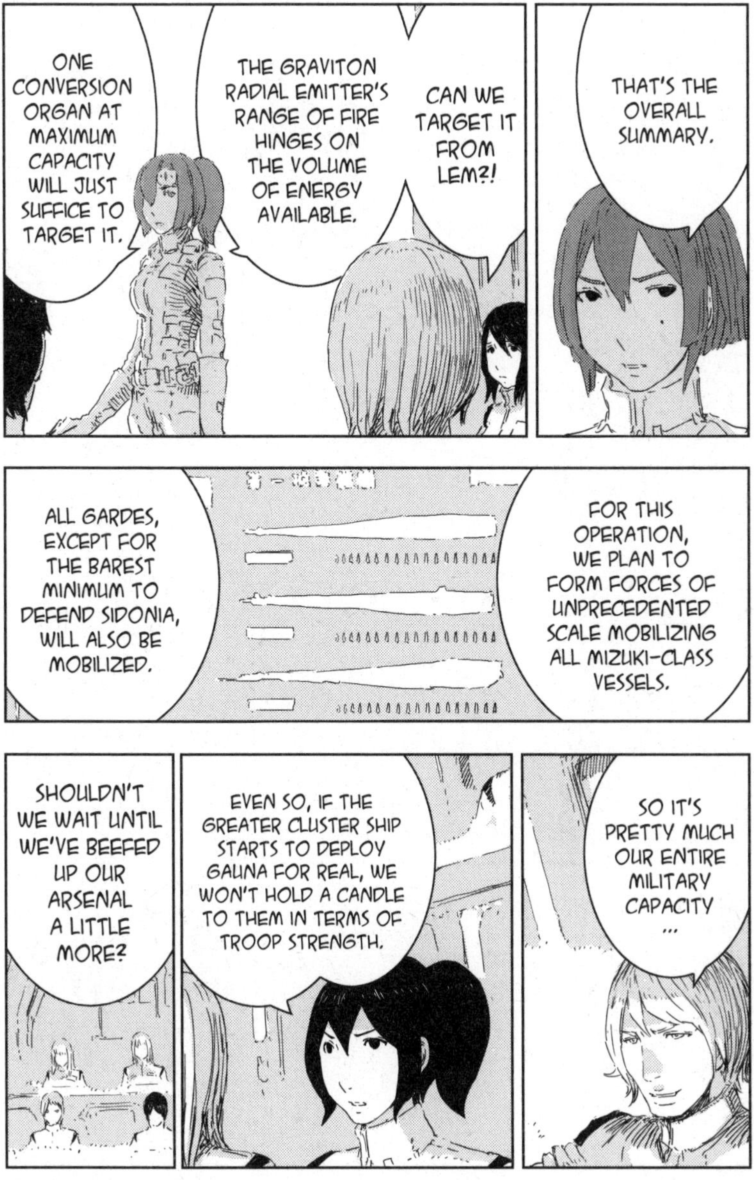
THAT'S THE OVERALL SUMMARY.
CAN WE TARGET IT FROM LEM?!
THE GRAVITON RADIAL EMITTER'S RANGE OF FIRE HINGES ON THE VOLUME OF ENERGY AVAILABLE.
ONE CONVERSION ORGAN AT MAXIMUM CAPACITY WILL JUST SUFFICE TO TARGET IT.
FOR THIS OPERATION, WE PLAN TO FORM FORCES OF UNPRECEDENTED SCALE MOBILIZING ALL MIZUKI-CLASS VESSELS.
ALL GARDES, EXCEPT FOR THE BAREST MINIMUM TO DEFEND SIDONIA, WILL ALSO BE MOBILIZED.
SO IT'S PRETTY MUCH OUR ENTIRE MILITARY CAPACITY ...
EVEN SO, IF THE GREATER CLUSTER SHIP STARTS TO DEPLOY GAUNA FOR REAL, WE WON'T HOLD A CANDLE TO THEM IN TERMS OF TROOP STRENGTH.
SHOULDN'T WE WAIT UNTIL WE'VE BEEFED UP OUR ARSENAL A LITTLE MORE?

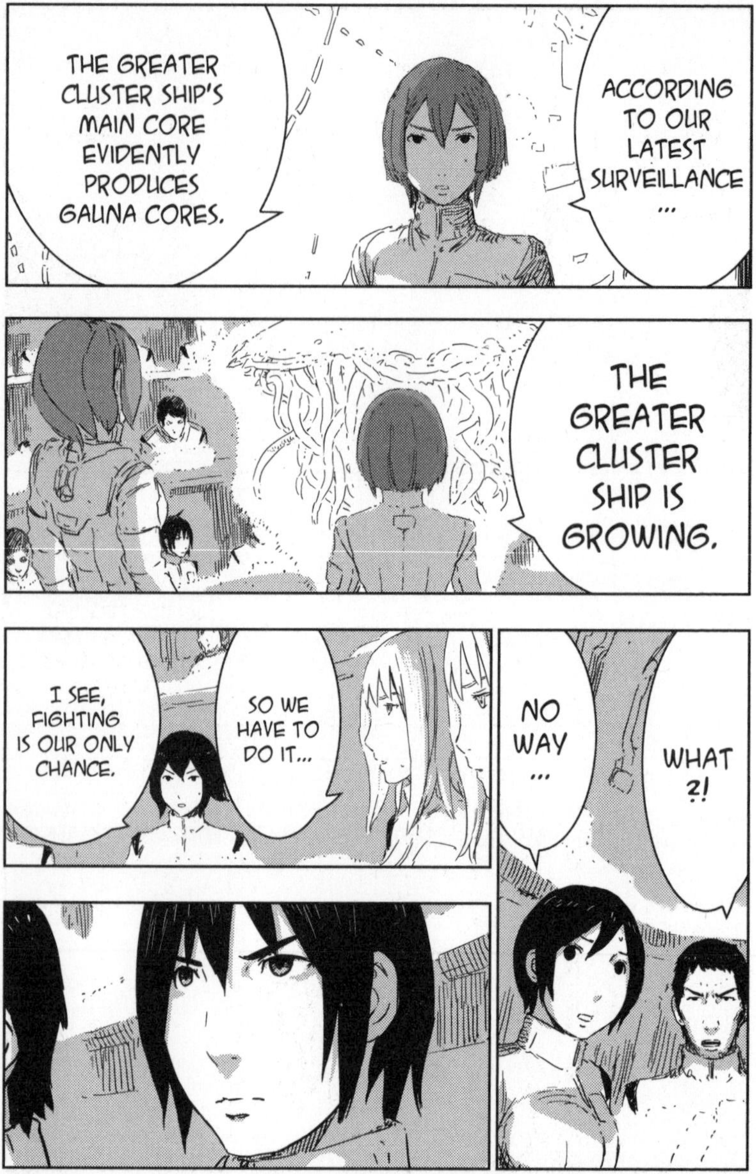
ACCORDING TO OUR LATEST SURVEILLANCE ...
THE GREATER CLUSTER SHIP'S MAIN CORE EVIDENTLY PRODUCES GAUNA CORES.
THE GREATER CLUSTER SHIP IS GROWING.
WHAT ?!
NO WAY ...
SO WE HAVE TO DO IT...
I SEE, FIGHTING IS OUR ONLY CHANCE.

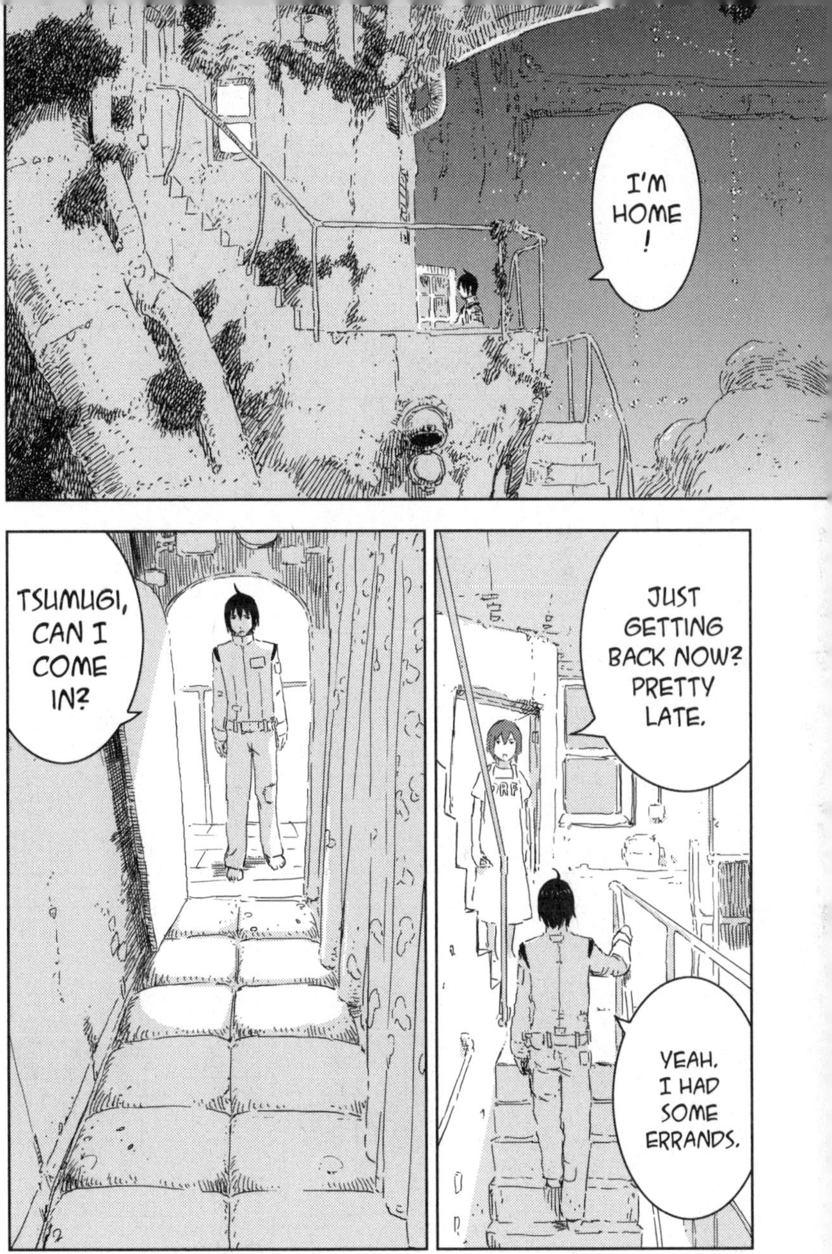
I'M HOME!
JUST GETTING BACK NOW? PRETTY LATE.
YEAH. I HAD SOME ERRANDS.
TSUMUGI, CAN I COME IN?

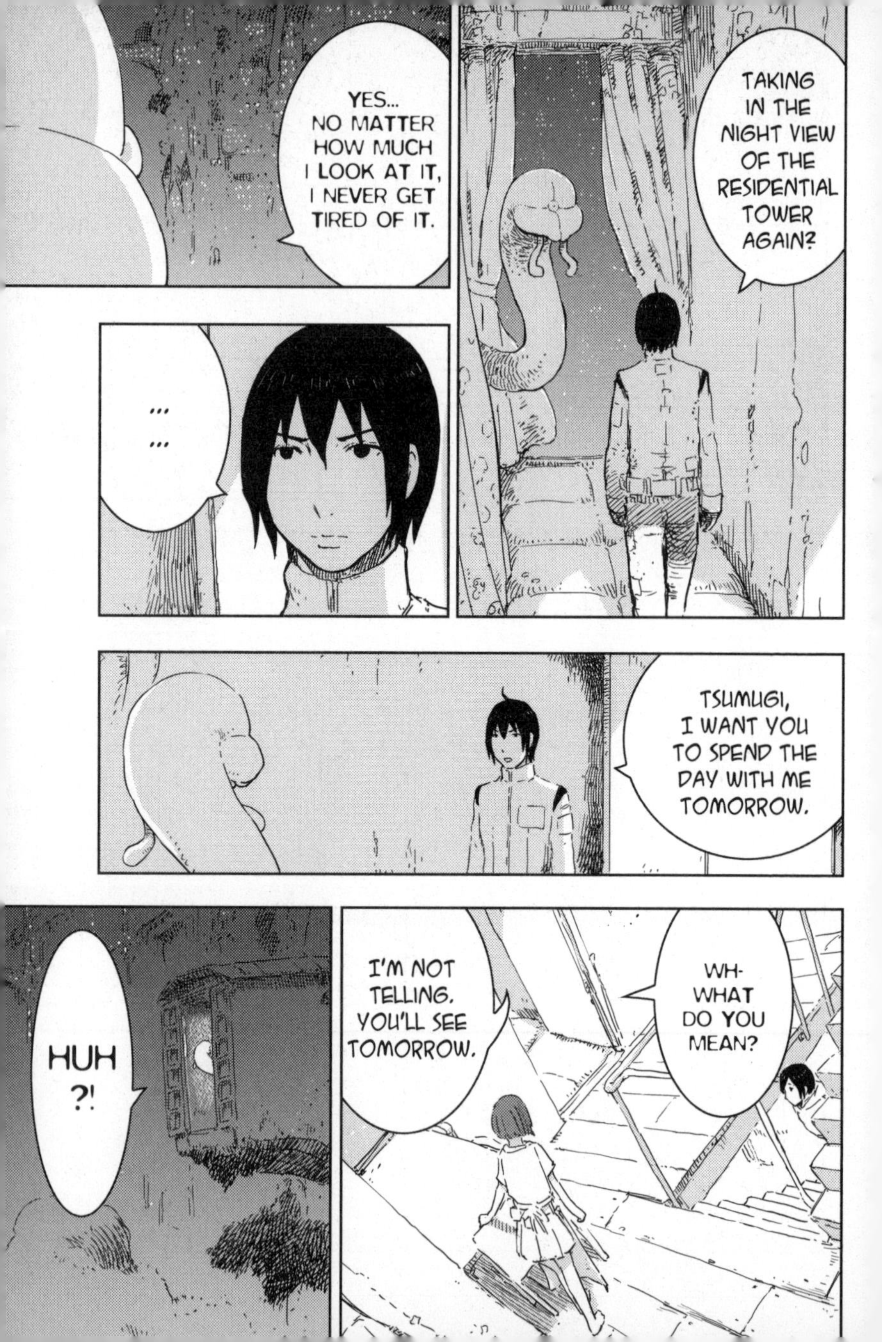
TAKING IN THE NIGHT VIEW OF THE RESIDENTIAL TOWER AGAIN?
YES... NO MATTER HOW MUCH I LOOK AT IT, I NEVER GET TIRED OF IT.
... ...
TSUMUGI, I WANT YOU TO SPEND THE DAY WITH ME TOMORROW.
WH- WHAT DO YOU MEAN?
I'M NOT TELLING. YOU'LL SEE TOMORROW.
HUH ?!

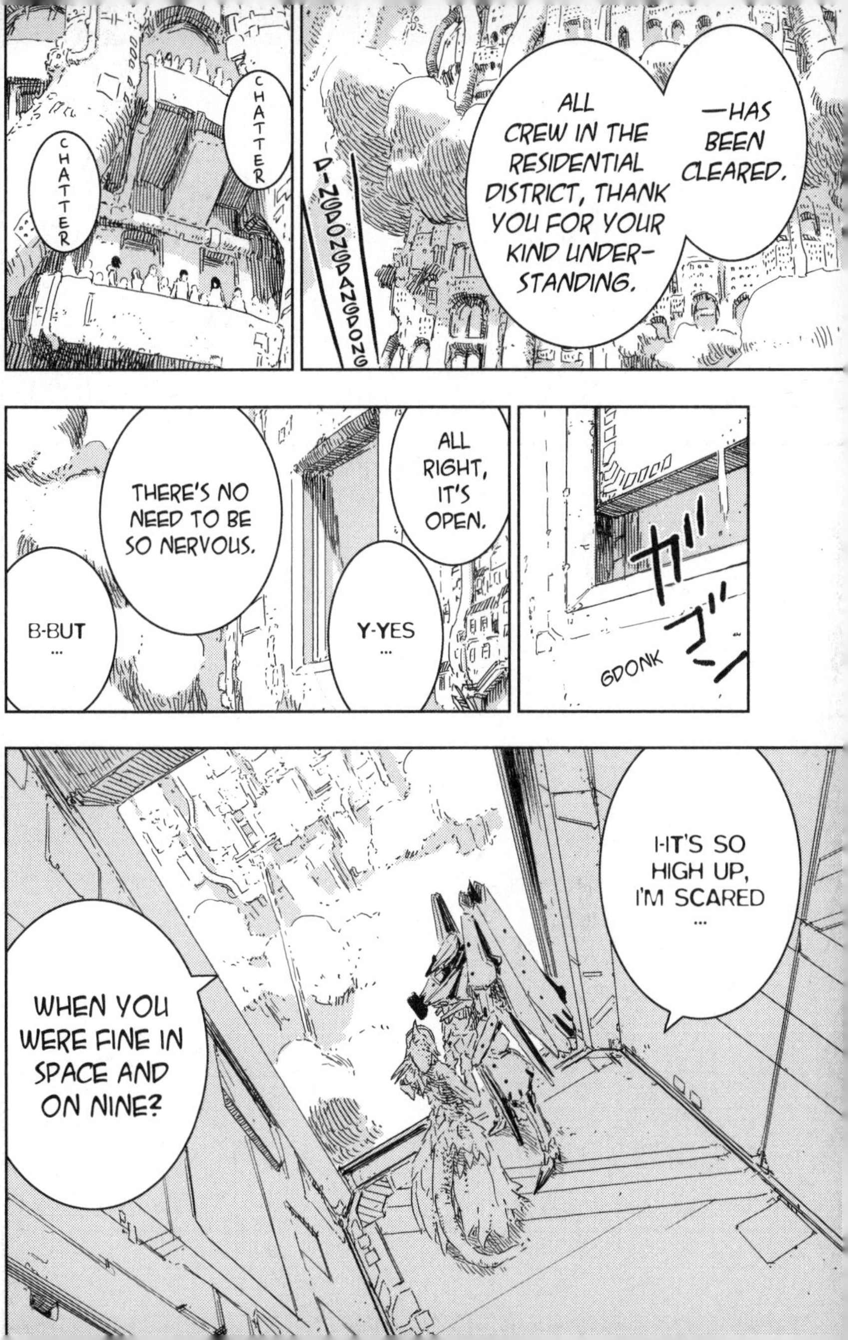
—HAS BEEN CLEARED.
ALL CREW IN THE RESIDENTIAL DISTRICT, THANK YOU FOR YOUR KIND UNDERSTANDING.
D-INGDONGDANGDONG
CHATTER
CHATTER
ガゴン
GDONK
ALL RIGHT, IT'S OPEN.
Y-YES ...
THERE'S NO NEED TO BE SO NERVOUS.
B-BUT ...
I-IT'S SO HIGH UP, I'M SCARED ...
WHEN YOU WERE FINE IN SPACE AND ON NINE?

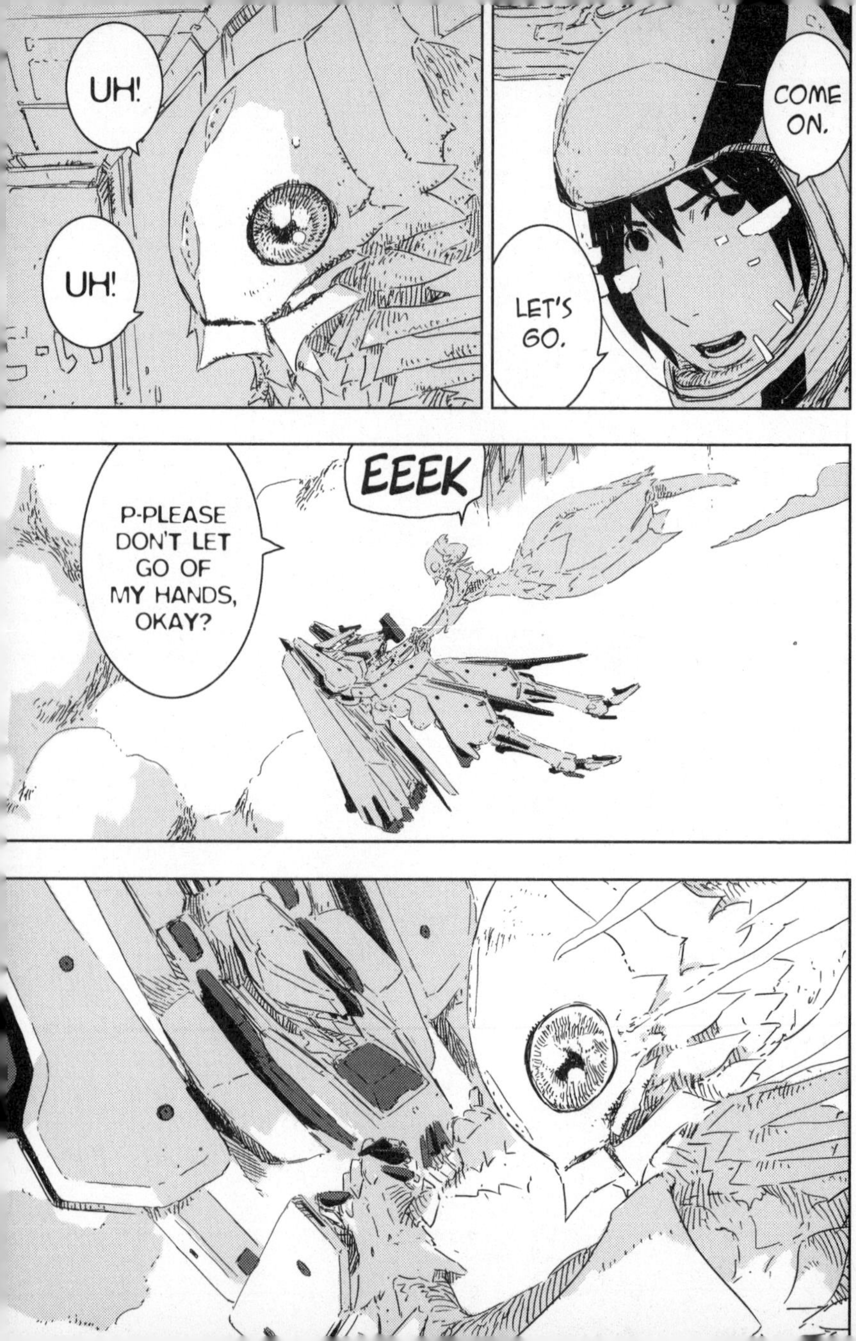
COME ON.
LET'S GO.
UH!
UH!
EEEK
P-PLEASE DON'T LET GO OF MY HANDS, OKAY?

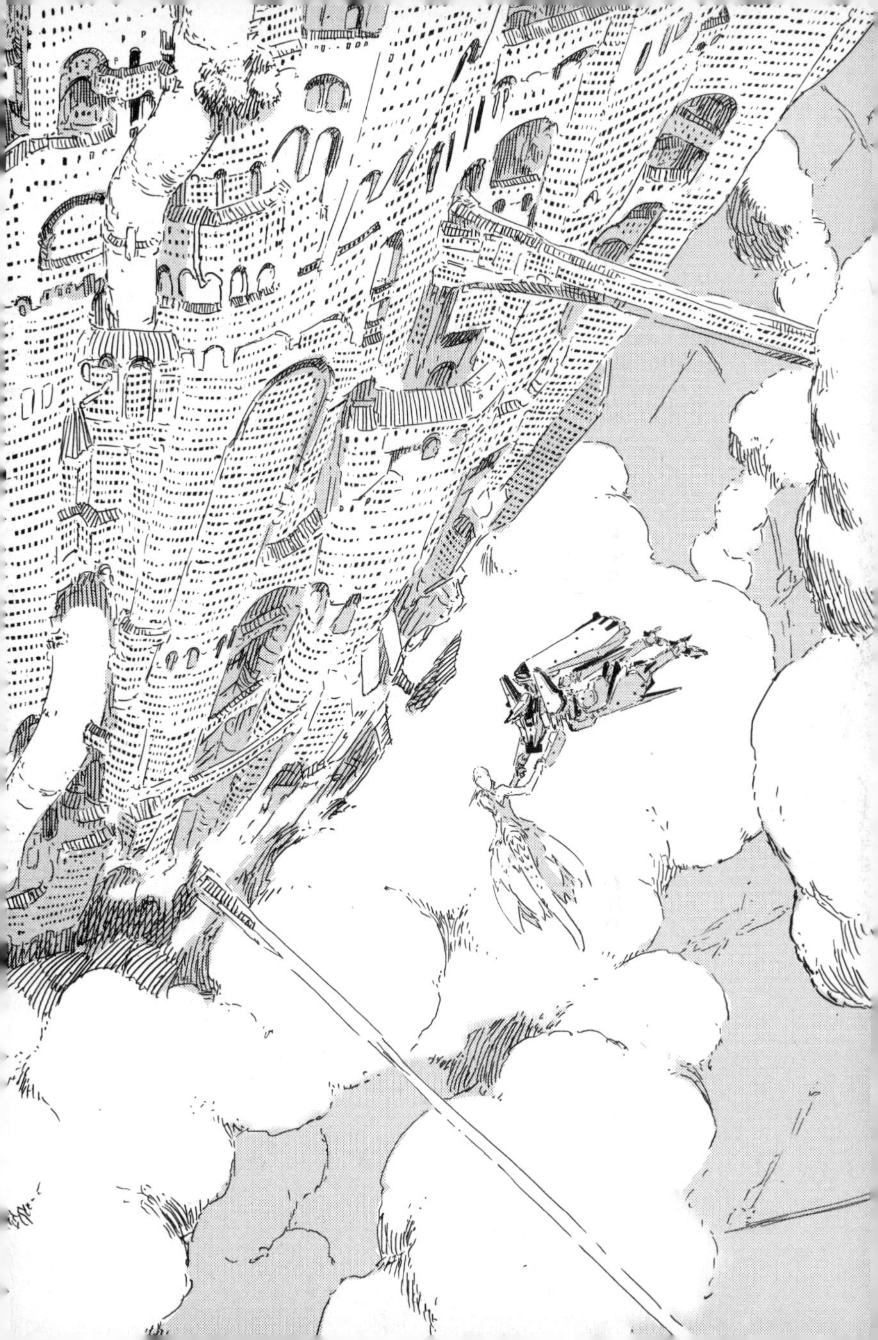

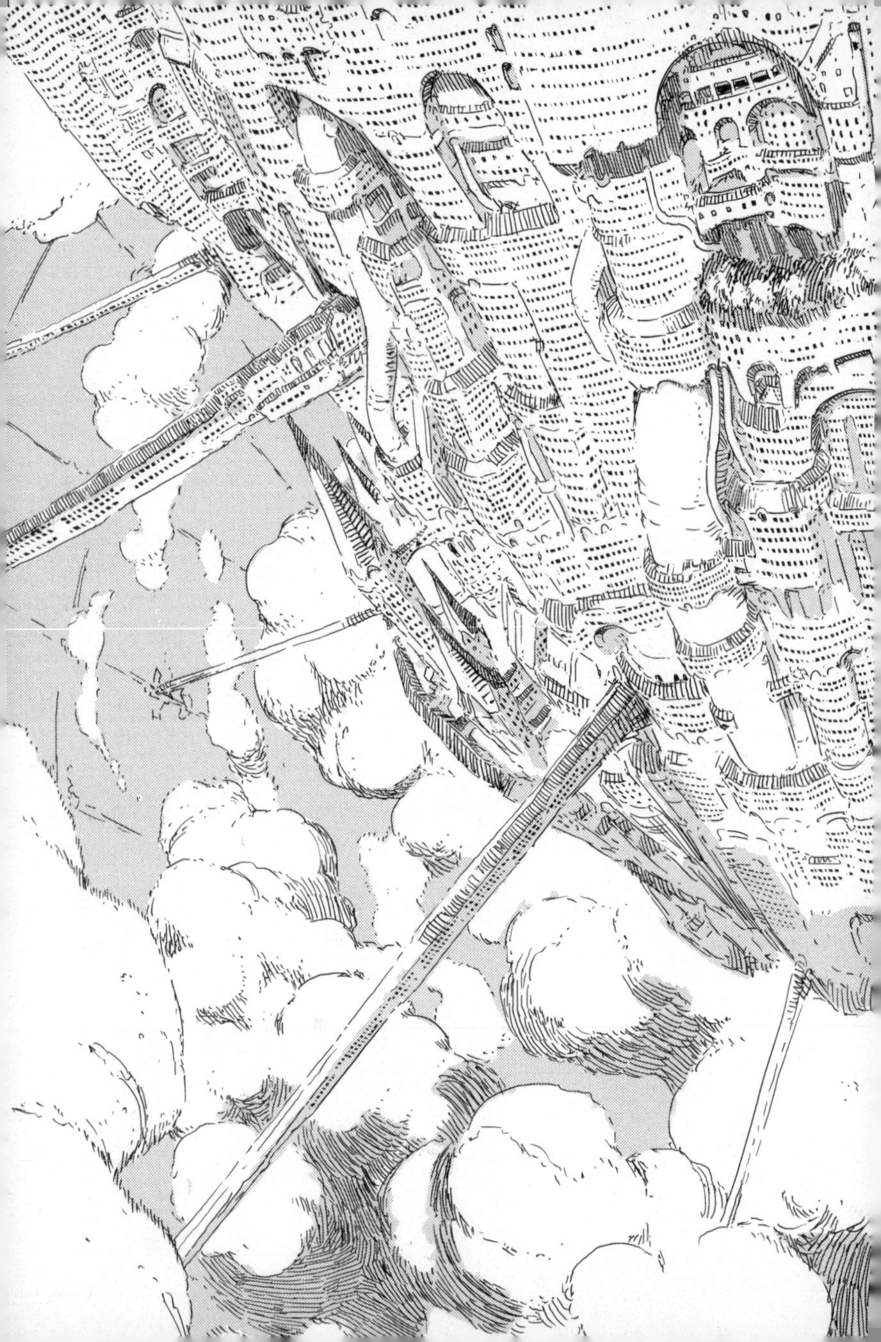

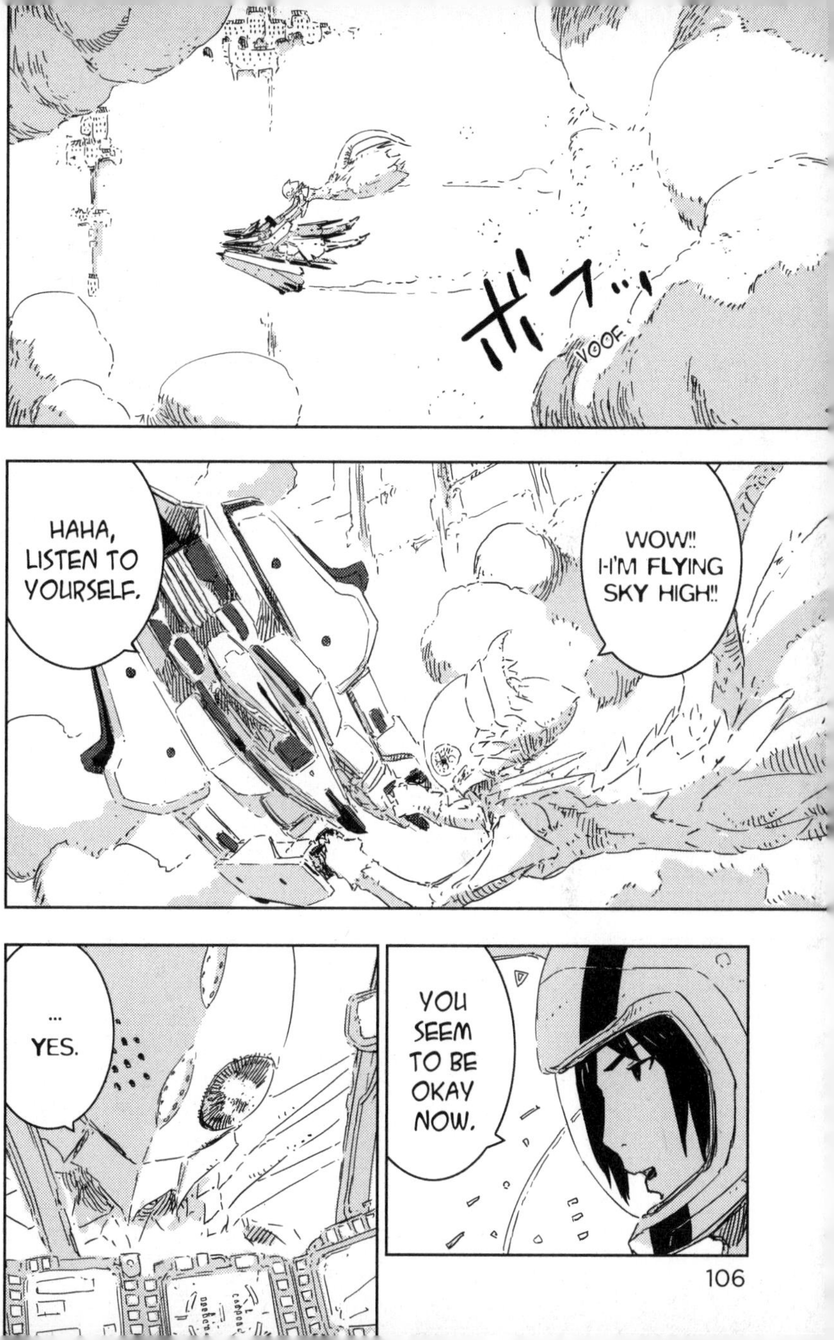
ボフッ
VOOF
WOW!! I-I'M FLYING SKY HIGH!!
HAHA, LISTEN TO YOURSELF.
YOU SEEM TO BE OKAY NOW.
... YES.

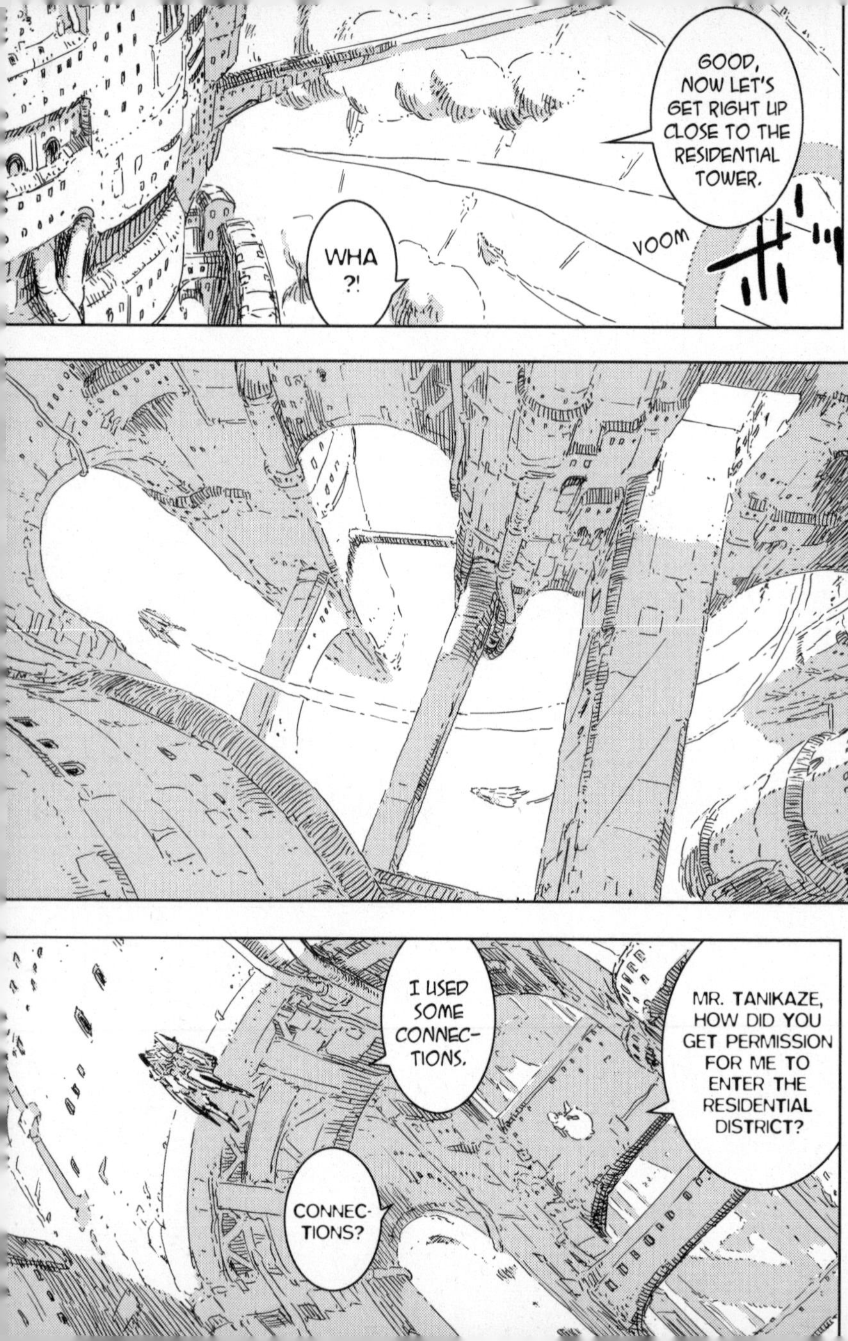
GOOD, NOW LET'S GET RIGHT UP CLOSE TO THE RESIDENTIAL TOWER.
VOOM
WHA ?!
MR. TANIKAZE, HOW DID YOU GET PERMISSION FOR ME TO ENTER THE RESIDENTIAL DISTRICT?
I USED SOME CONNEC-TIONS.
CONNEC-TIONS?

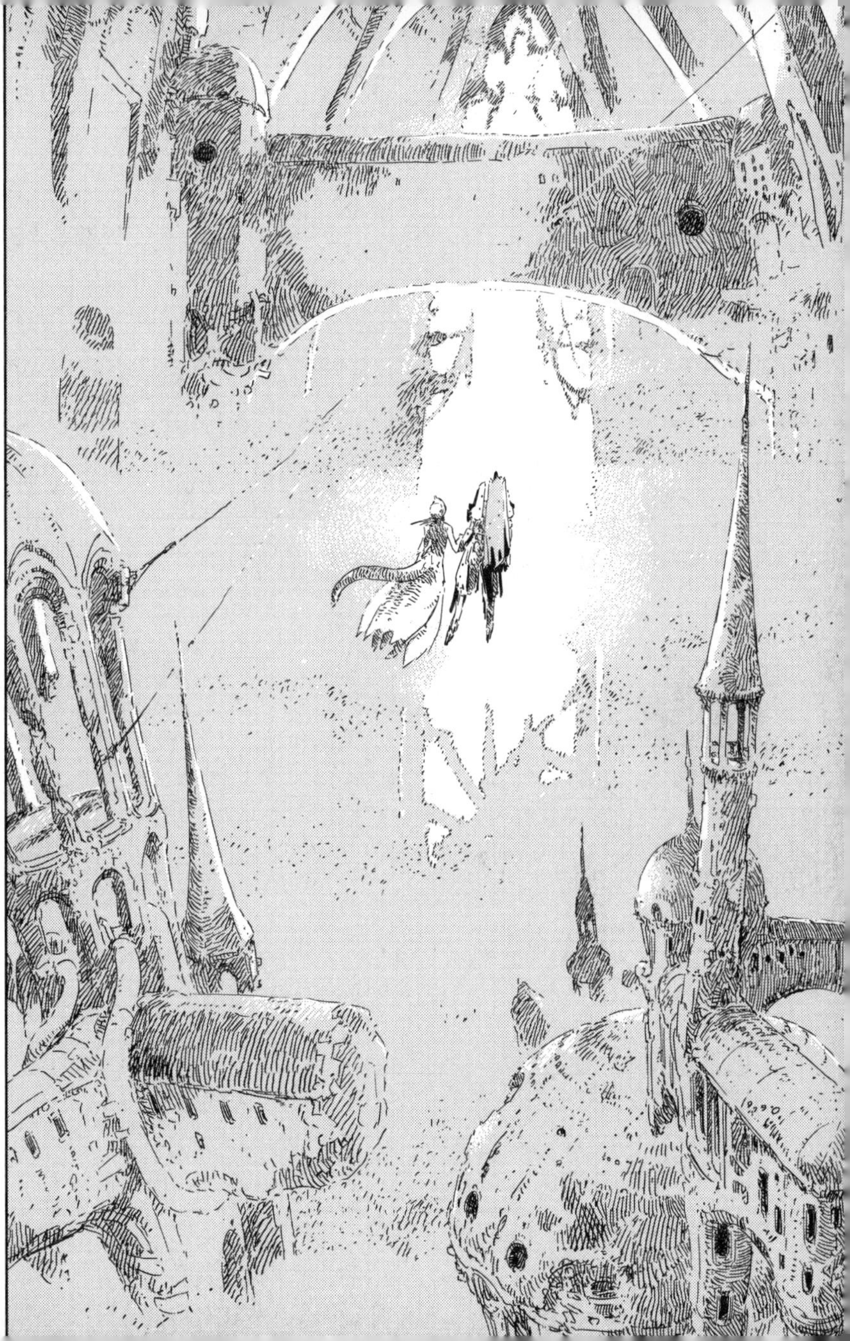

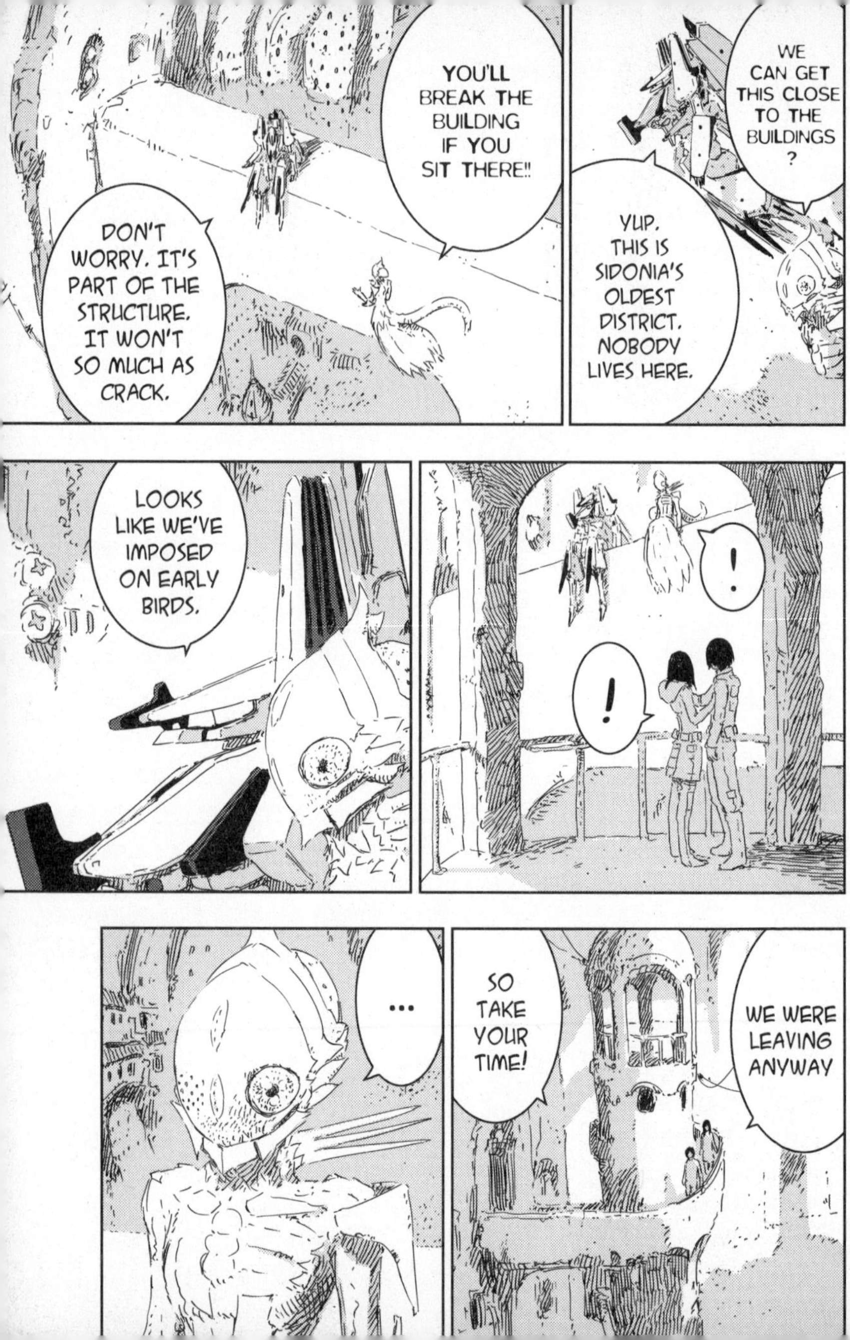
WE CAN GET THIS CLOSE TO THE BUILDINGS?
YUP. THIS IS SIDONIA'S OLDEST DISTRICT. NOBODY LIVES HERE.
YOU'LL BREAK THE BUILDING IF YOU SIT THERE!!
DON'T WORRY. IT'S PART OF THE STRUCTURE. IT WON'T SO MUCH AS CRACK.
!
!
LOOKS LIKE WE'VE IMPOSED ON EARLY BIRDS.
WE WERE LEAVING ANYWAY
SO TAKE YOUR TIME!
...

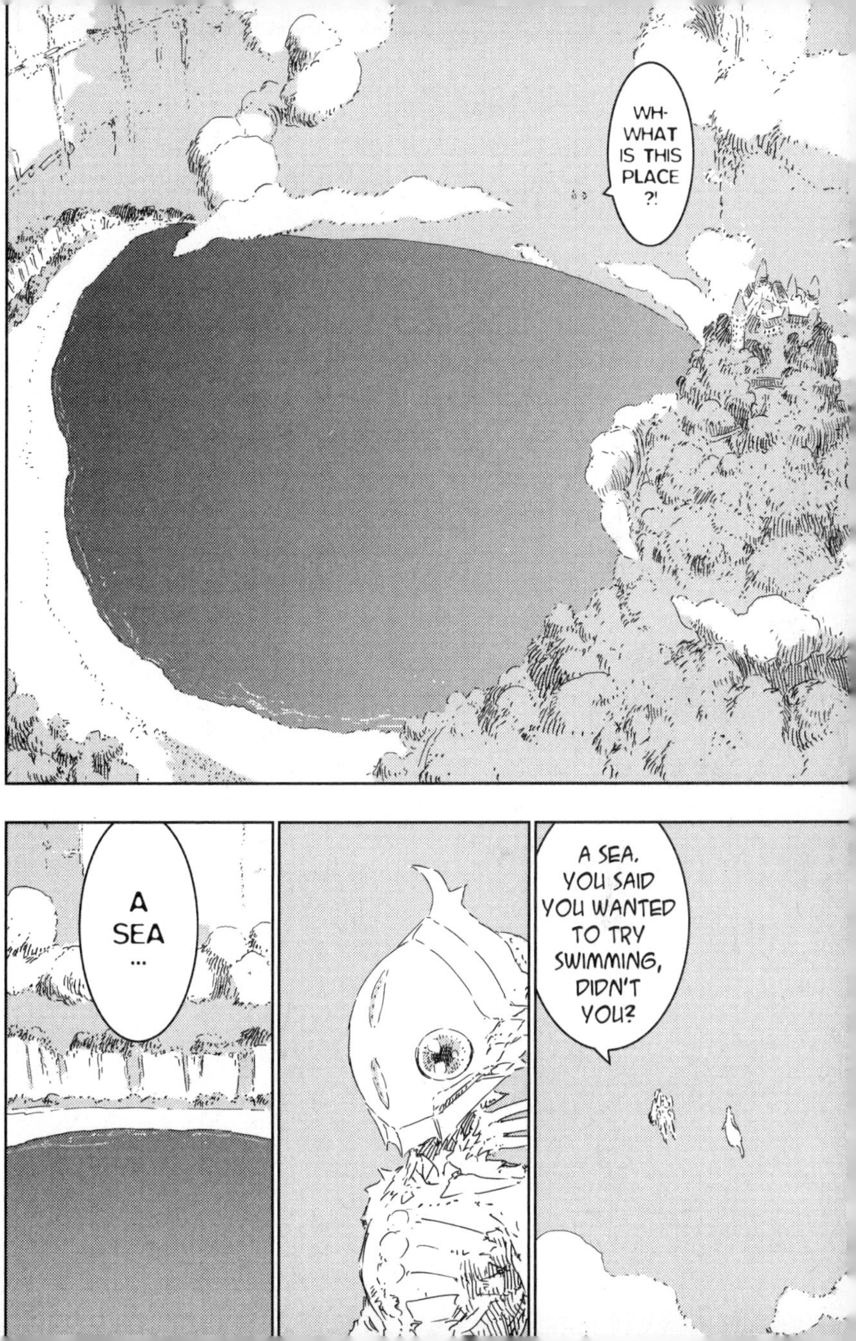
WH- WHAT IS THIS PLACE?!
A SEA. YOU SAID YOU WANTED TO TRY SWIMMING, DIDN'T YOU?
A SEA...

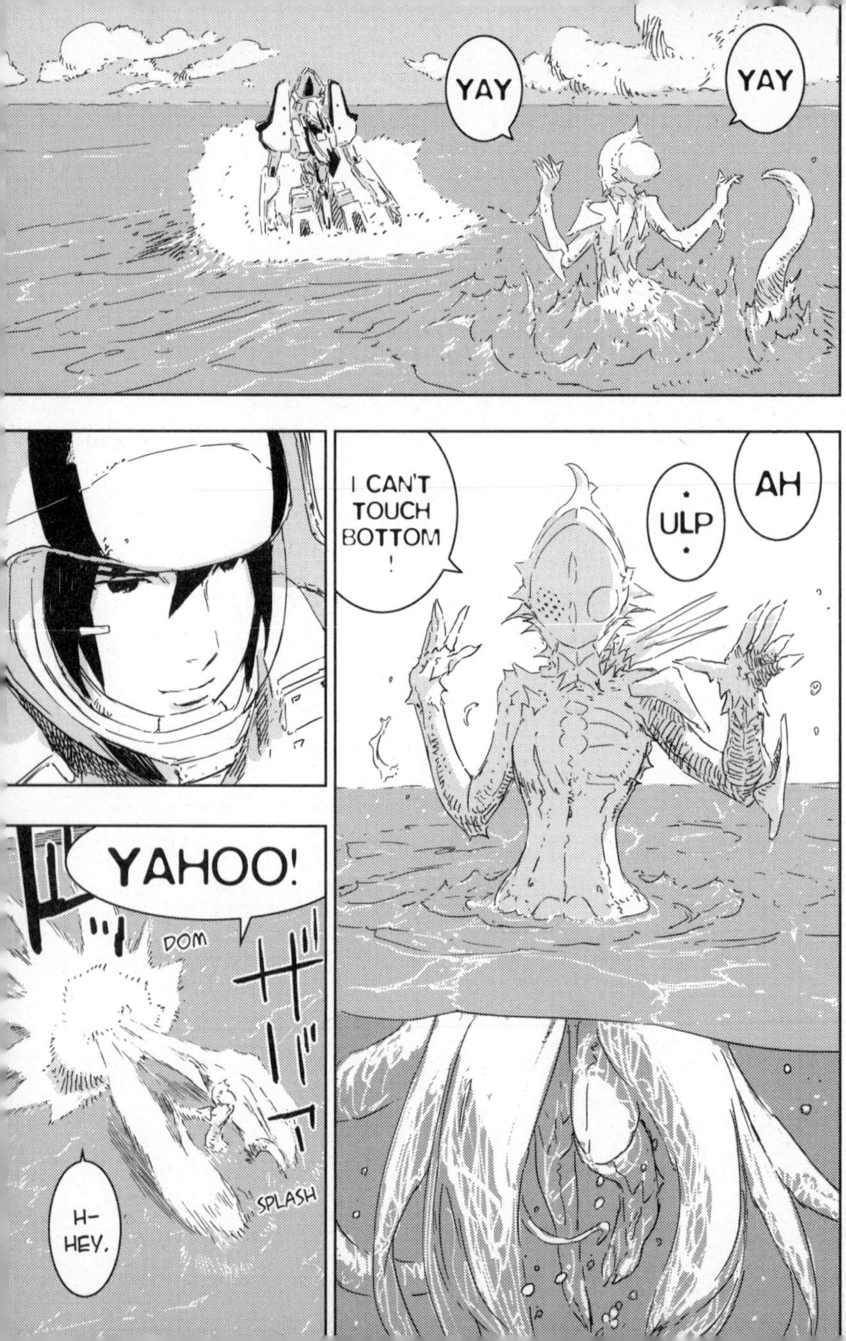
YAY
YAY
AH
ULP
I CAN'T TOUCH BOTTOM!
YAHOO!
DOM
SPLASH
H-HEY.

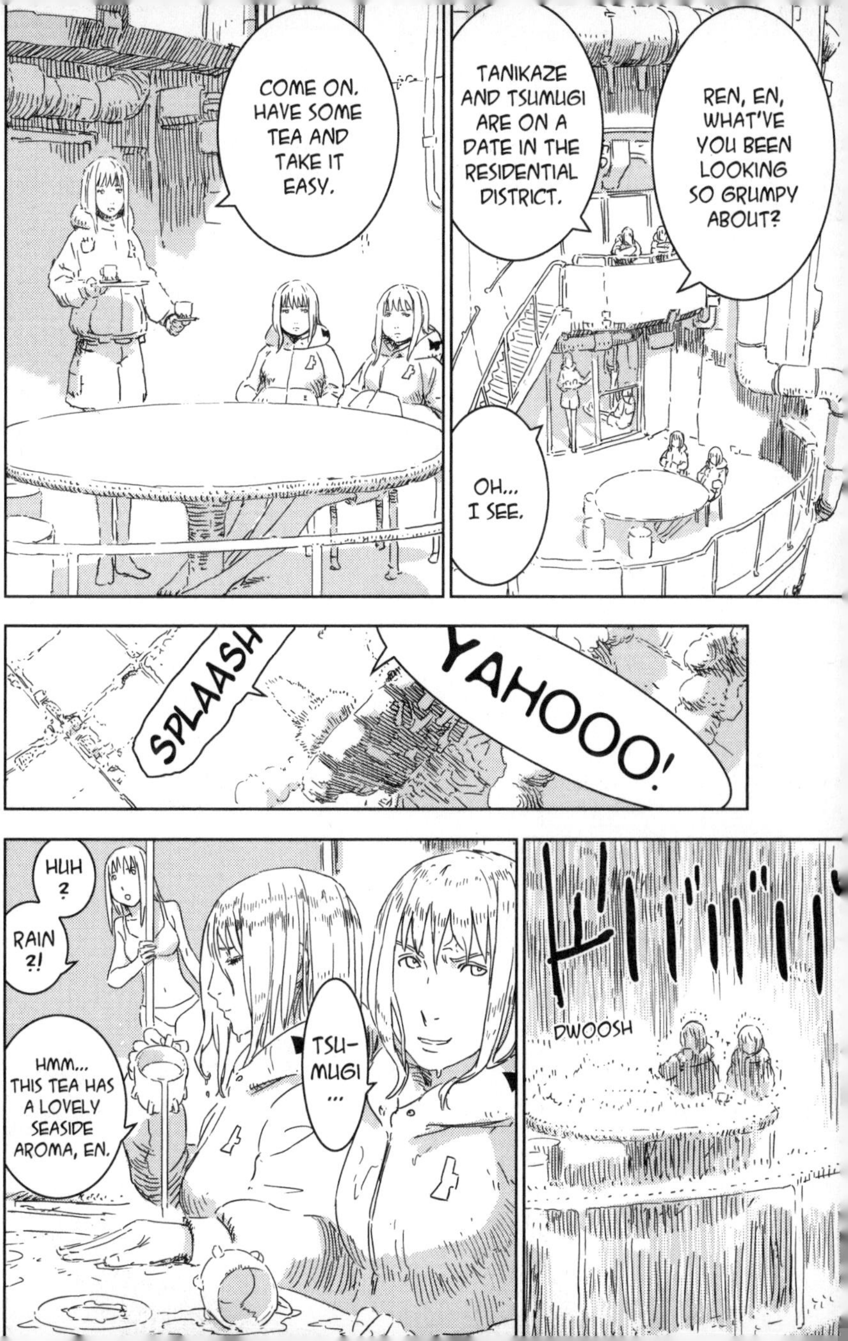
REN, EN, WHAT'VE YOU BEEN LOOKING SO GRUMPY ABOUT?
TANIKAZE AND TSUMUGI ARE ON A DATE IN THE RESIDENTIAL DISTRICT.
OH... I SEE.
COME ON. HAVE SOME TEA AND TAKE IT EASY.
YAHOOO!
SPLAASH
DWOOSH
HUH?
RAIN?!
TSU-MUGI...
HMM... THIS TEA HAS A LOVELY SEASIDE AROMA, EN.

ZAZAW

SURF

YES.

SHALL WE REST A BIT?

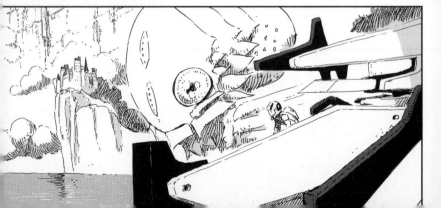

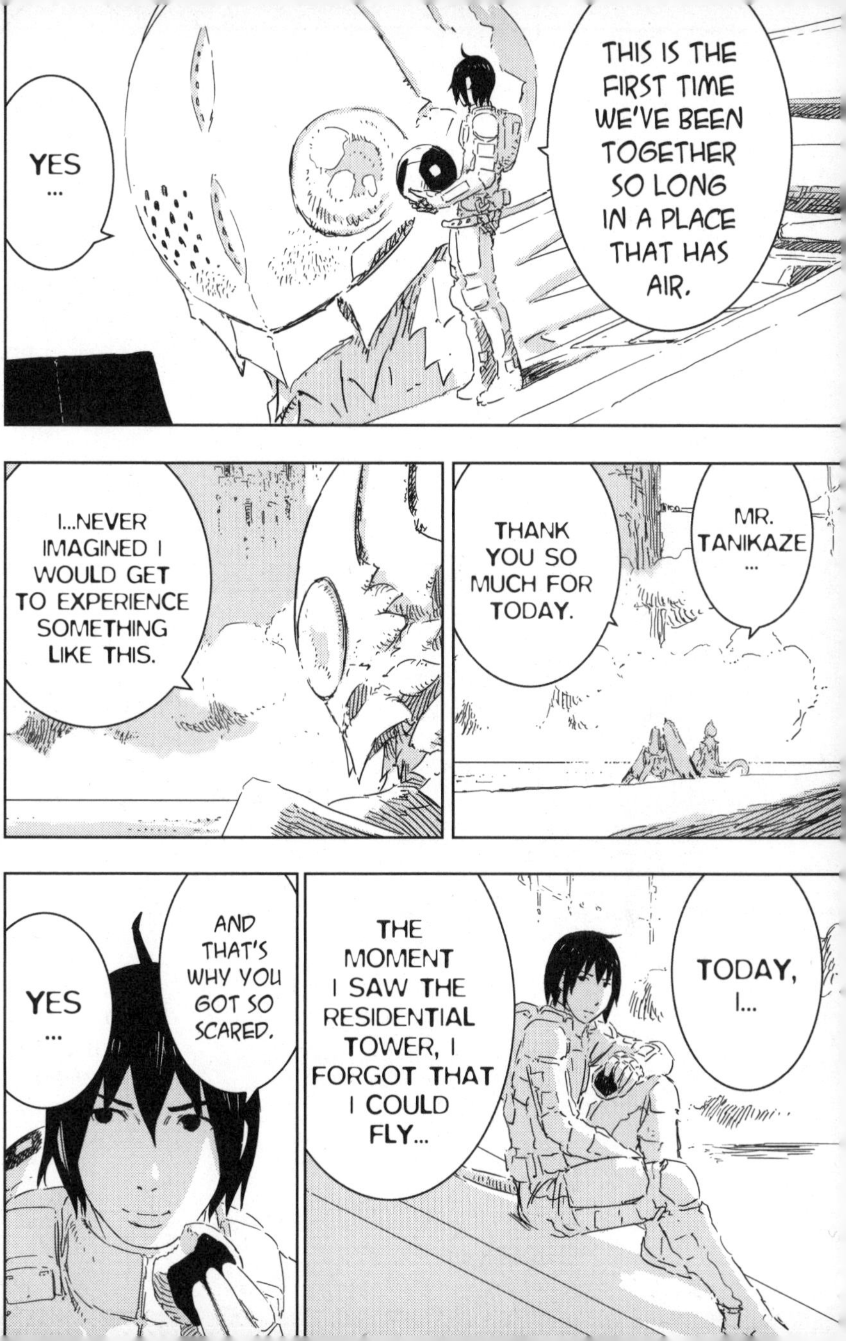
THIS IS THE FIRST TIME WE'VE BEEN TOGETHER SO LONG IN A PLACE THAT HAS AIR.
YES...
MR. TANIKAZE...
THANK YOU SO MUCH FOR TODAY.
I...NEVER IMAGINED I WOULD GET TO EXPERIENCE SOMETHING LIKE THIS.
TODAY, I...
THE MOMENT I SAW THE RESIDENTIAL TOWER, I FORGOT THAT I COULD FLY...
AND THAT'S WHY YOU GOT SO SCARED.
YES...

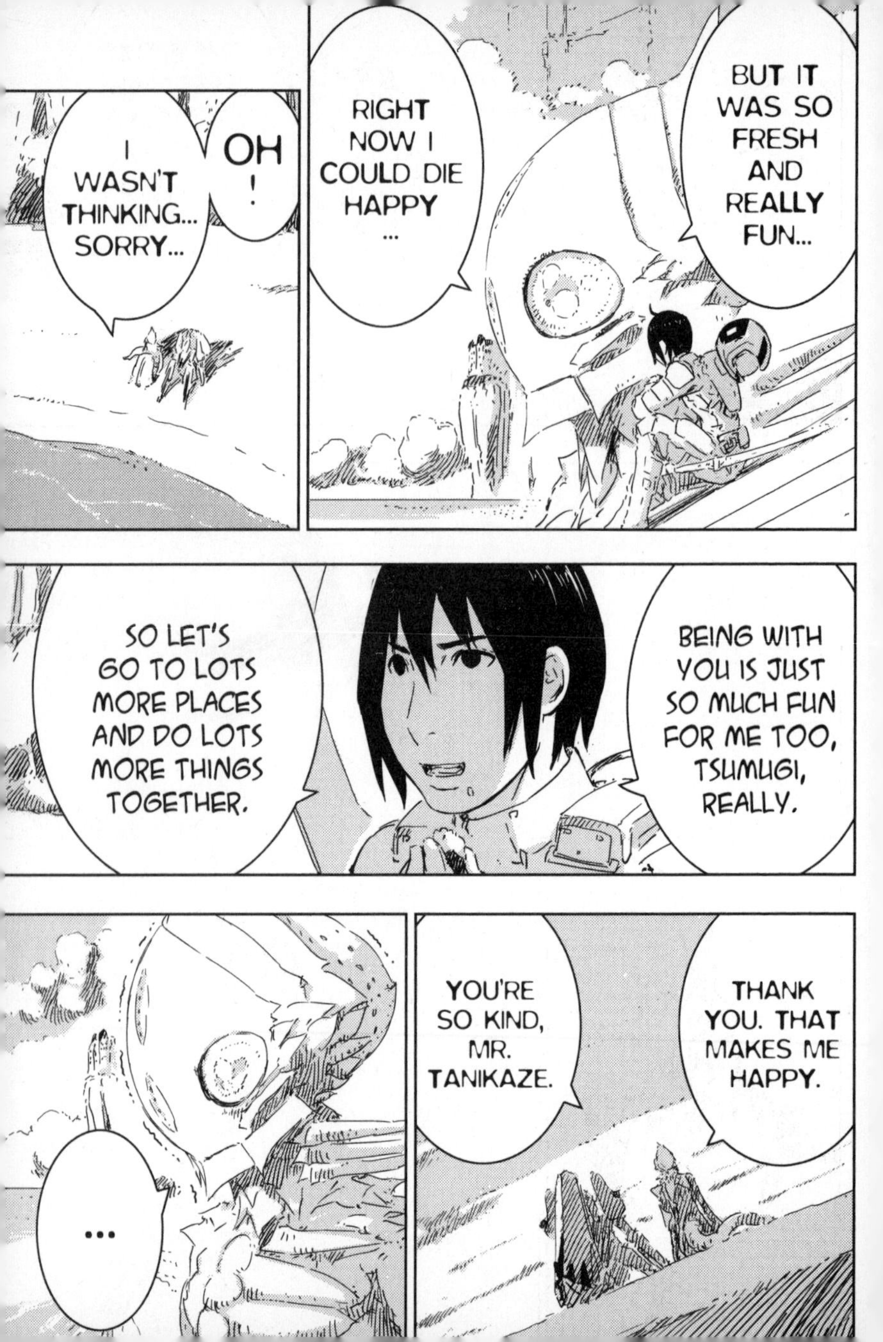
BUT IT WAS SO FRESH AND REALLY FUN...
RIGHT NOW I COULD DIE HAPPY ...
OH!
I WASN'T THINKING... SORRY...
BEING WITH YOU IS JUST SO MUCH FUN FOR ME TOO, TSUMUGI, REALLY.
SO LET'S GO TO LOTS MORE PLACES AND DO LOTS MORE THINGS TOGETHER.
THANK YOU. THAT MAKES ME HAPPY.
YOU'RE SO KIND, MR. TANIKAZE.
...

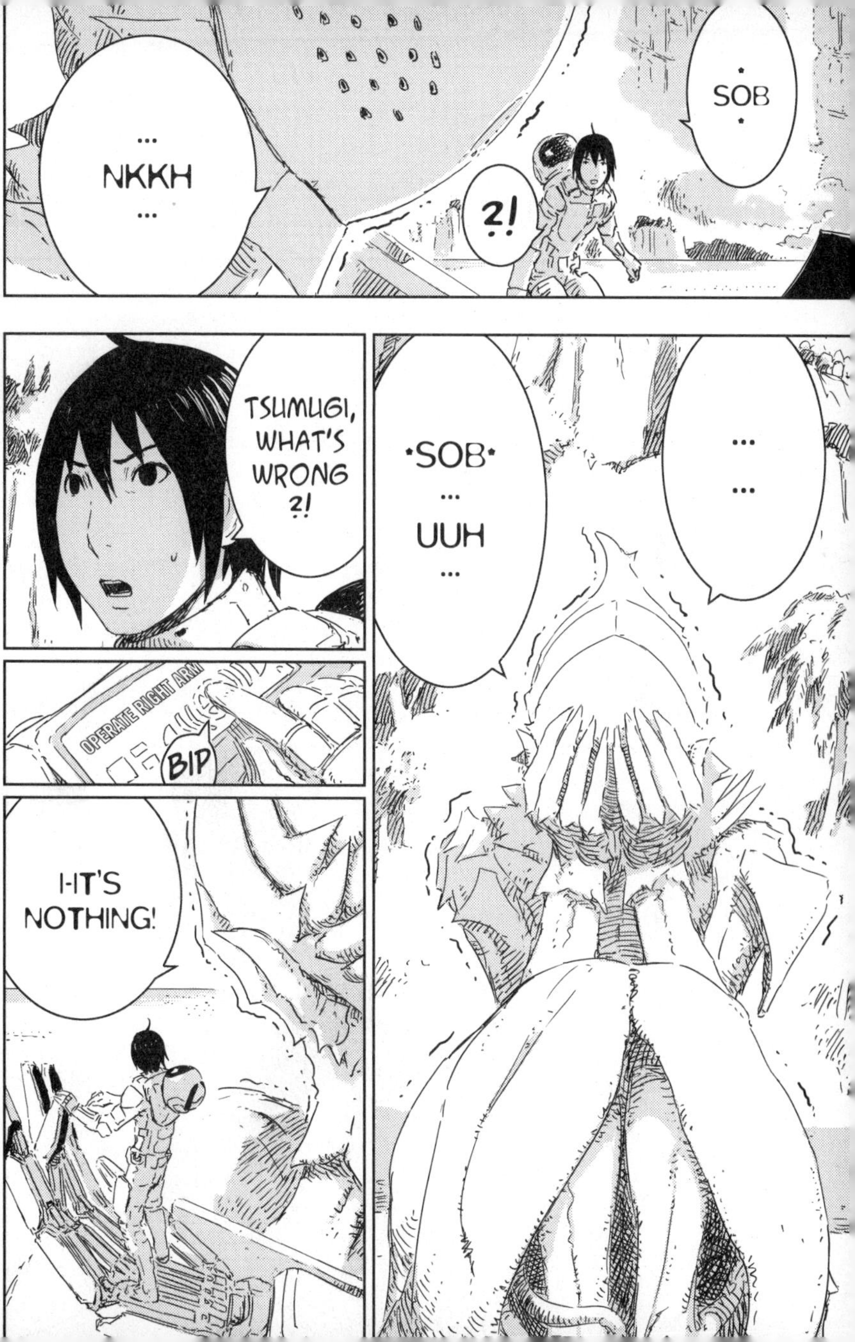
SOB
?!
... NKKH ...
... ...
SOB ... UUH ...
TSUMUGI, WHAT'S WRONG?!
OPERATE RIGHT ARM
BIP
I-IT'S NOTHING!

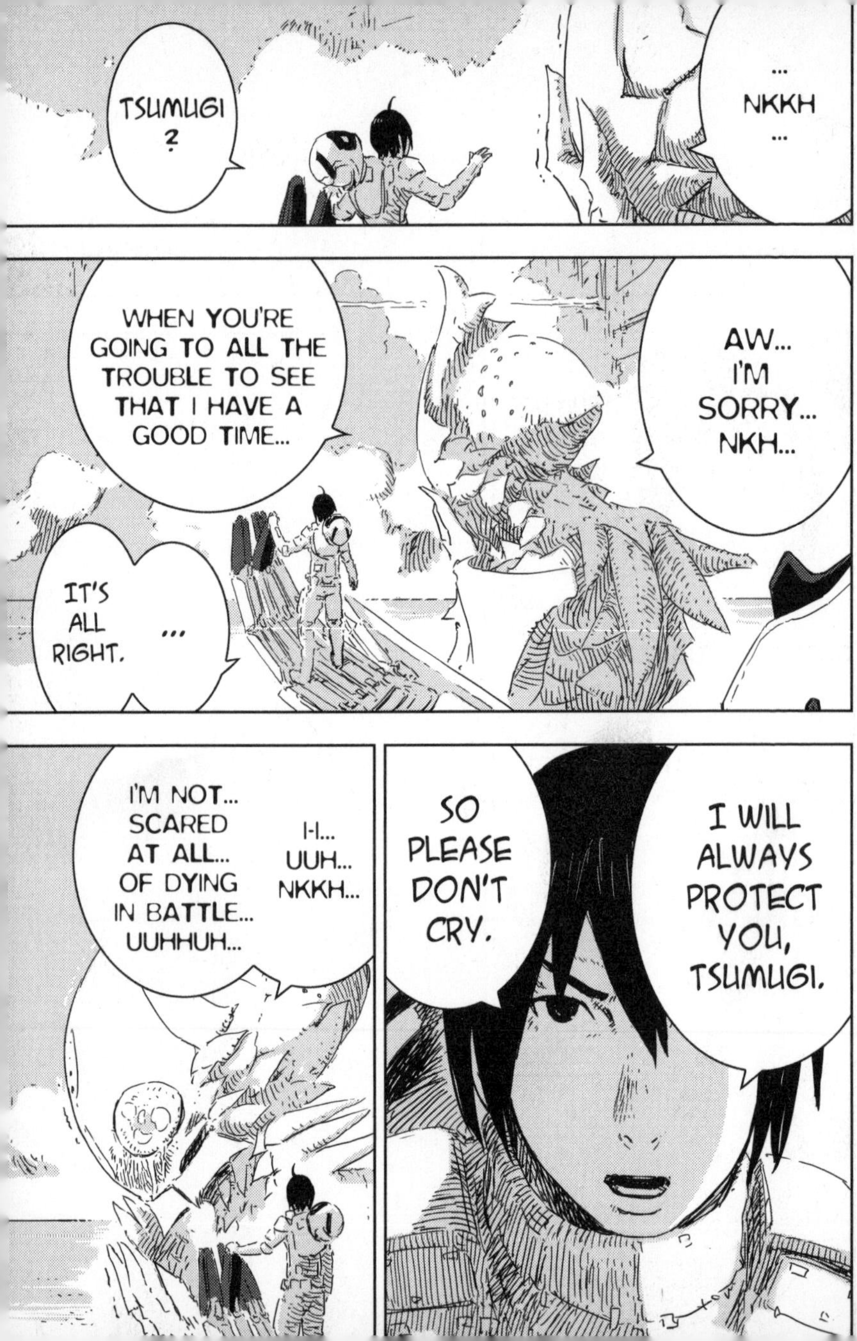
... NKKH ...
TSUMUGI ?
AW... I'M SORRY... NKH...
WHEN YOU'RE GOING TO ALL THE TROUBLE TO SEE THAT I HAVE A GOOD TIME...
IT'S ALL RIGHT. ...
I WILL ALWAYS PROTECT YOU, TSUMUGI.
SO PLEASE DON'T CRY.
I'M NOT... SCARED AT ALL... OF DYING IN BATTLE... UUHHUH...
I-I... UUH... NKKH...

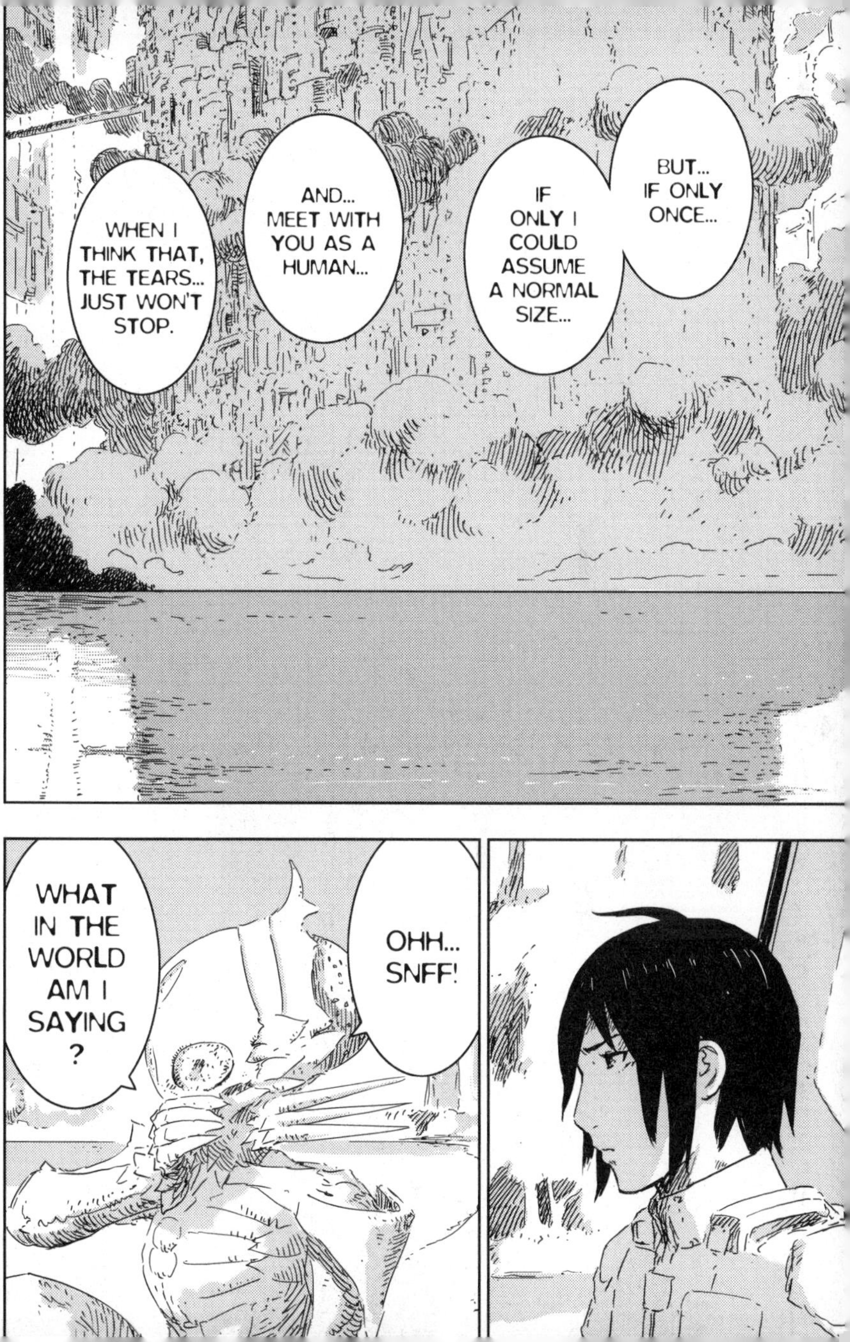
BUT... IF ONLY ONCE...
IF ONLY I COULD ASSUME A NORMAL SIZE...
AND... MEET WITH YOU AS A HUMAN...
WHEN I THINK THAT, THE TEARS... JUST WON'T STOP.
OHH... SNFF!
WHAT IN THE WORLD AM I SAYING?

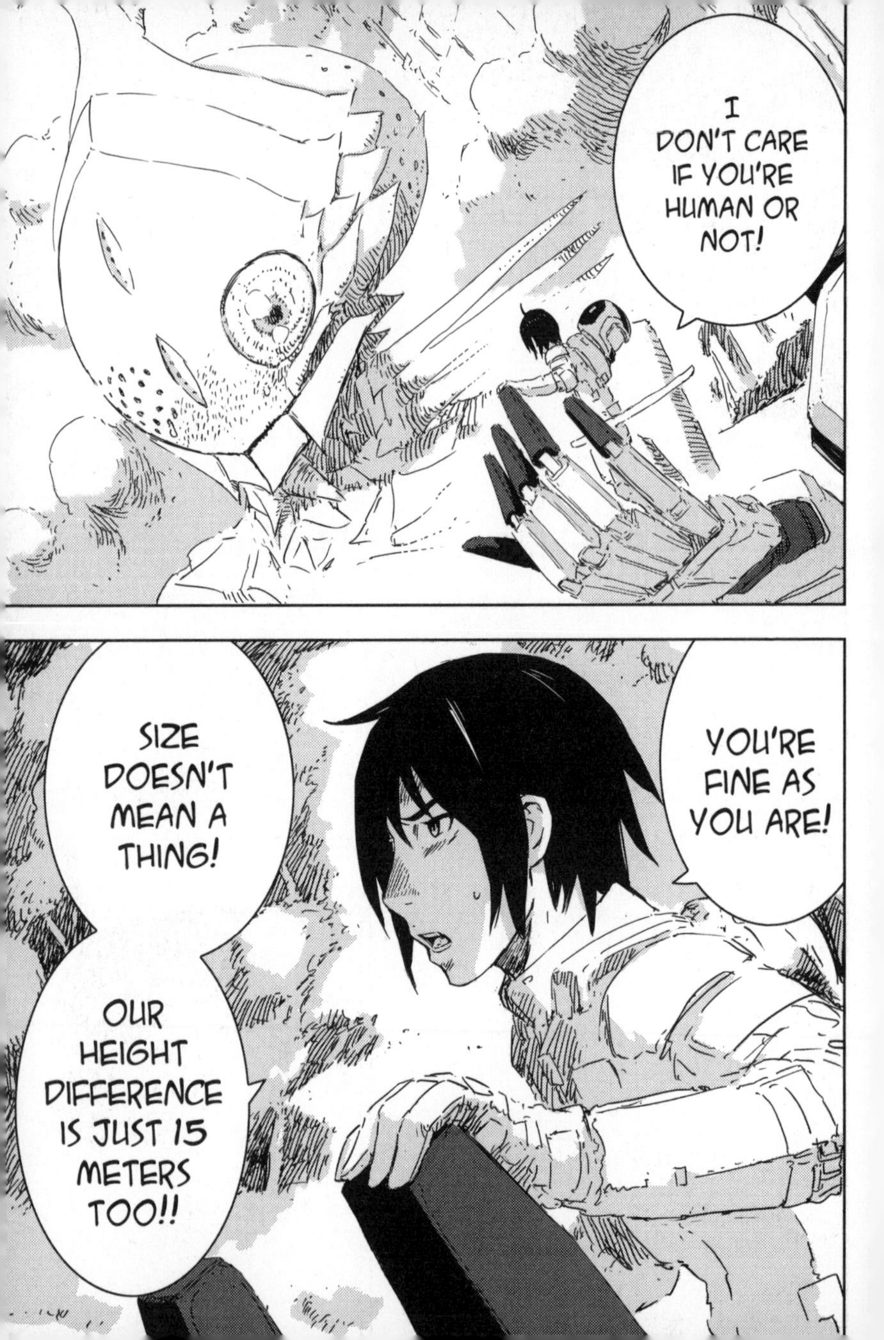
I DON'T CARE IF YOU'RE HUMAN OR NOT!
YOU'RE FINE AS YOU ARE!
SIZE DOESN'T MEAN A THING!
OUR HEIGHT DIFFERENCE IS JUST 15 METERS TOO!!

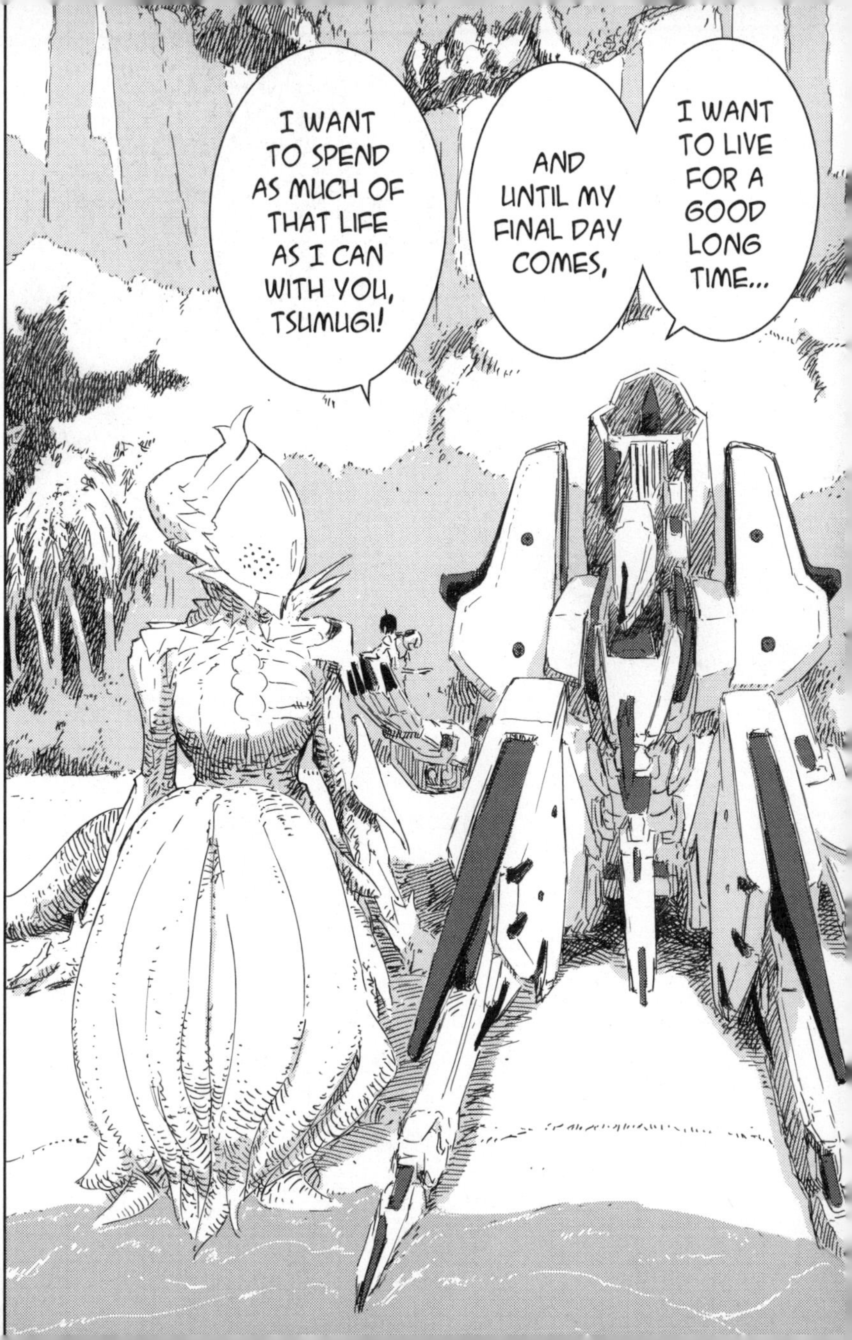
I WANT TO LIVE FOR A GOOD LONG TIME...
AND UNTIL MY FINAL DAY COMES,
I WANT TO SPEND AS MUCH OF THAT LIFE AS I CAN WITH YOU, TSUMUGI!

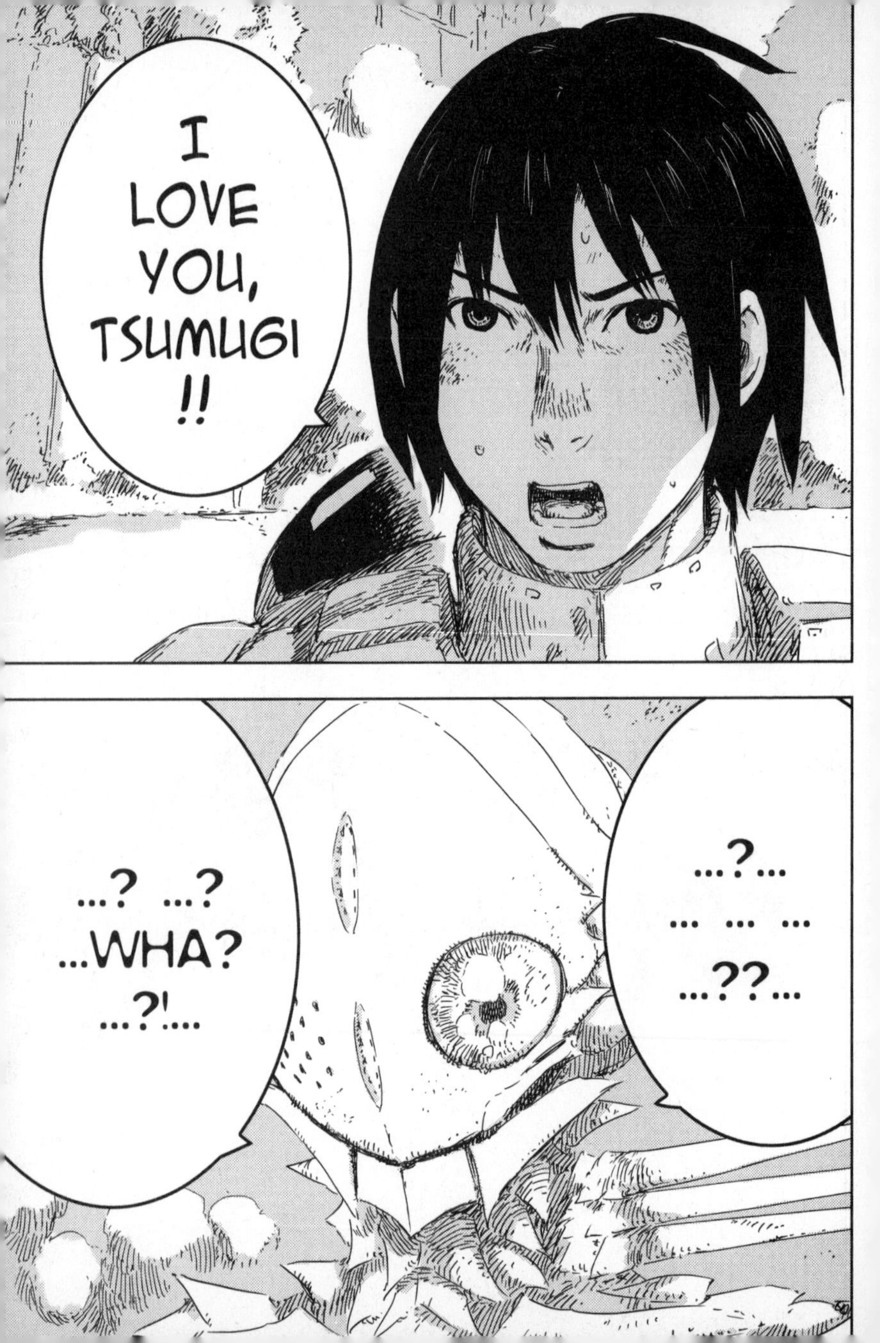
I LOVE YOU, TSUMUGI !!
...?... ... ...??...
...? ...? ...WHA? ...?!...

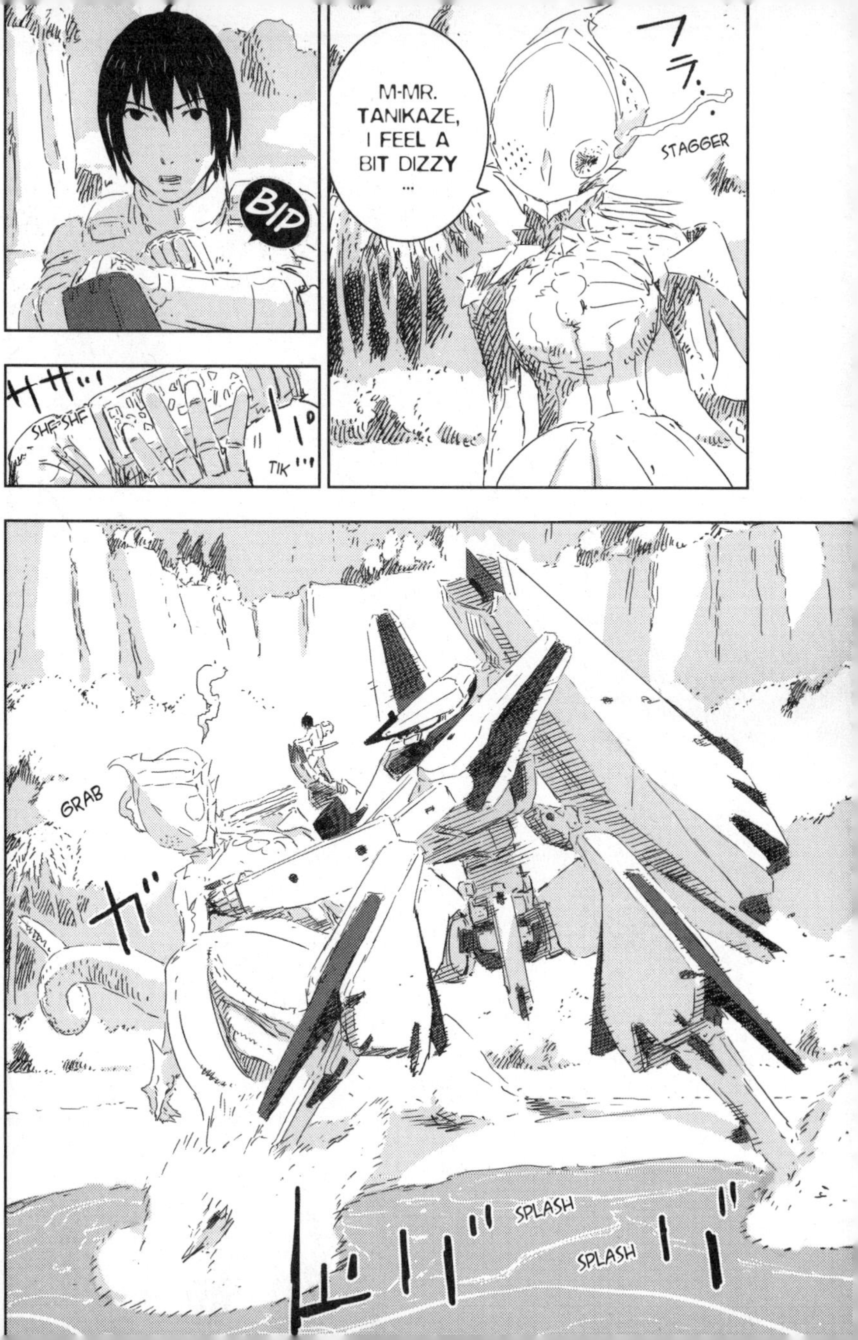
M-MR. TANIKAZE, I FEEL A BIT DIZZY ...
STAGGER
BIP
SHF SHF
TIK
GRAB
SPLASH
SPLASH

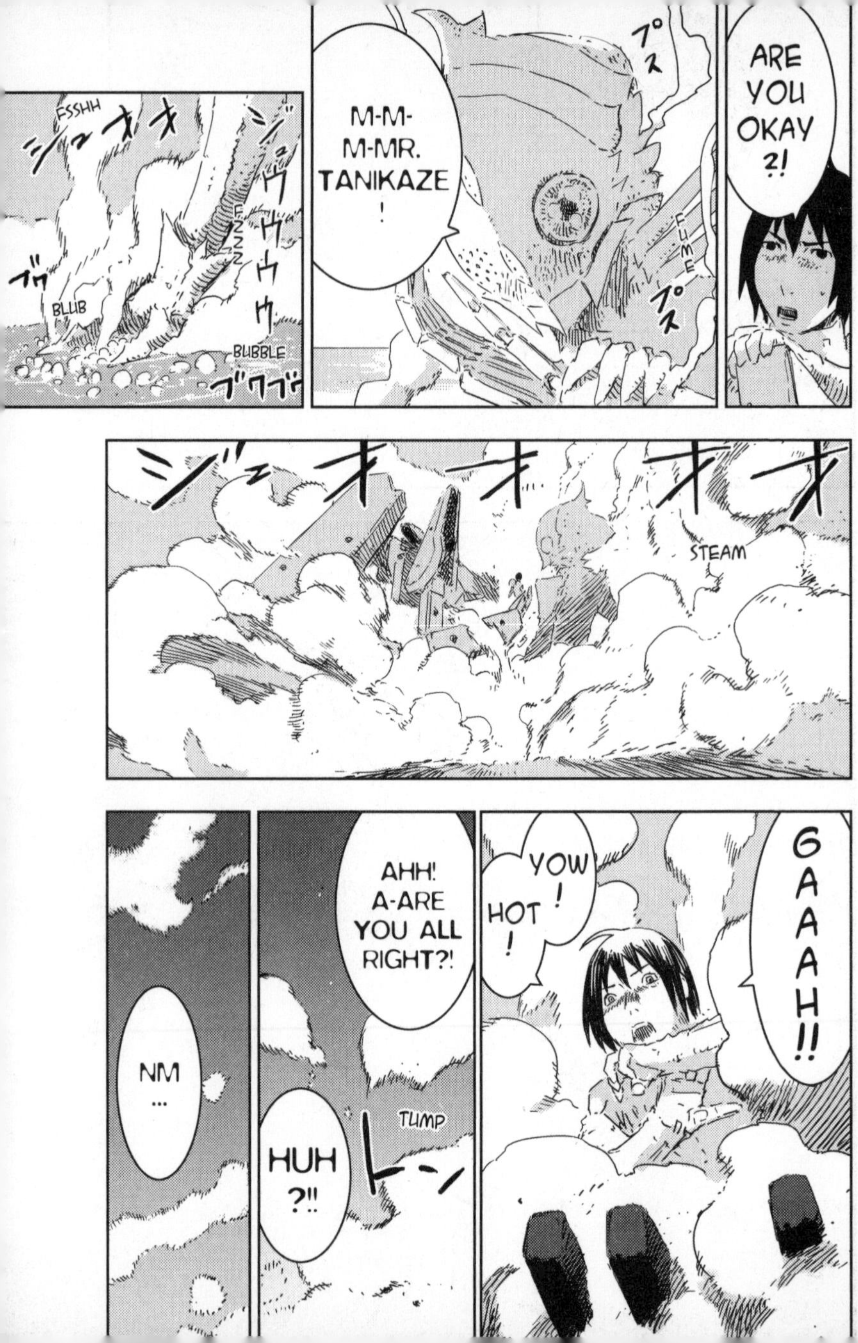
ARE YOU OKAY ?!
M-M-M-MR. TANIKAZE !
FUME
FSSHH
FZZZ
BLUB
BUBBLE
STEAM
GAAAAH!!
YOW !
HOT !
AHH! A-ARE YOU ALL RIGHT?!
TUMP
HUH ?!!
NM ...

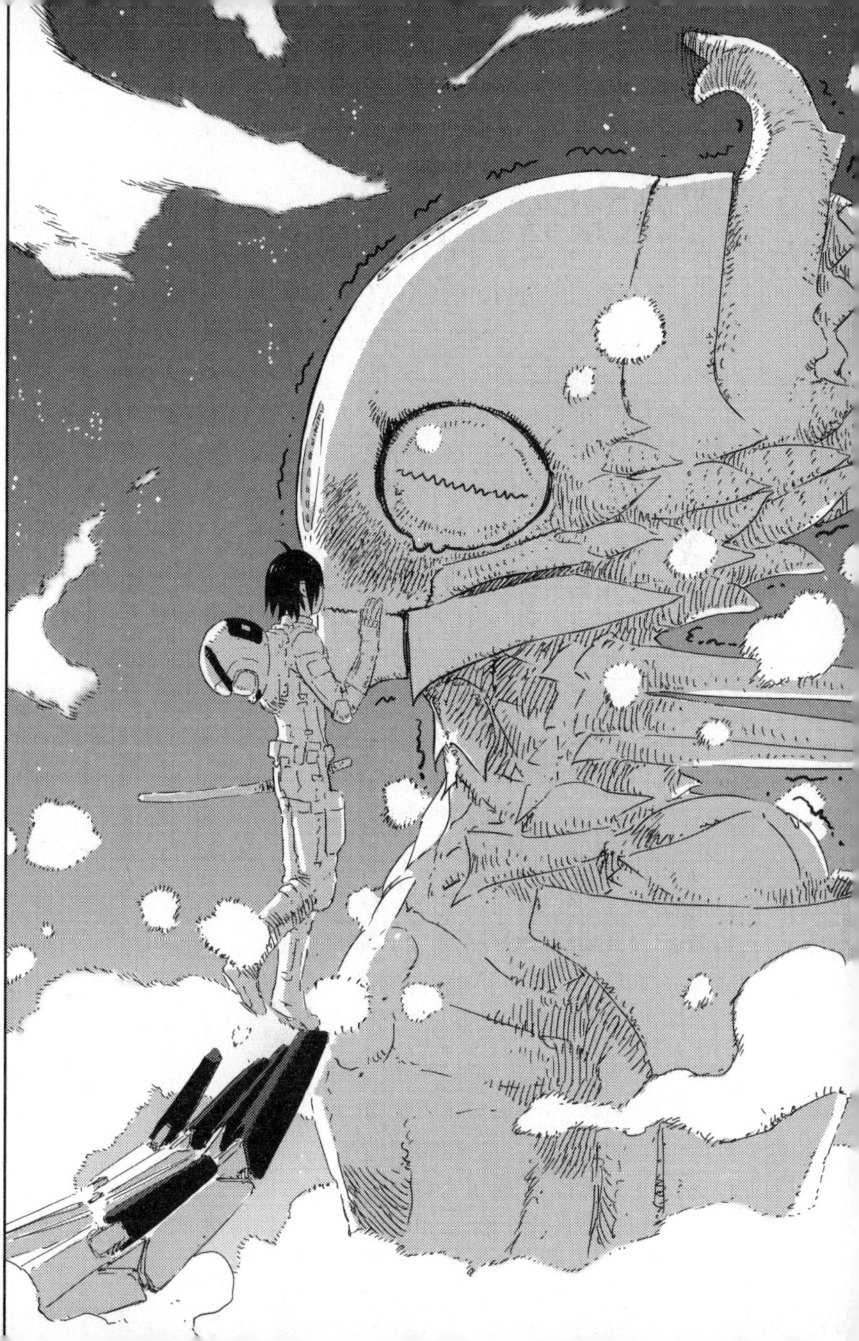

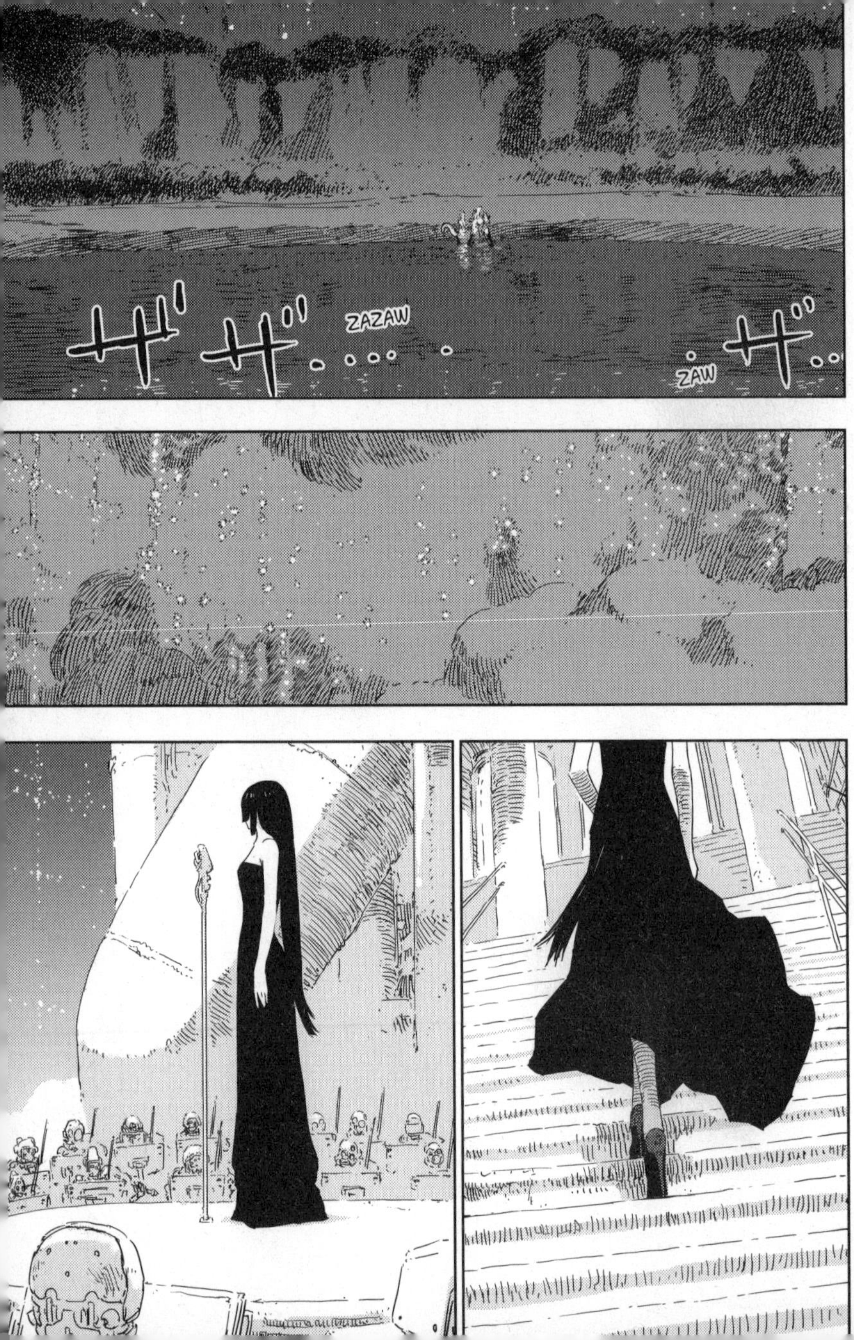
ザザ…
ZAZAW
ZAW
ザザ…

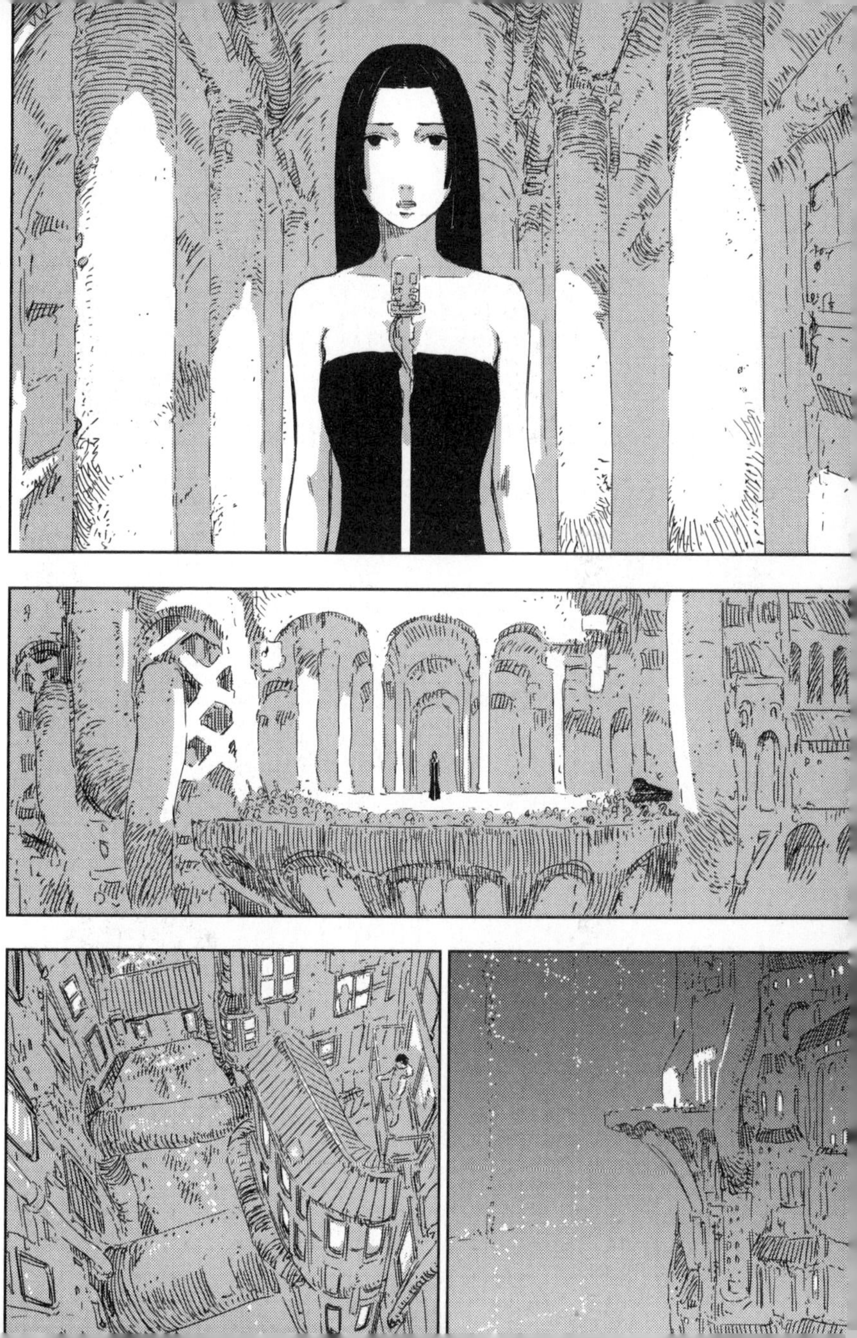

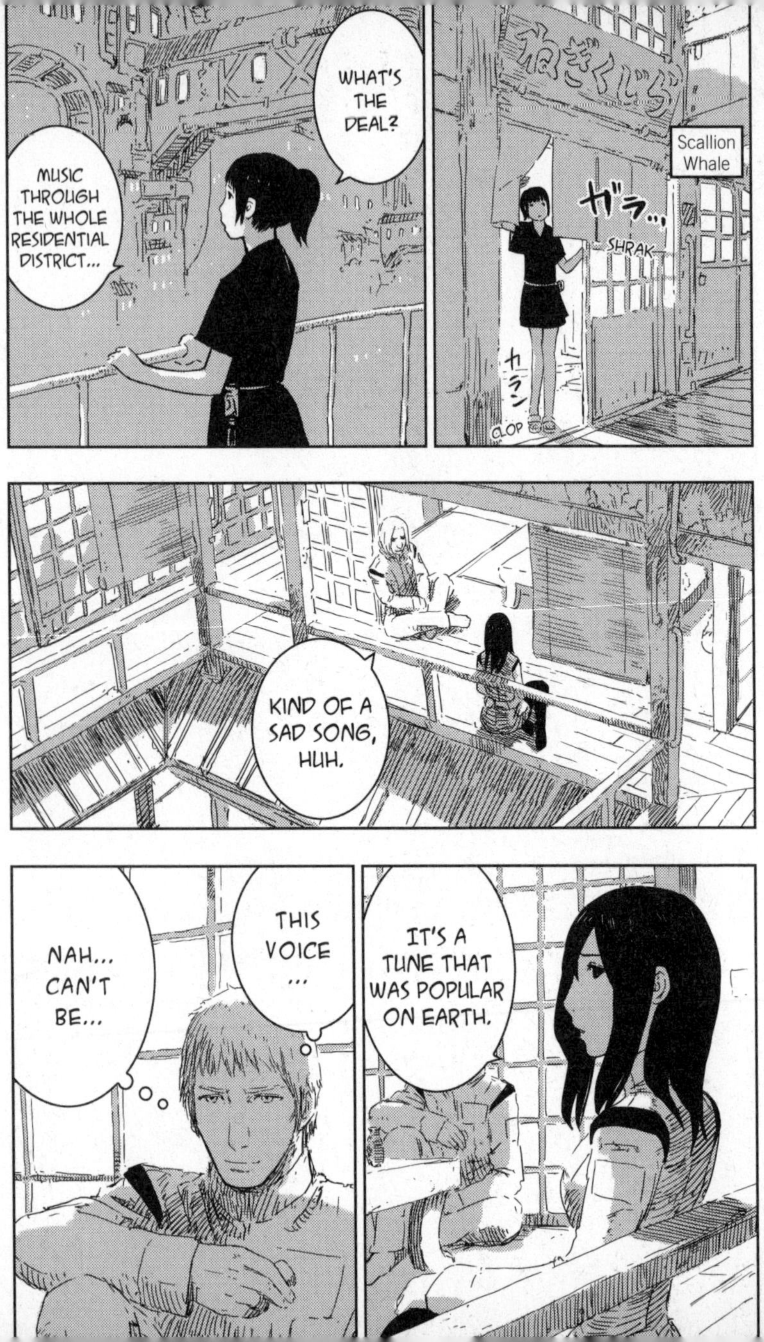
ねぎくじら
Scallion Whale
ガラ…
SHRAK
カラン
CLOP
WHAT'S THE DEAL?
MUSIC THROUGH THE WHOLE RESIDENTIAL DISTRICT...
KIND OF A SAD SONG, HUH.
IT'S A TUNE THAT WAS POPULAR ON EARTH.
THIS VOICE ...
NAH... CAN'T BE...

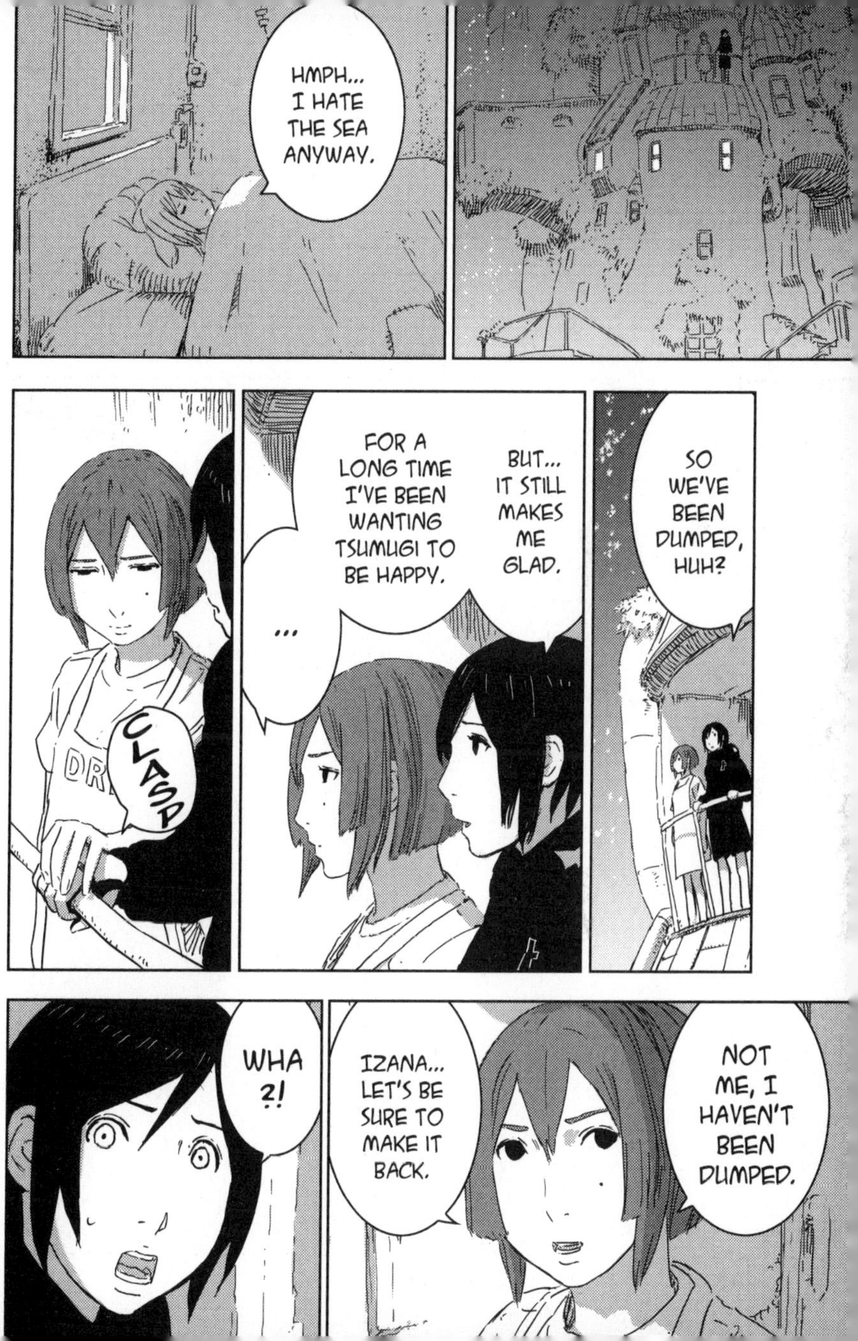
HMPH... I HATE THE SEA ANYWAY.
SO WE'VE BEEN DUMPED, HUH?
BUT... IT STILL MAKES ME GLAD.
FOR A LONG TIME I'VE BEEN WANTING TSUMUGI TO BE HAPPY.
...
CLASP
NOT ME, I HAVEN'T BEEN DUMPED.
IZANA... LET'S BE SURE TO MAKE IT BACK.
WHA ?!

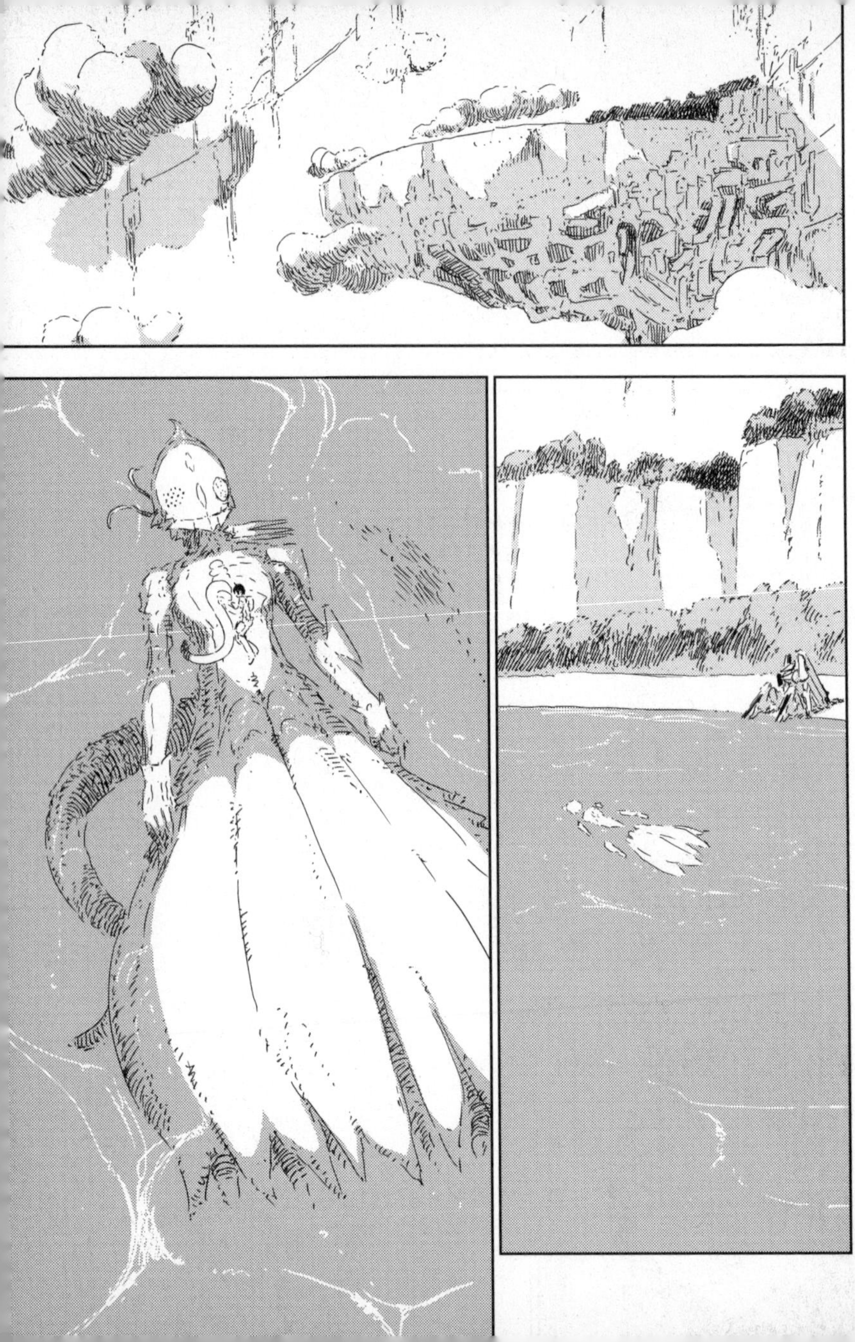

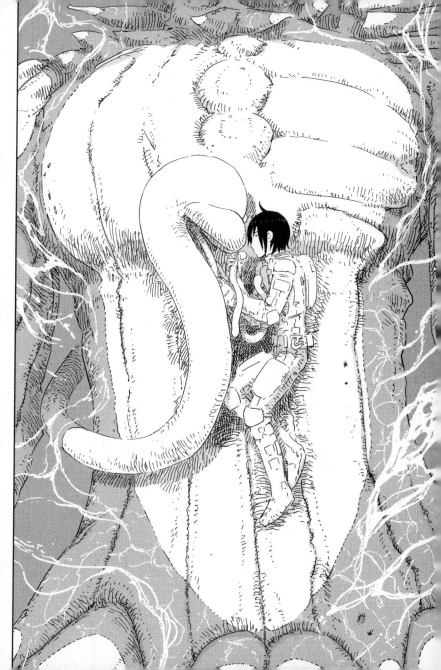

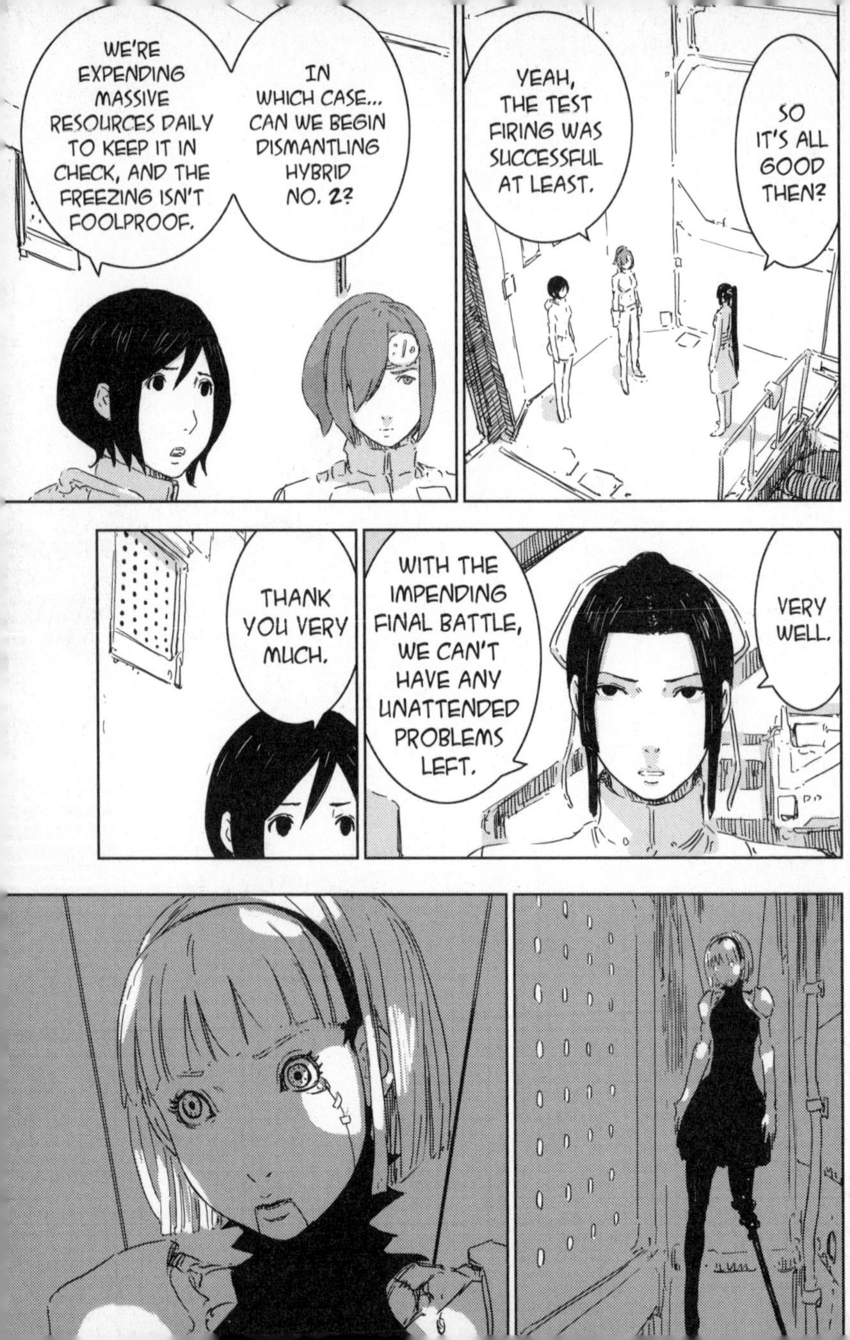
SO IT'S ALL GOOD THEN?
YEAH, THE TEST FIRING WAS SUCCESSFUL AT LEAST.
IN WHICH CASE... CAN WE BEGIN DISMANTLING HYBRID NO. 2?
WE'RE EXPENDING MASSIVE RESOURCES DAILY TO KEEP IT IN CHECK, AND THE FREEZING ISN'T FOOLPROOF.
VERY WELL.
WITH THE IMPENDING FINAL BATTLE, WE CAN'T HAVE ANY UNATTENDED PROBLEMS LEFT.
THANK YOU VERY MUCH.

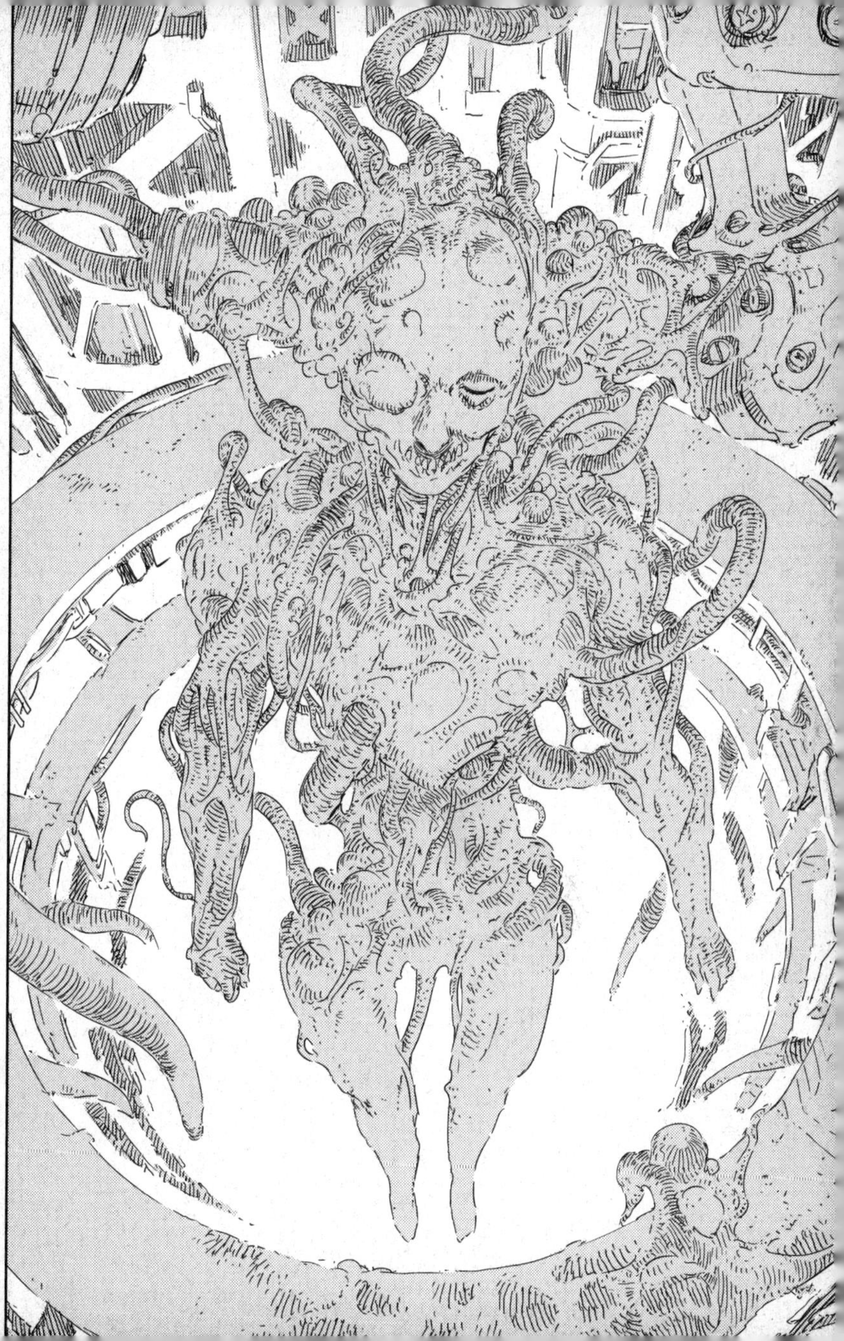

Chapter 63: END

シドニアの騎士

KNIGHTS OF SIDONIA

Tsugumori Mark II

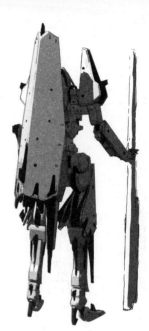

Tsugumori Mark II head

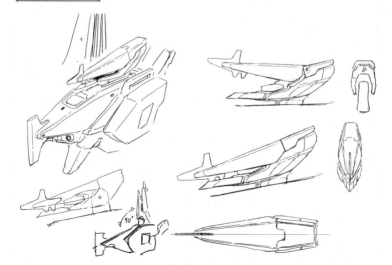

90°

Chapter 64: Kanata's Dismantlement

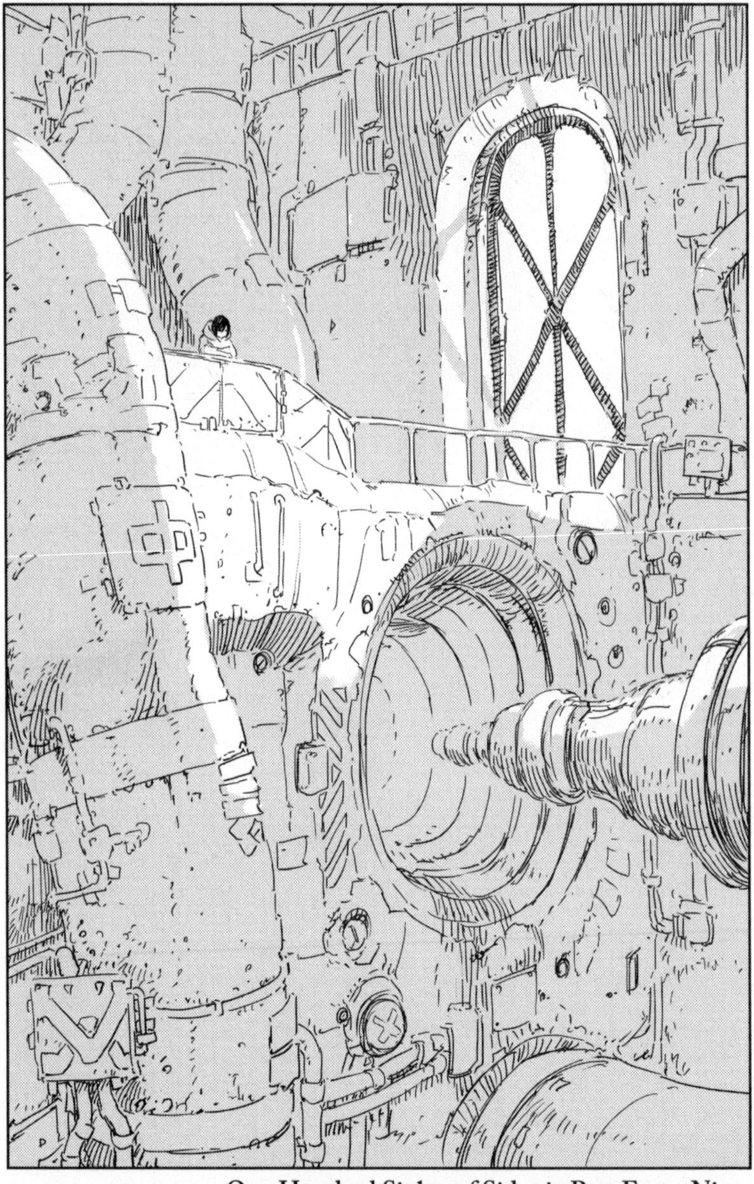

One Hundred Sights of Sidonia Part Forty-Nine:
Higgs Flow Channel Connection Terminal

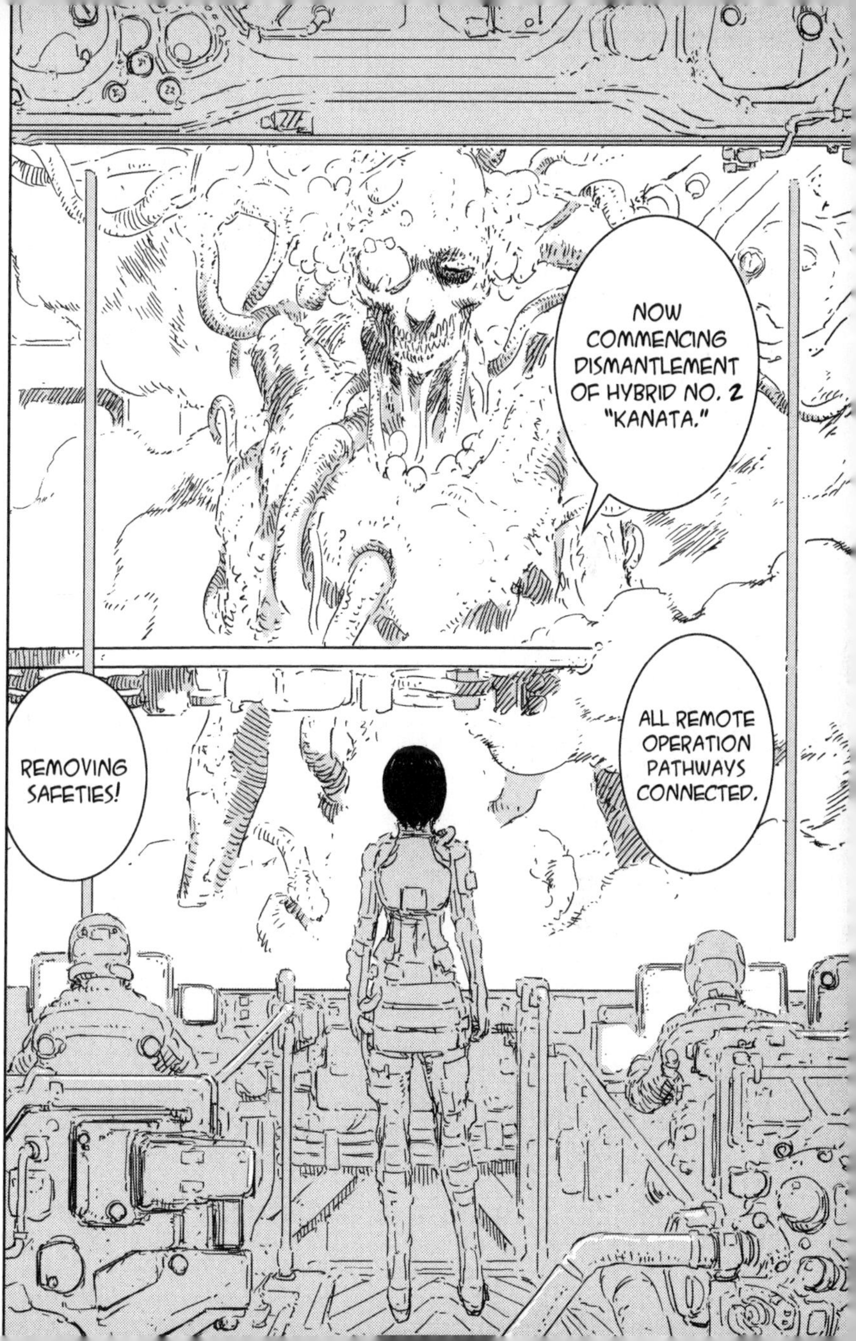
NOW COMMENCING DISMANTLEMENT OF HYBRID NO. 2 "KANATA."
ALL REMOTE OPERATION PATHWAYS CONNECTED.
REMOVING SAFETIES!

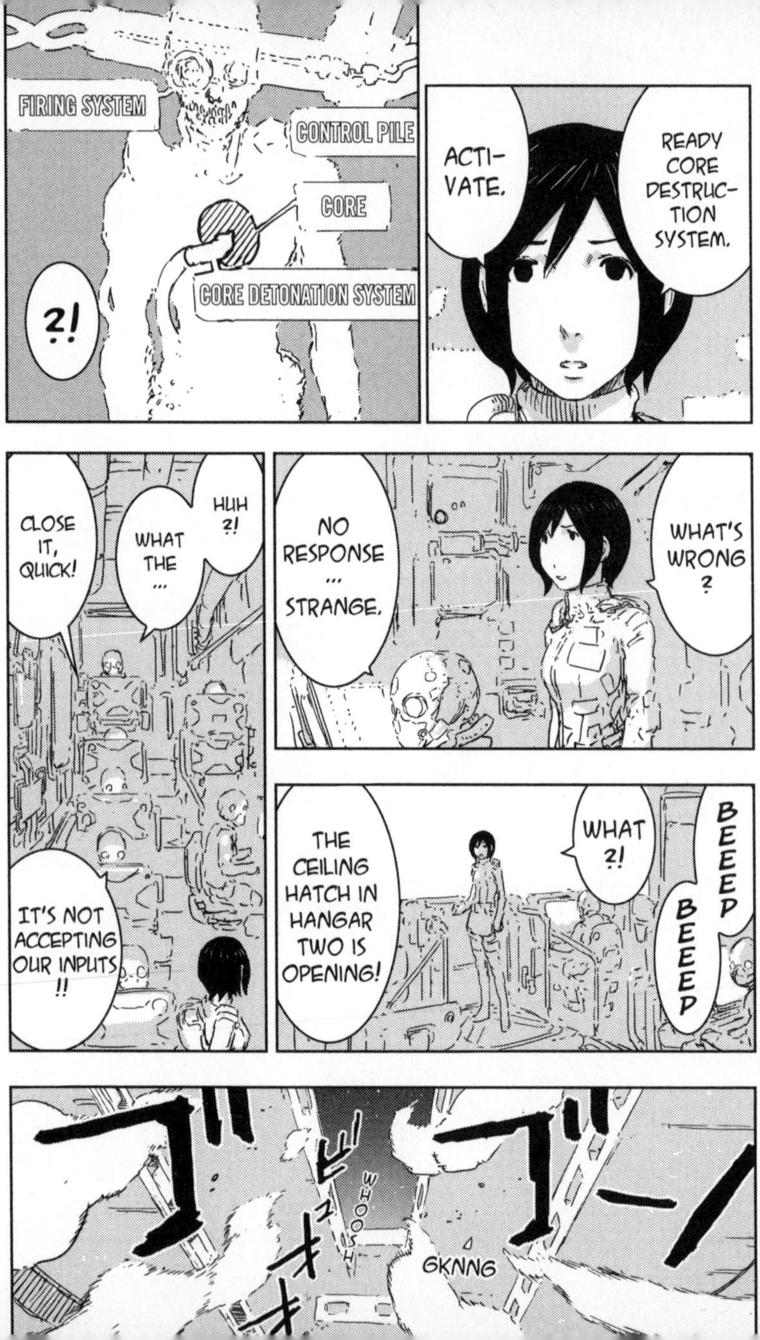
READY CORE DESTRUCTION SYSTEM.
ACTIVATE.
FIRING SYSTEM
CONTROL PILE
CORE
CORE DETONATION SYSTEM
?!
WHAT'S WRONG?
NO RESPONSE ... STRANGE.
BEEEP
BEEEP
WHAT?!
THE CEILING HATCH IN HANGAR TWO IS OPENING!
HUH ?!
WHAT THE ...
CLOSE IT, QUICK!
IT'S NOT ACCEPTING OUR INPUTS!!
WHOOSH
GKNNG

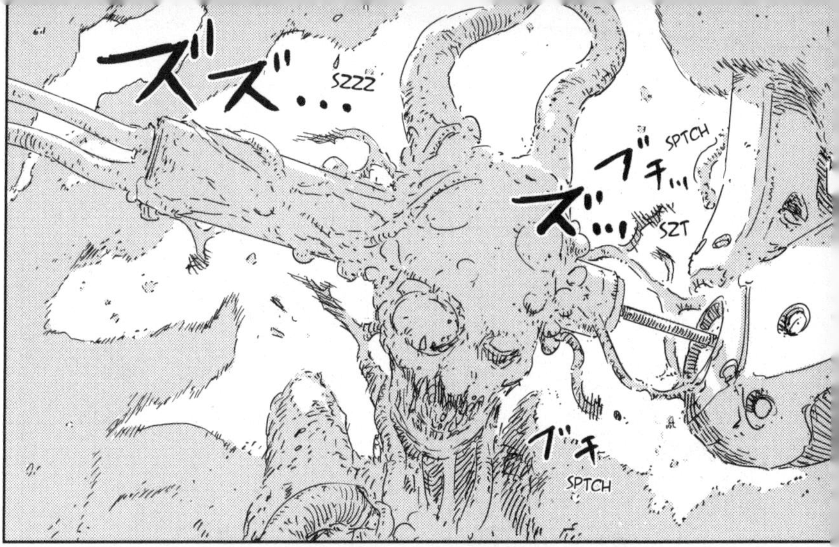
ズズ…
SZZZ
ブチ…
SPTCH
ズ…
SZT
ブチ
SPTCH

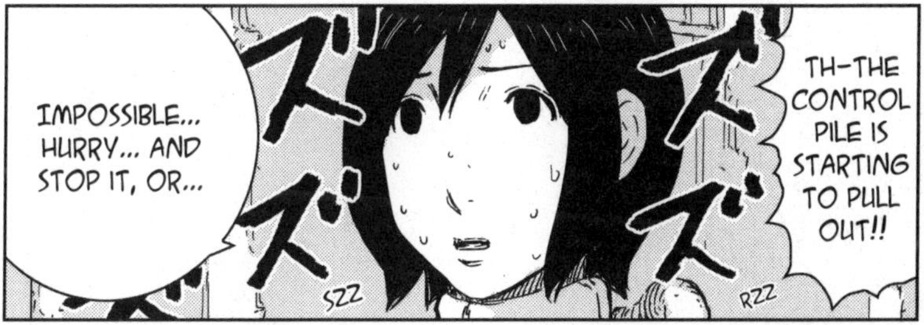
TH-THE CONTROL PILE IS STARTING TO PULL OUT!!
RZZ
IMPOSSIBLE... HURRY... AND STOP IT, OR...
SZZ

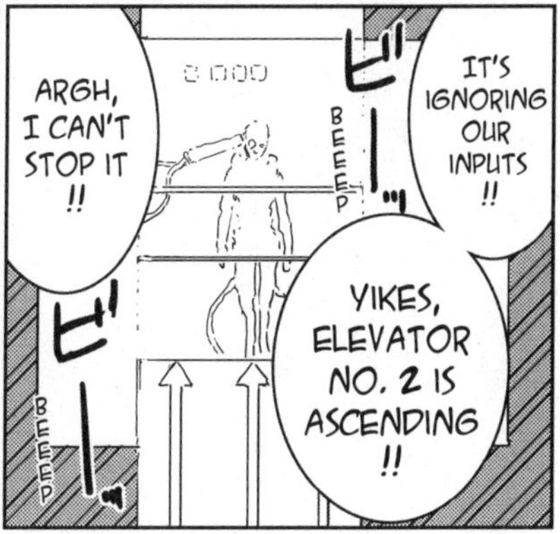
IT'S IGNORING OUR INPUTS!!
BEEEP
YIKES, ELEVATOR NO. 2 IS ASCENDING!!
ARGH, I CAN'T STOP IT!!
BEEEP

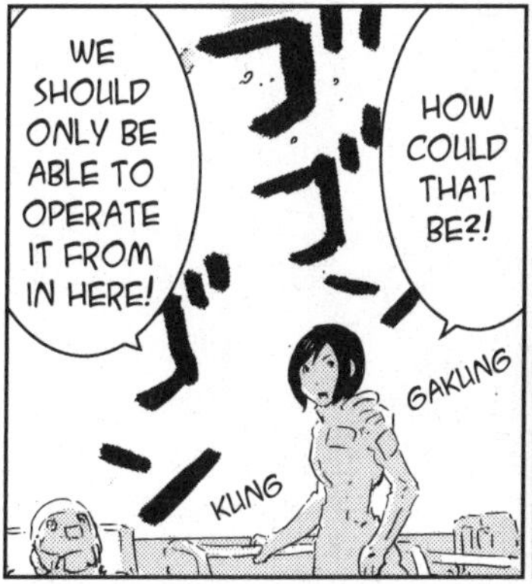
HOW COULD THAT BE?!
GAKUNG
WE SHOULD ONLY BE ABLE TO OPERATE IT FROM IN HERE!
KUNG

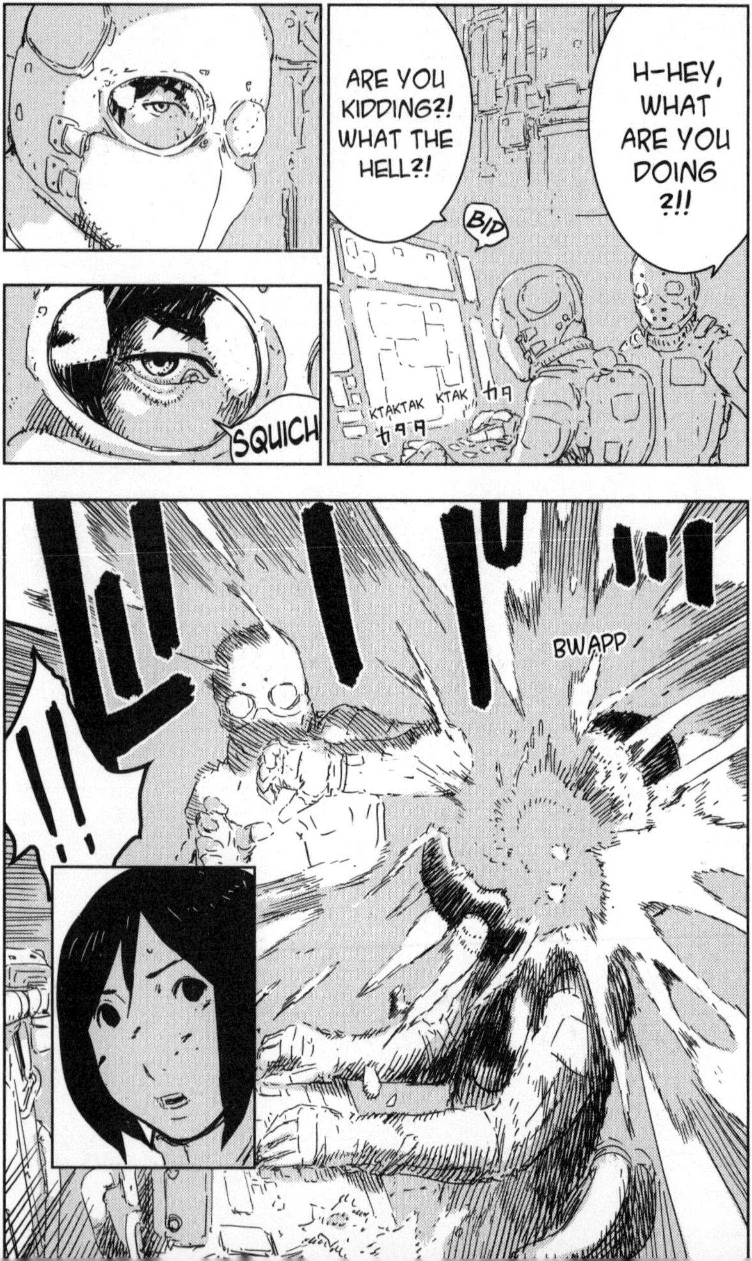
H-HEY, WHAT ARE YOU DOING ?!!
ARE YOU KIDDING?! WHAT THE HELL?!
BIP
KTAKTAK KTAK
SQUICH
BWAPP
!!!

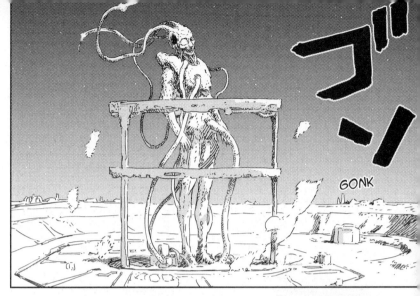

ゴン
GONK
EMERGENCY MESSAGE FROM THE SHINATOSE LABORATORY!
REQUEST FOR GARDE DEPLOYMENT TO OUTER SHELL OF KUNATO DEVELOPMENT!
WHAT IS UP ?!
THIS IS COMMAND. WHAT'S GOING ON OVER THERE ?!

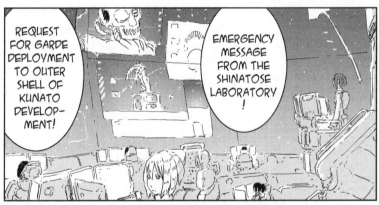

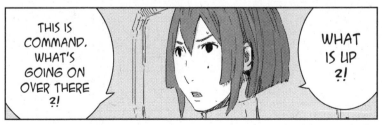

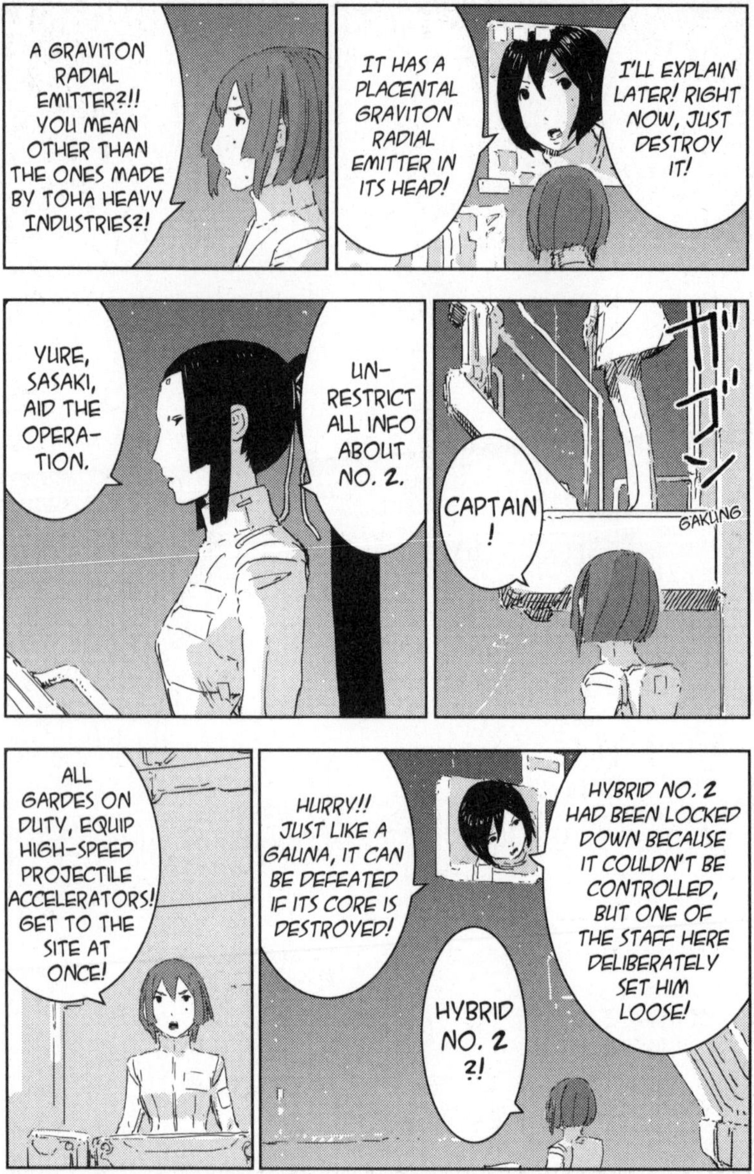
I'LL EXPLAIN LATER! RIGHT NOW, JUST DESTROY IT!
IT HAS A PLACENTAL GRAVITON RADIAL EMITTER IN ITS HEAD!
A GRAVITON RADIAL EMITTER?!! YOU MEAN OTHER THAN THE ONES MADE BY TOHA HEAVY INDUSTRIES?!
ガゴン
GAKUNG
CAPTAIN!
UN-RESTRICT ALL INFO ABOUT NO. 2.
YURE, SASAKI, AID THE OPERATION.
HYBRID NO. 2 HAD BEEN LOCKED DOWN BECAUSE IT COULDN'T BE CONTROLLED, BUT ONE OF THE STAFF HERE DELIBERATELY SET HIM LOOSE!
HYBRID NO. 2?!
HURRY!! JUST LIKE A GAUNA, IT CAN BE DEFEATED IF ITS CORE IS DESTROYED!
ALL GARDES ON DUTY, EQUIP HIGH-SPEED PROJECTILE ACCELERATORS! GET TO THE SITE AT ONCE!

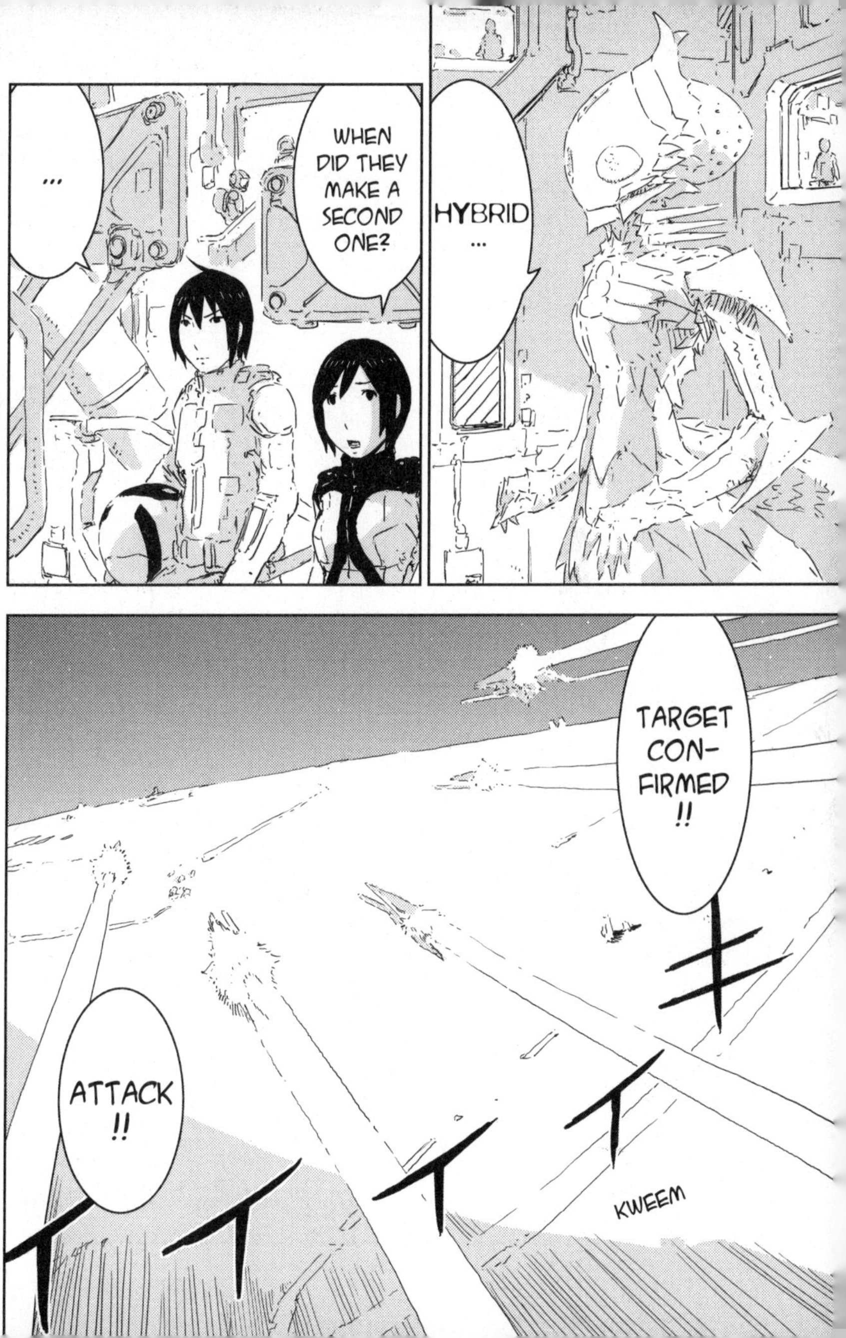
HYBRID ...
WHEN DID THEY MAKE A SECOND ONE?
...
TARGET CON-FIRMED !!
ATTACK !!
KWEEM

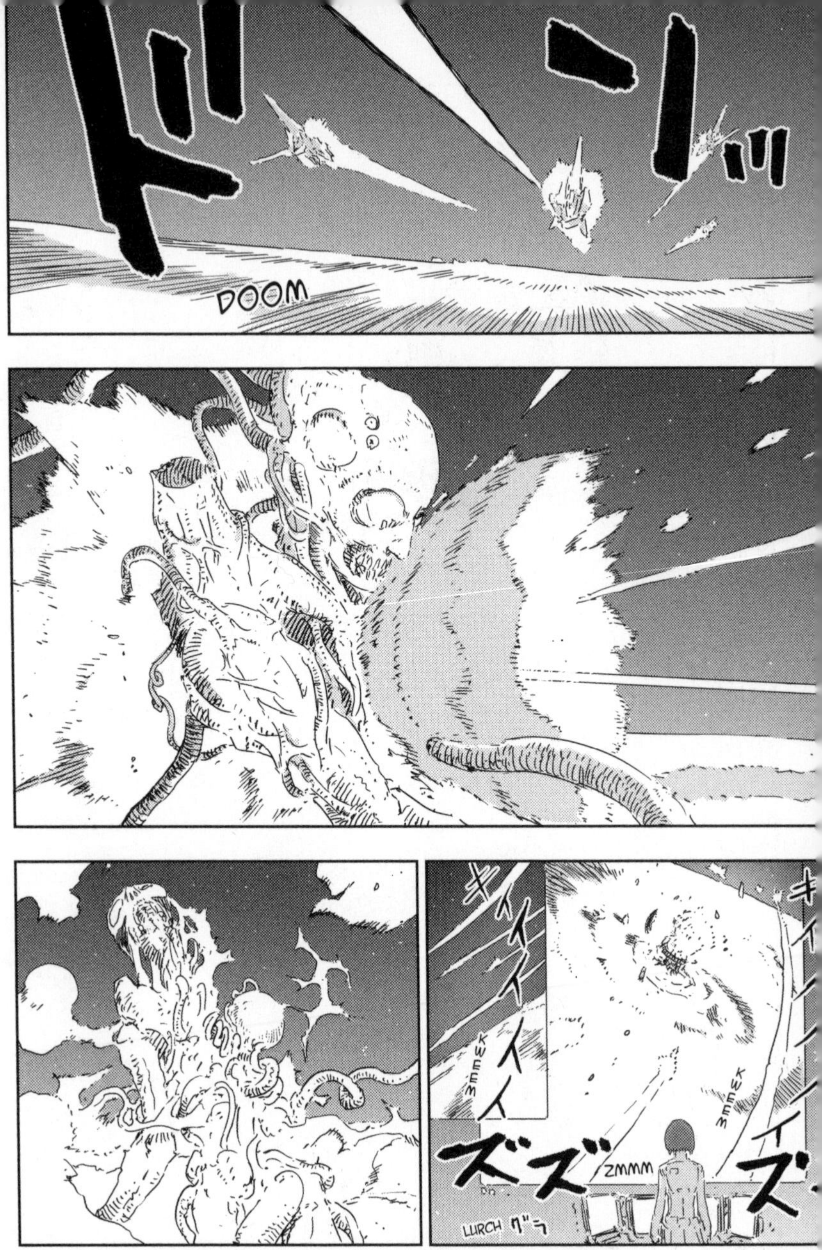
DOOM
KWEEEK
KWEEEK
ZMMM
LURCH

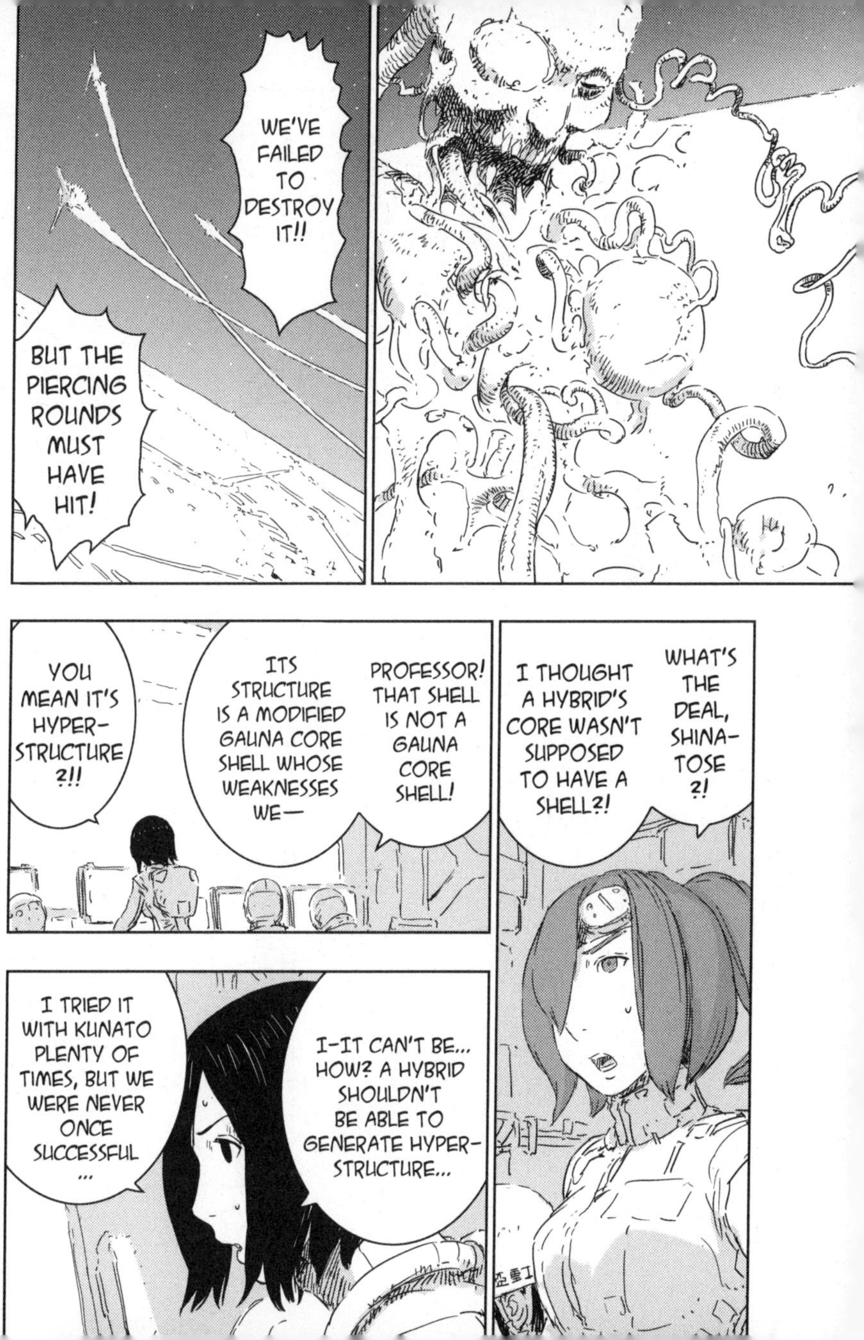
WE'VE FAILED TO DESTROY IT!!
BUT THE PIERCING ROUNDS MUST HAVE HIT!
WHAT'S THE DEAL, SHINATOSE?!
I THOUGHT A HYBRID'S CORE WASN'T SUPPOSED TO HAVE A SHELL?!
PROFESSOR! THAT SHELL IS NOT A GAUNA CORE SHELL!
ITS STRUCTURE IS A MODIFIED GAUNA CORE SHELL WHOSE WEAKNESSES WE—
YOU MEAN IT'S HYPER-STRUCTURE?!!
I-IT CAN'T BE... HOW? A HYBRID SHOULDN'T BE ABLE TO GENERATE HYPER-STRUCTURE...
I TRIED IT WITH KUNATO PLENTY OF TIMES, BUT WE WERE NEVER ONCE SUCCESSFUL...

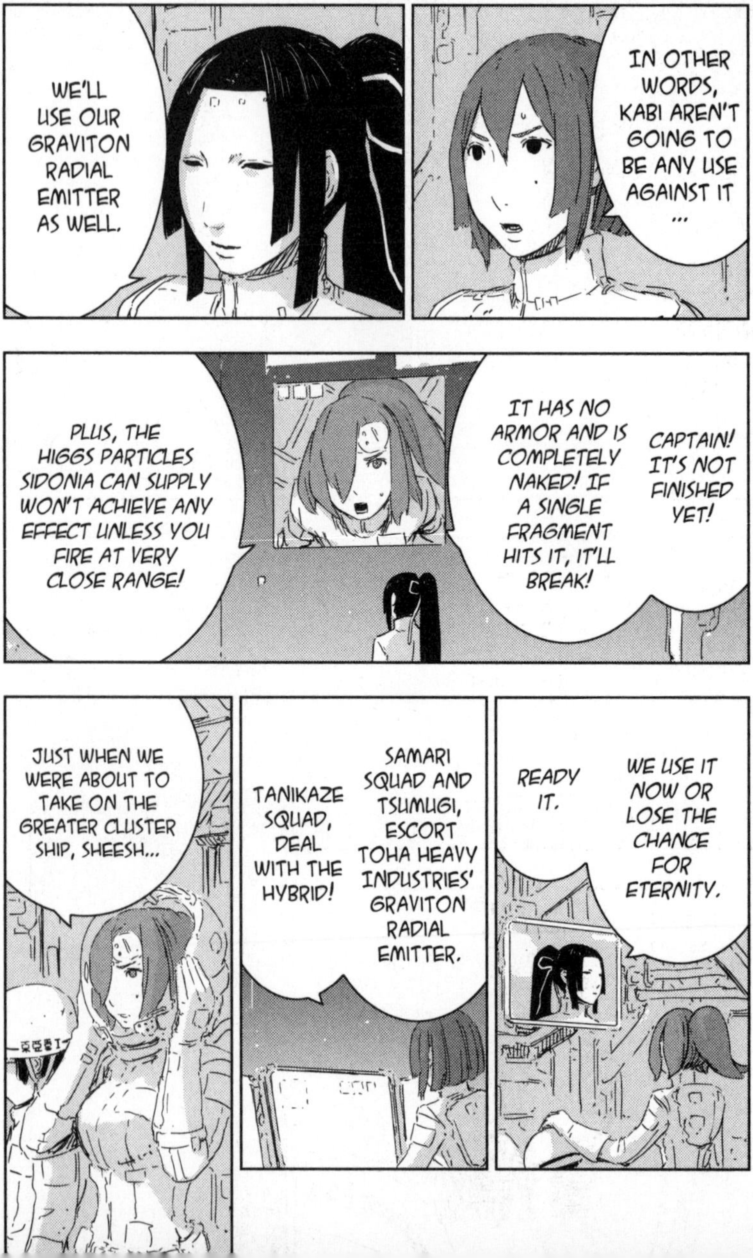
IN OTHER WORDS, KABI AREN'T GOING TO BE ANY USE AGAINST IT ...
WE'LL USE OUR GRAVITON RADIAL EMITTER AS WELL.
CAPTAIN! IT'S NOT FINISHED YET!
IT HAS NO ARMOR AND IS COMPLETELY NAKED! IF A SINGLE FRAGMENT HITS IT, IT'LL BREAK!
PLUS, THE HIGGS PARTICLES SIDONIA CAN SUPPLY WON'T ACHIEVE ANY EFFECT UNLESS YOU FIRE AT VERY CLOSE RANGE!
WE USE IT NOW OR LOSE THE CHANCE FOR ETERNITY.
READY IT.
SAMARI SQUAD AND TSUMUGI, ESCORT TOHA HEAVY INDUSTRIES' GRAVITON RADIAL EMITTER.
TANIKAZE SQUAD, DEAL WITH THE HYBRID!
JUST WHEN WE WERE ABOUT TO TAKE ON THE GREATER CLUSTER SHIP, SHEESH...

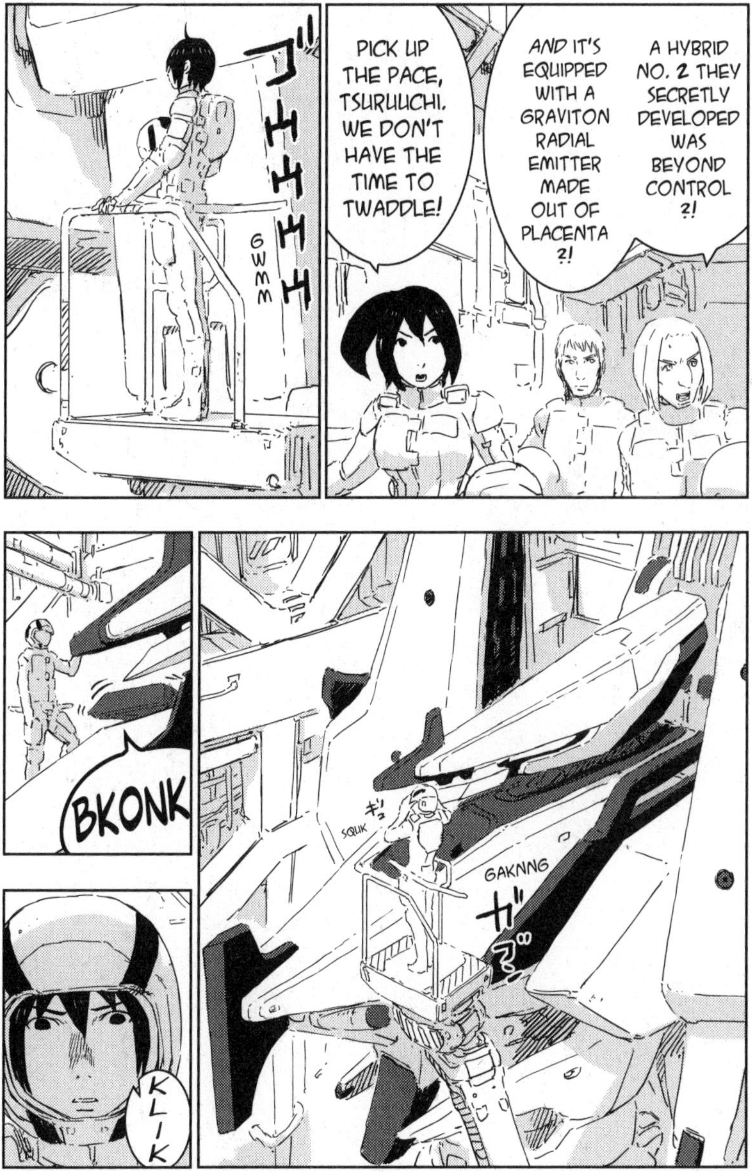
A HYBRID NO. 2 THEY SECRETLY DEVELOPED WAS BEYOND CONTROL ?!
AND IT'S EQUIPPED WITH A GRAVITON RADIAL EMITTER MADE OUT OF PLACENTA ?!
PICK UP THE PACE, TSURUUCHI. WE DON'T HAVE THE TIME TO TWADDLE!
GWMM
SQUK
GAKNNG
BKONK
KLIK

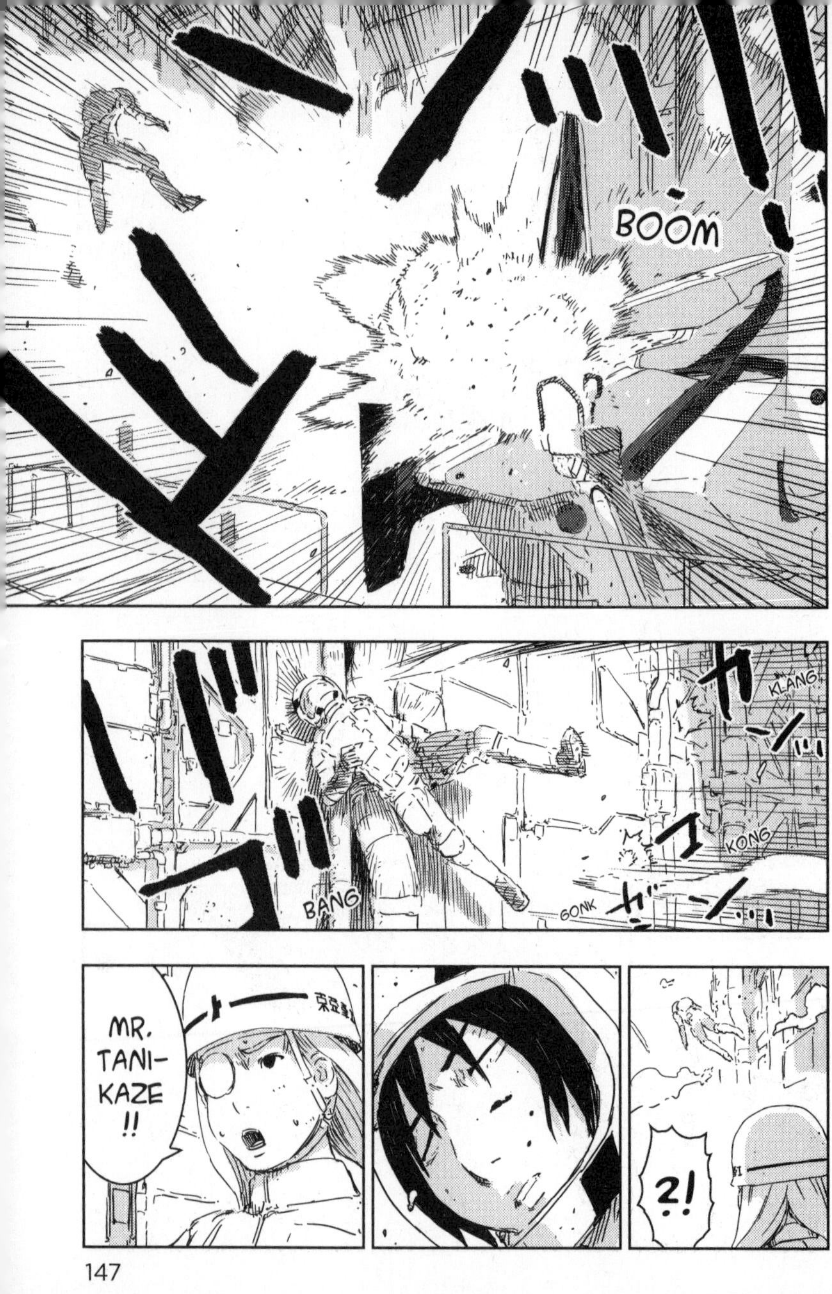
BOOM
KLANG
KONG
GONK
BANG
?!
MR. TANI-KAZE!!

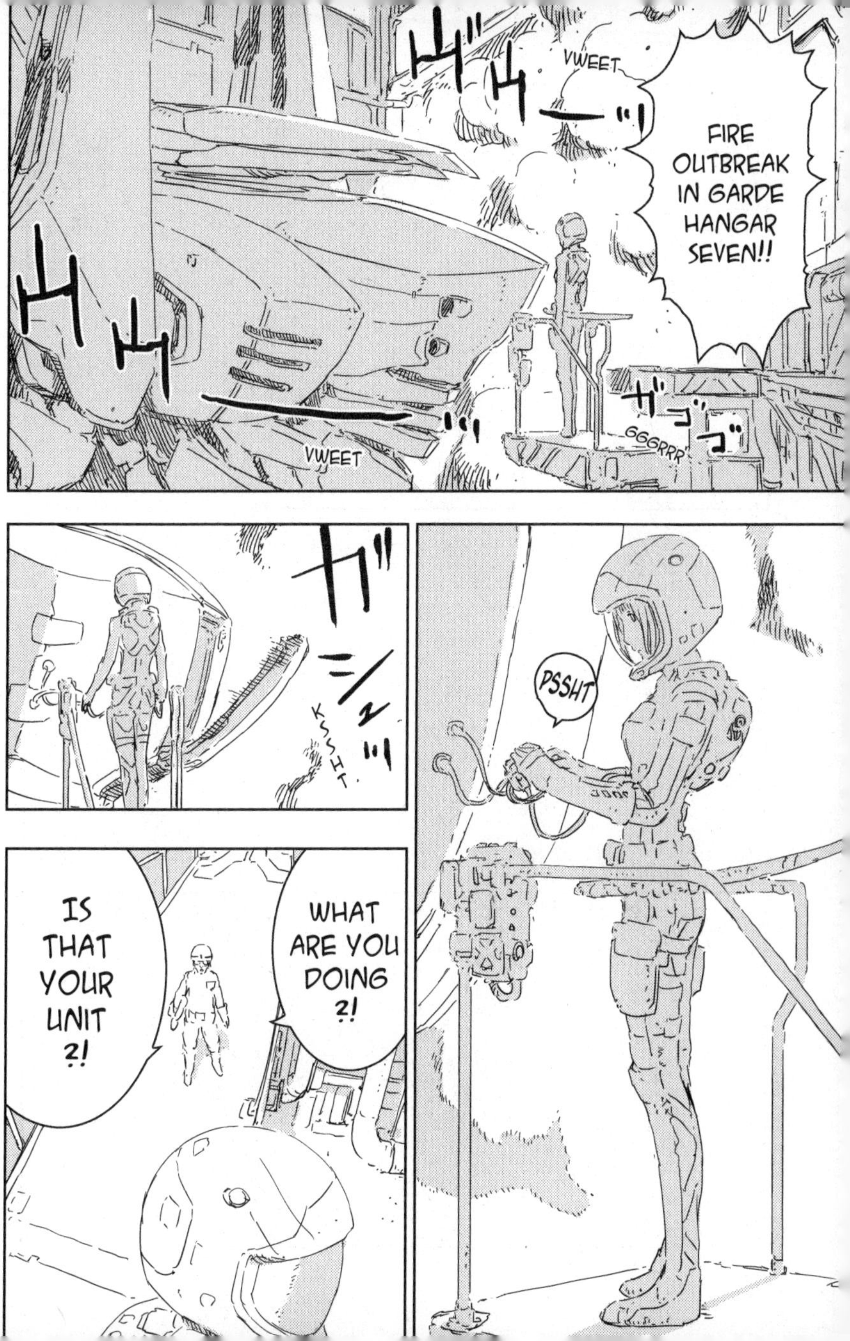
VWEET
FIRE OUTBREAK IN GARDE HANGAR SEVEN!!
VWEET
GGGRRR
PSSHT
KSSHT
WHAT ARE YOU DOING ?!
IS THAT YOUR UNIT ?!

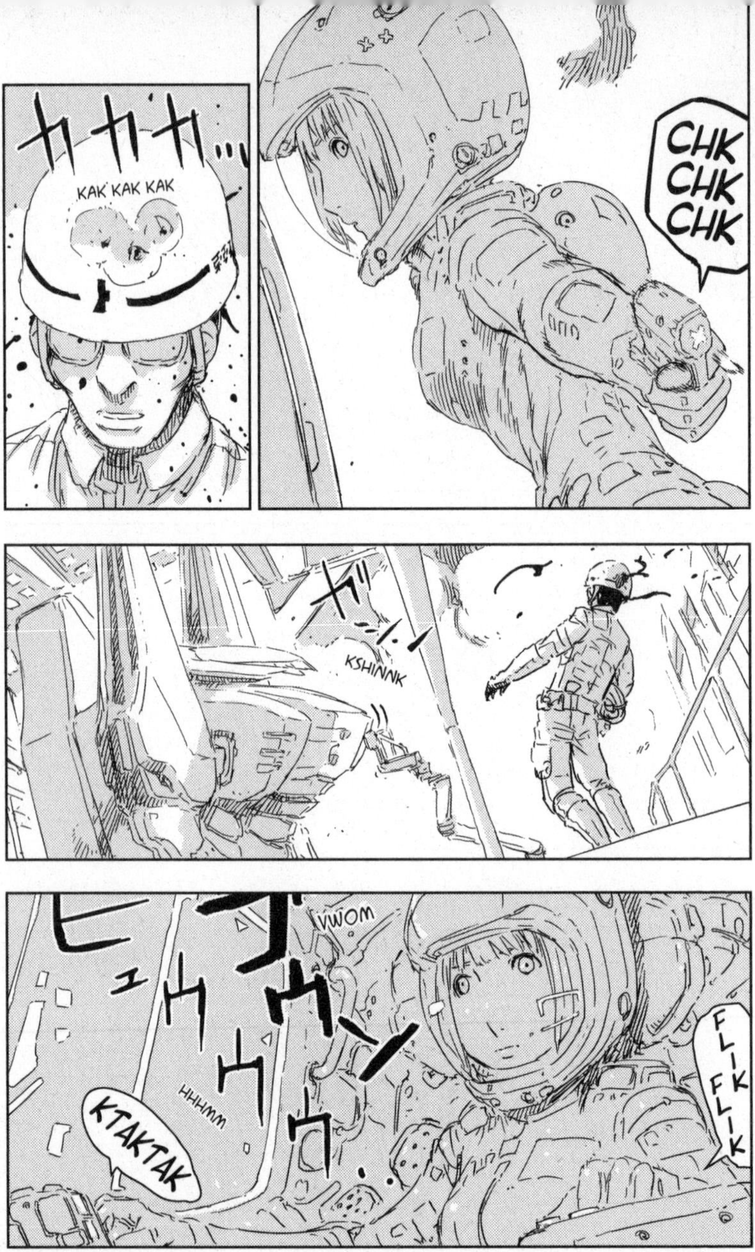
CHK CHK CHK
カカカ…
KAK KAK KAK
KSHINNK
FLIK FLIK
VWOM
HHHMM
KTAKTAK

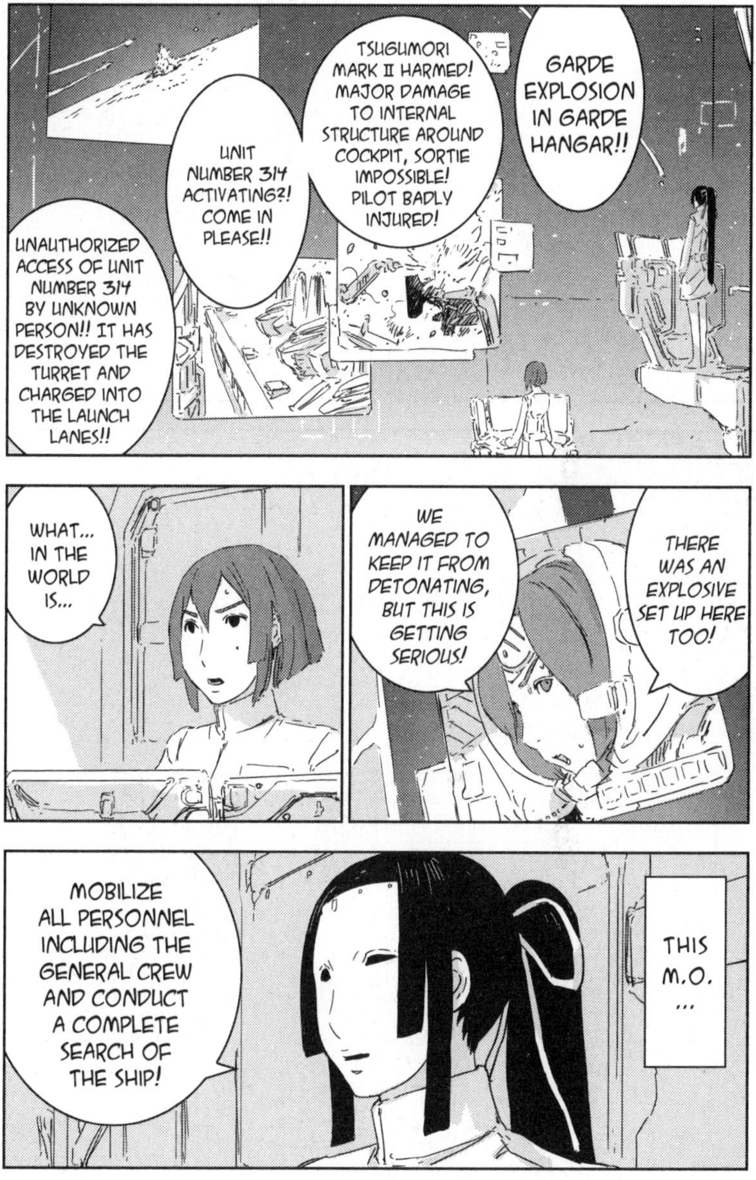
GARDE EXPLOSION IN GARDE HANGAR!!
TSUGUMORI MARK II HARMED! MAJOR DAMAGE TO INTERNAL STRUCTURE AROUND COCKPIT, SORTIE IMPOSSIBLE! PILOT BADLY INJURED!
UNIT NUMBER 314 ACTIVATING?! COME IN PLEASE!!
UNAUTHORIZED ACCESS OF UNIT NUMBER 314 BY UNKNOWN PERSON!! IT HAS DESTROYED THE TURRET AND CHARGED INTO THE LAUNCH LANES!!
THERE WAS AN EXPLOSIVE SET UP HERE TOO!
WE MANAGED TO KEEP IT FROM DETONATING, BUT THIS IS GETTING SERIOUS!
WHAT... IN THE WORLD IS...
THIS M.O. ...
MOBILIZE ALL PERSONNEL INCLUDING THE GENERAL CREW AND CONDUCT A COMPLETE SEARCH OF THE SHIP!

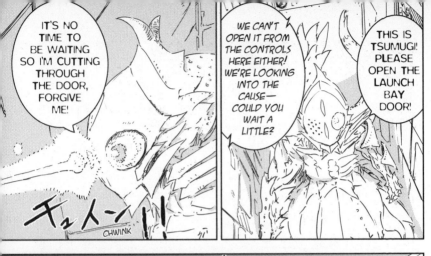

THIS IS TSUMUGI! PLEASE OPEN THE LAUNCH BAY DOOR!
WE CAN'T OPEN IT FROM THE CONTROLS HERE EITHER! WE'RE LOOKING INTO THE CAUSE— COULD YOU WAIT A LITTLE?
IT'S NO TIME TO BE WAITING SO I'M CUTTING THROUGH THE DOOR, FORGIVE ME!
CHWINK
WHOMF
IZANA, HOW'S MR. TANIKAZE ?!
HIS LIFE'S NOT IN DANGER BUT HE'S BADLY INJURED ...
I- I SEE ...

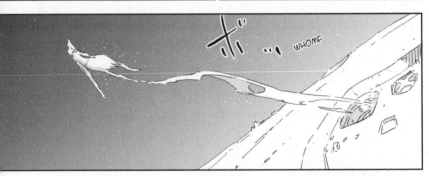

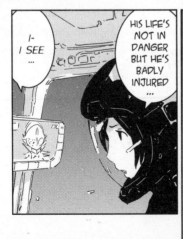

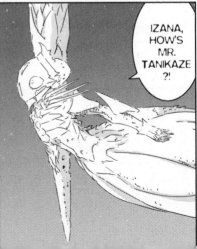

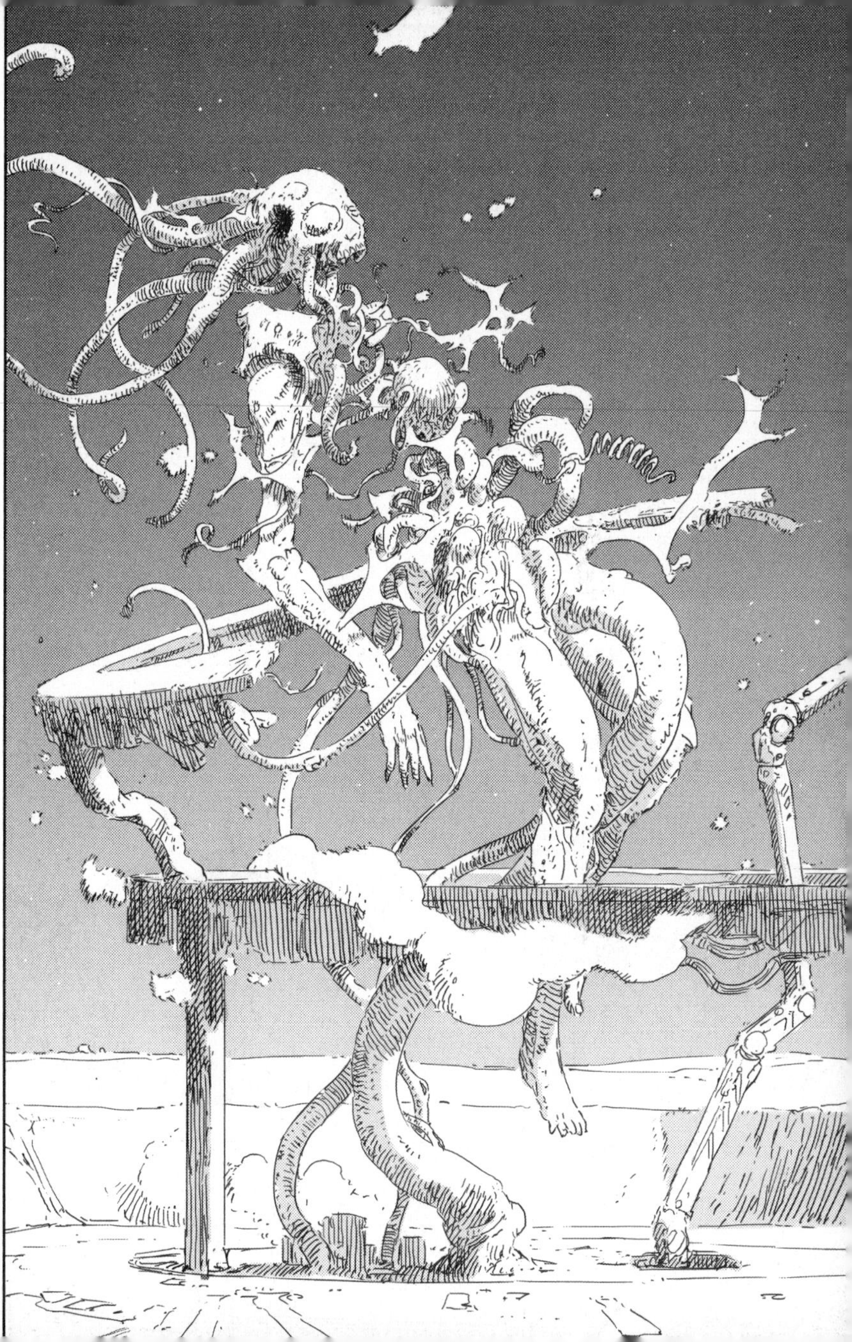

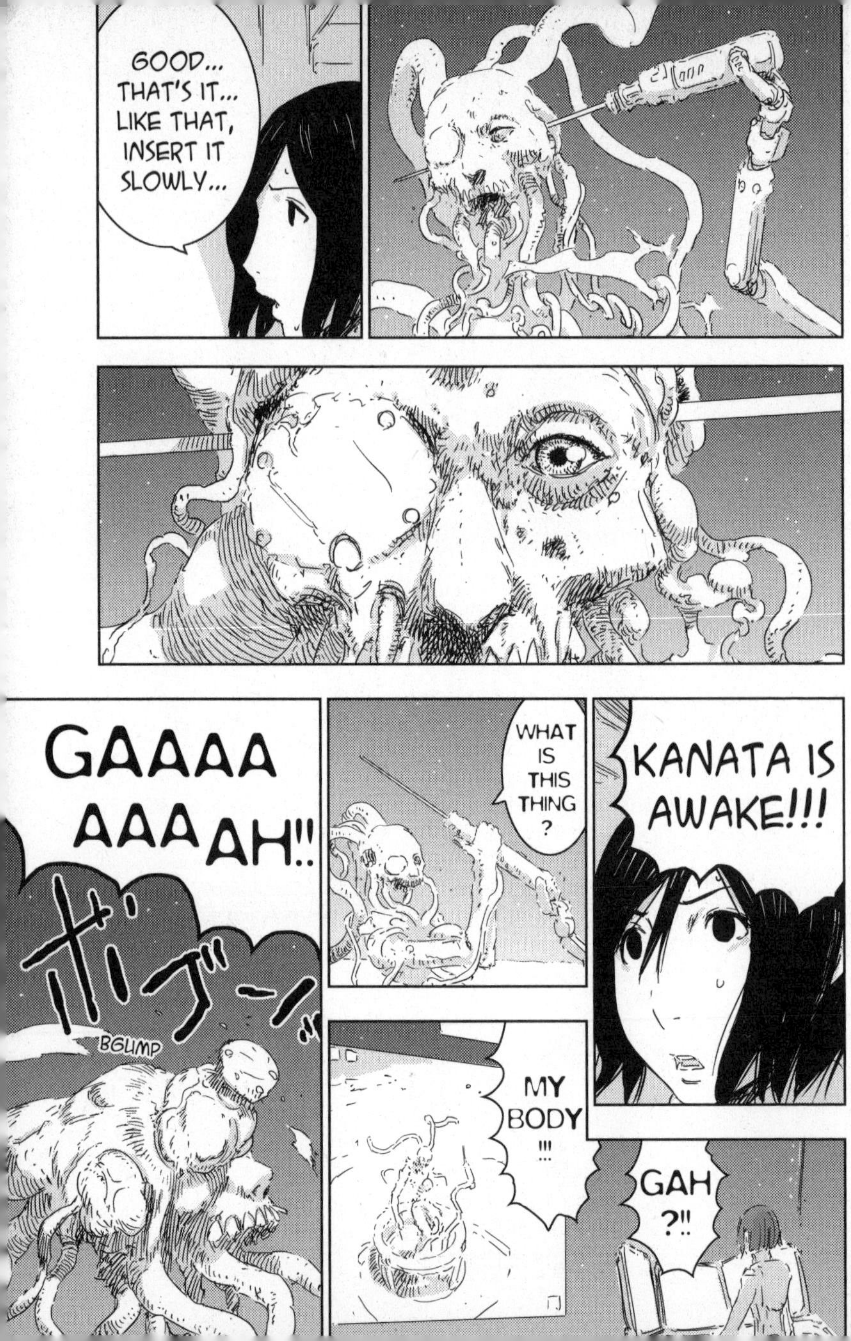
GOOD... THAT'S IT... LIKE THAT, INSERT IT SLOWLY...
KANATA IS AWAKE!!!
GAH ?!!
WHAT IS THIS THING ?
MY BODY !!!
GAAAA AAAAAH!!
BGUMP

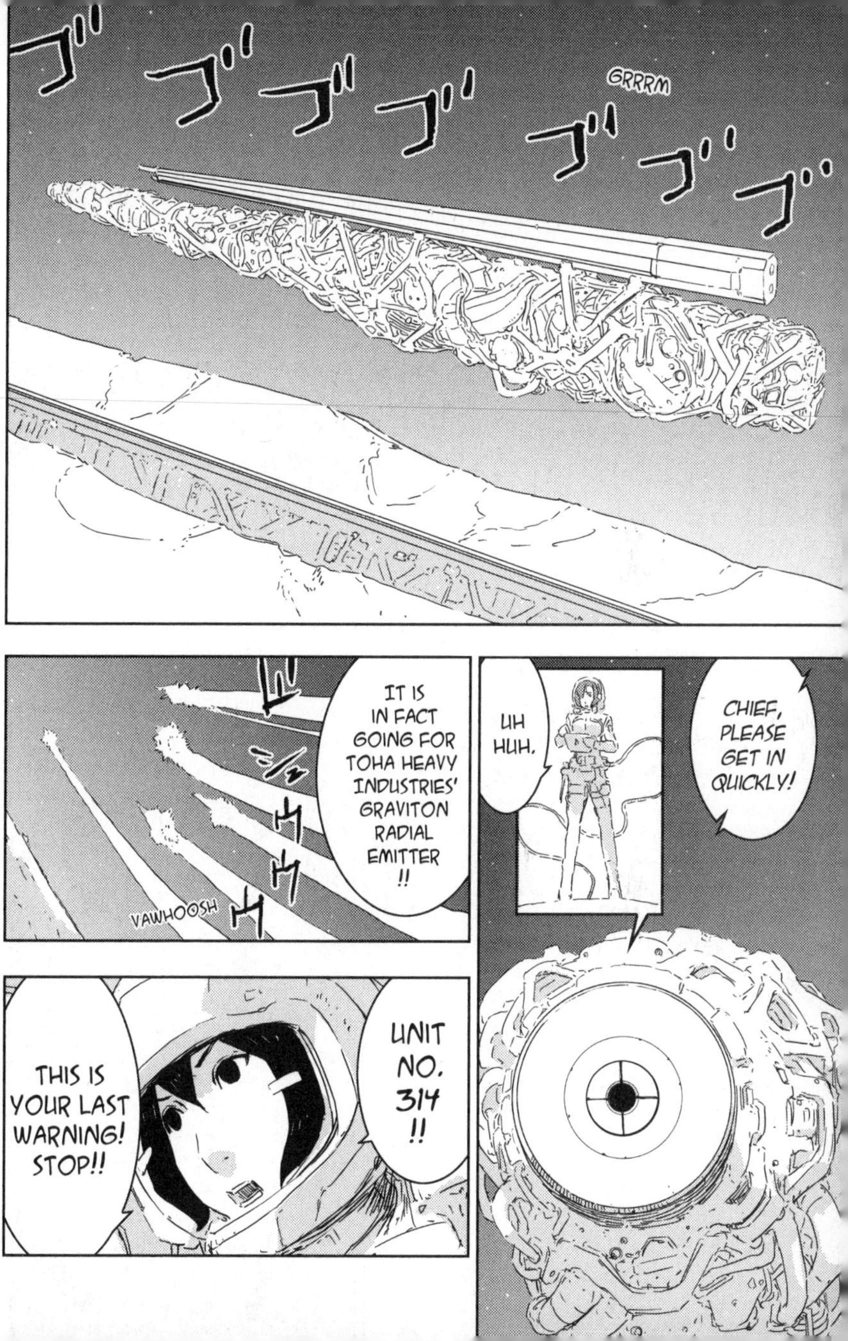
GRRRM
CHIEF, PLEASE GET IN QUICKLY!
UH HUH.
IT IS IN FACT GOING FOR TOHA HEAVY INDUSTRIES' GRAVITON RADIAL EMITTER !!
VAWHOOSH
UNIT NO. 314 !!
THIS IS YOUR LAST WARNING! STOP!!

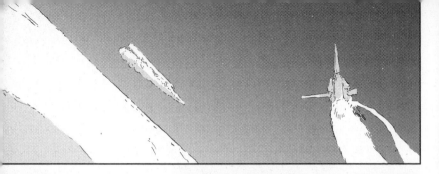

SHANNK

THIS IS SAMARI SQUAD! UNIT NO. 314 HAS BEEN DE-STROYED ...

BGWOO

NKK !

CHANK

DOOM

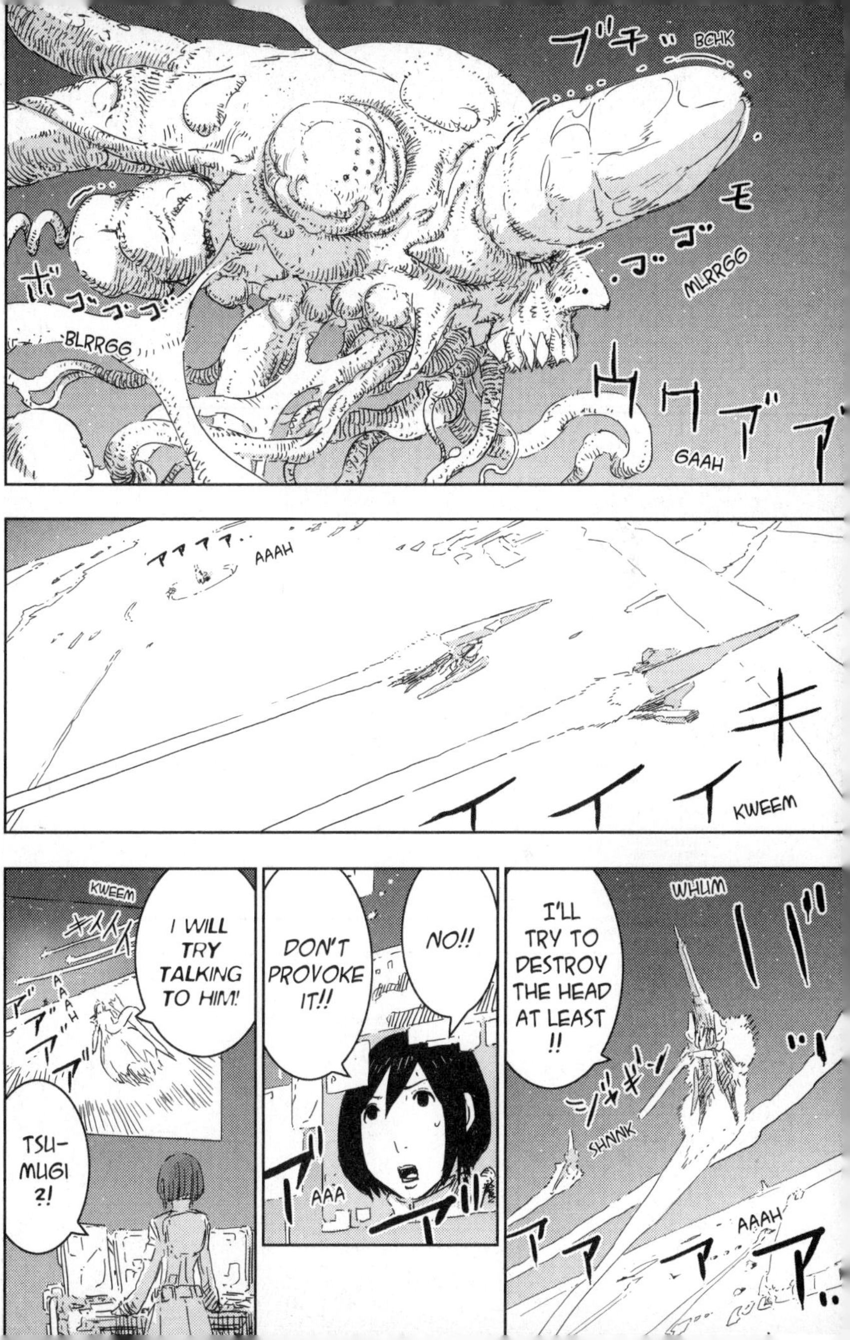
BCHK
MLRRGG
GAAH
BLRRGG
KWEEM
AAAH
WHUM
I'LL TRY TO DESTROY THE HEAD AT LEAST!!
SHNNK
AAAH
NO!!
DON'T PROVOKE IT!!
AAA
KWEEM
I WILL TRY TALKING TO HIM!
AAAH
TSU-MUGI?!

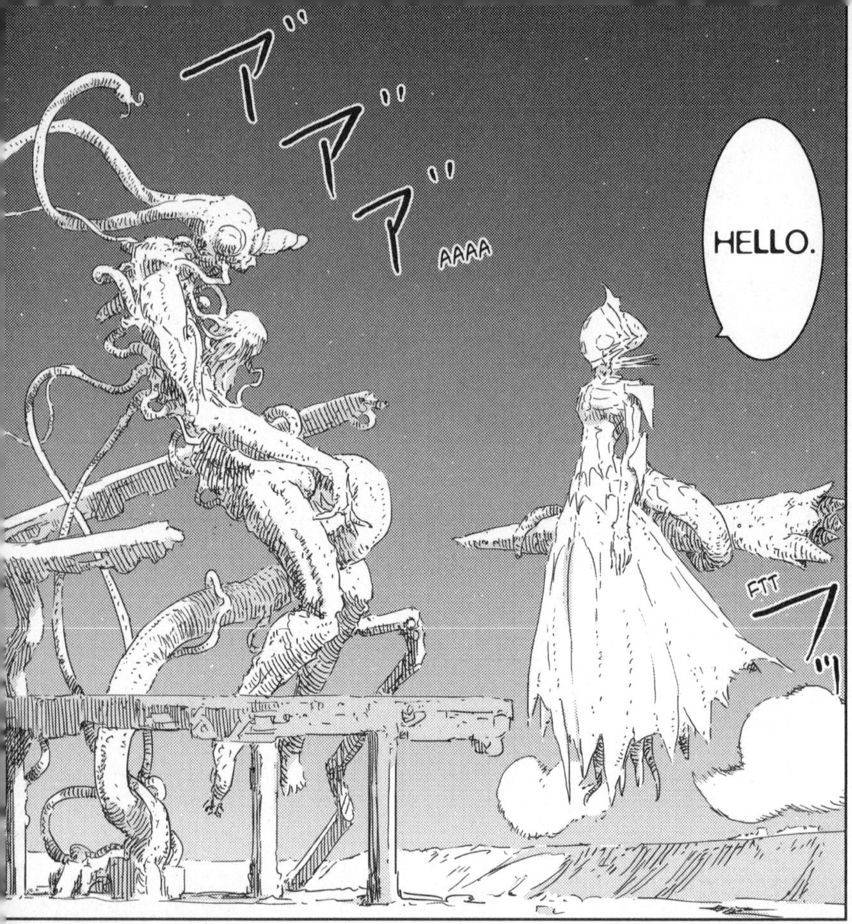
HELLO.
AAAA
FTT

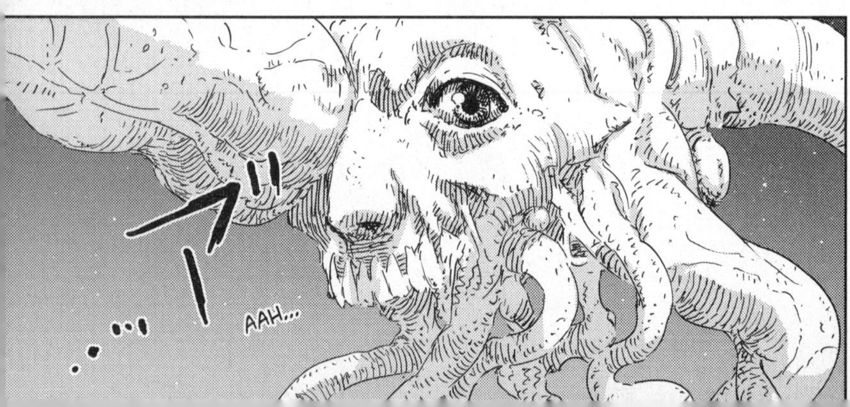
AAH...
...

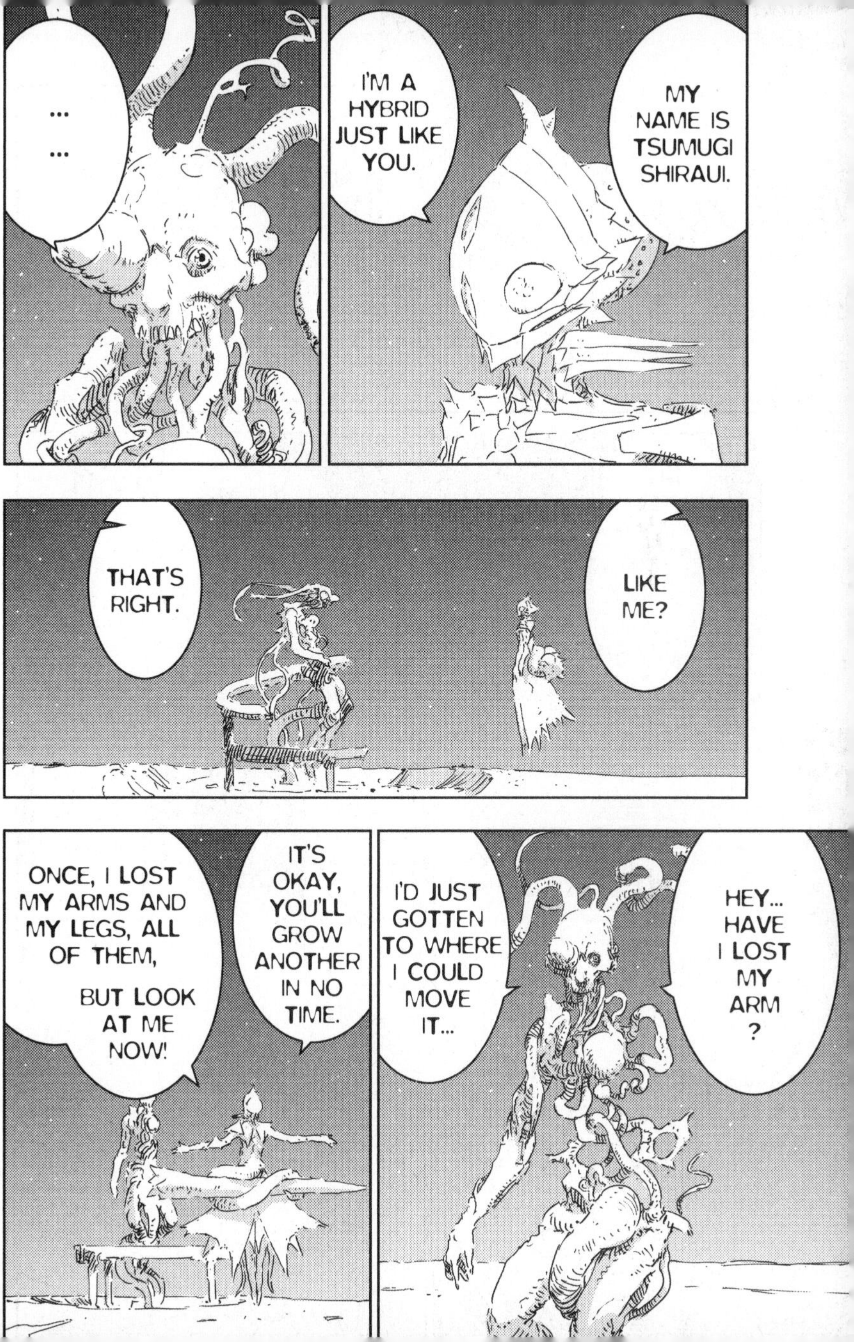
MY NAME IS TSUMUGI SHIRAUI.
I'M A HYBRID JUST LIKE YOU.
... ...
LIKE ME?
THAT'S RIGHT.
HEY... HAVE I LOST MY ARM?
I'D JUST GOTTEN TO WHERE I COULD MOVE IT...
IT'S OKAY, YOU'LL GROW ANOTHER IN NO TIME.
ONCE, I LOST MY ARMS AND MY LEGS, ALL OF THEM,
BUT LOOK AT ME NOW!

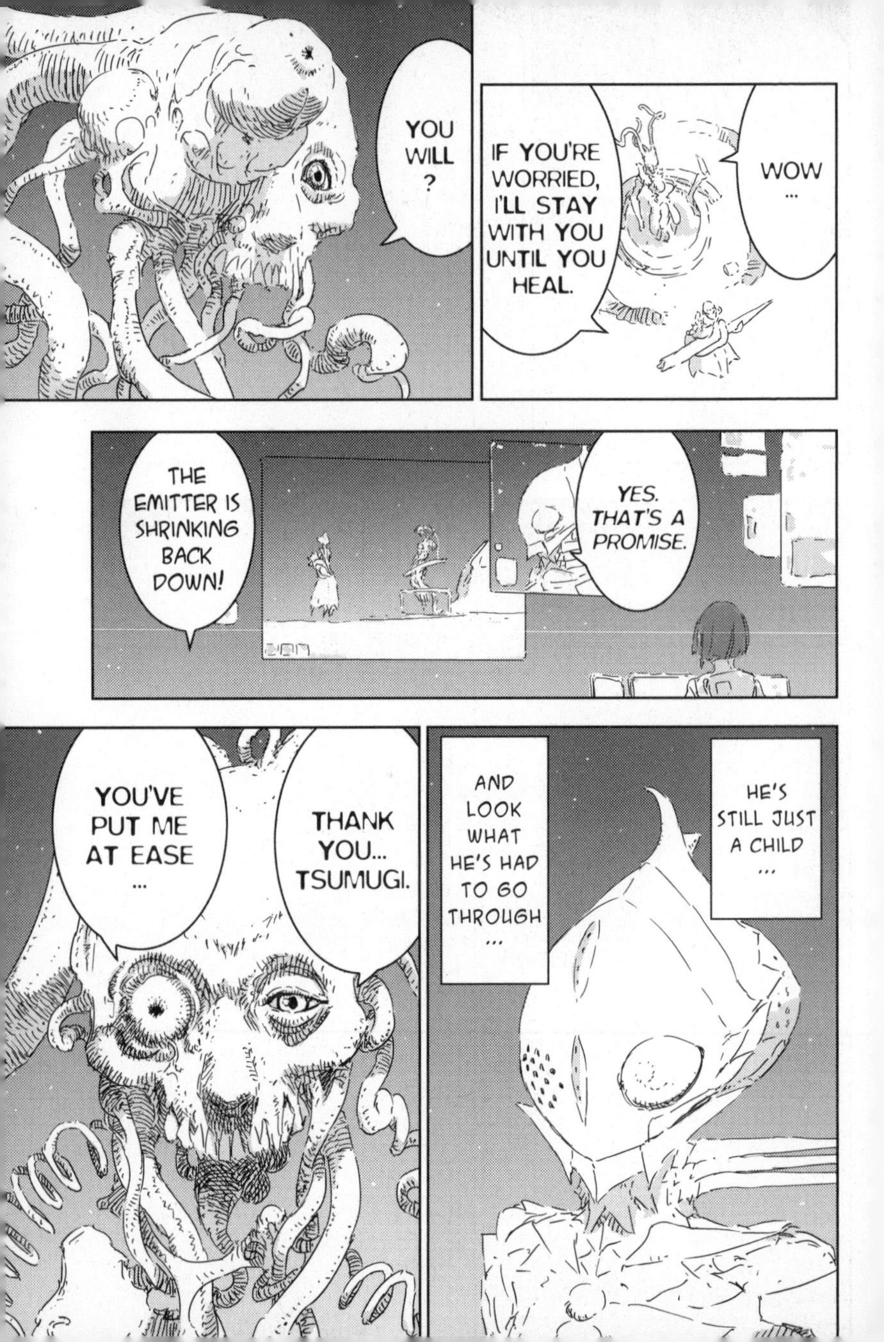
WOW ...
IF YOU'RE WORRIED, I'LL STAY WITH YOU UNTIL YOU HEAL.
YOU WILL ?
YES. THAT'S A PROMISE.
THE EMITTER IS SHRINKING BACK DOWN!
HE'S STILL JUST A CHILD ...
AND LOOK WHAT HE'S HAD TO GO THROUGH ...
THANK YOU... TSUMUGI.
YOU'VE PUT ME AT EASE ...

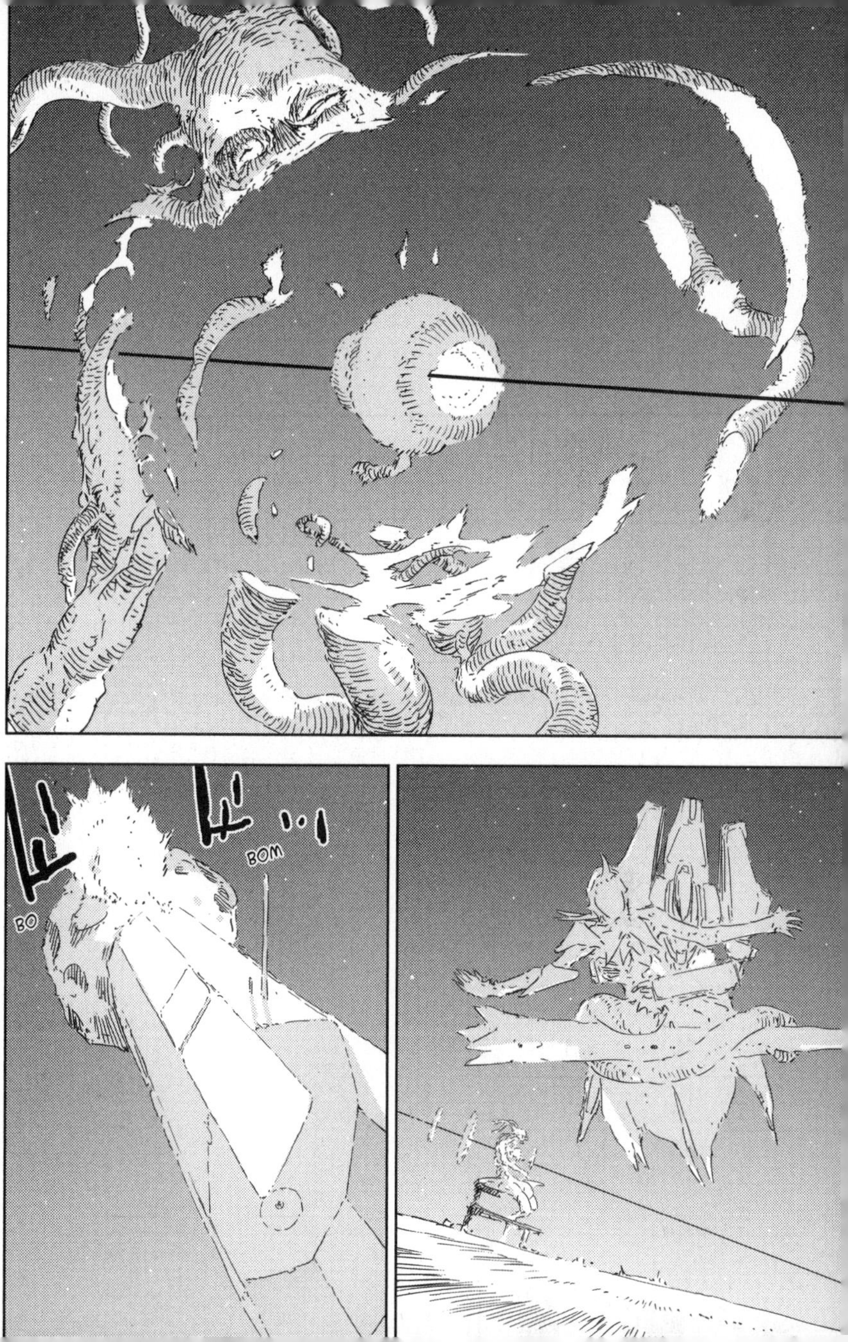
BOM
BO

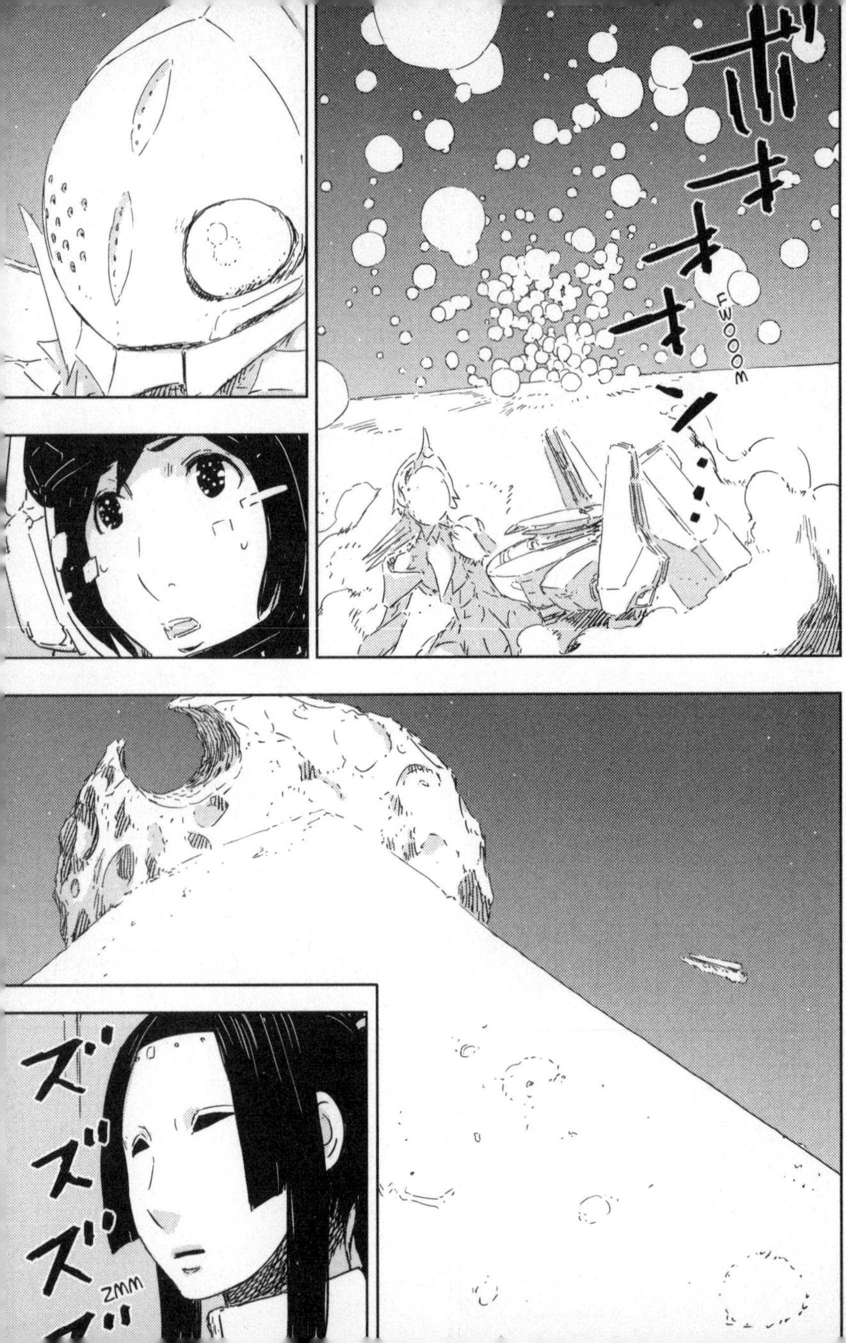
ボォォォン…
FWOOOM
ズズズズ
ZMM

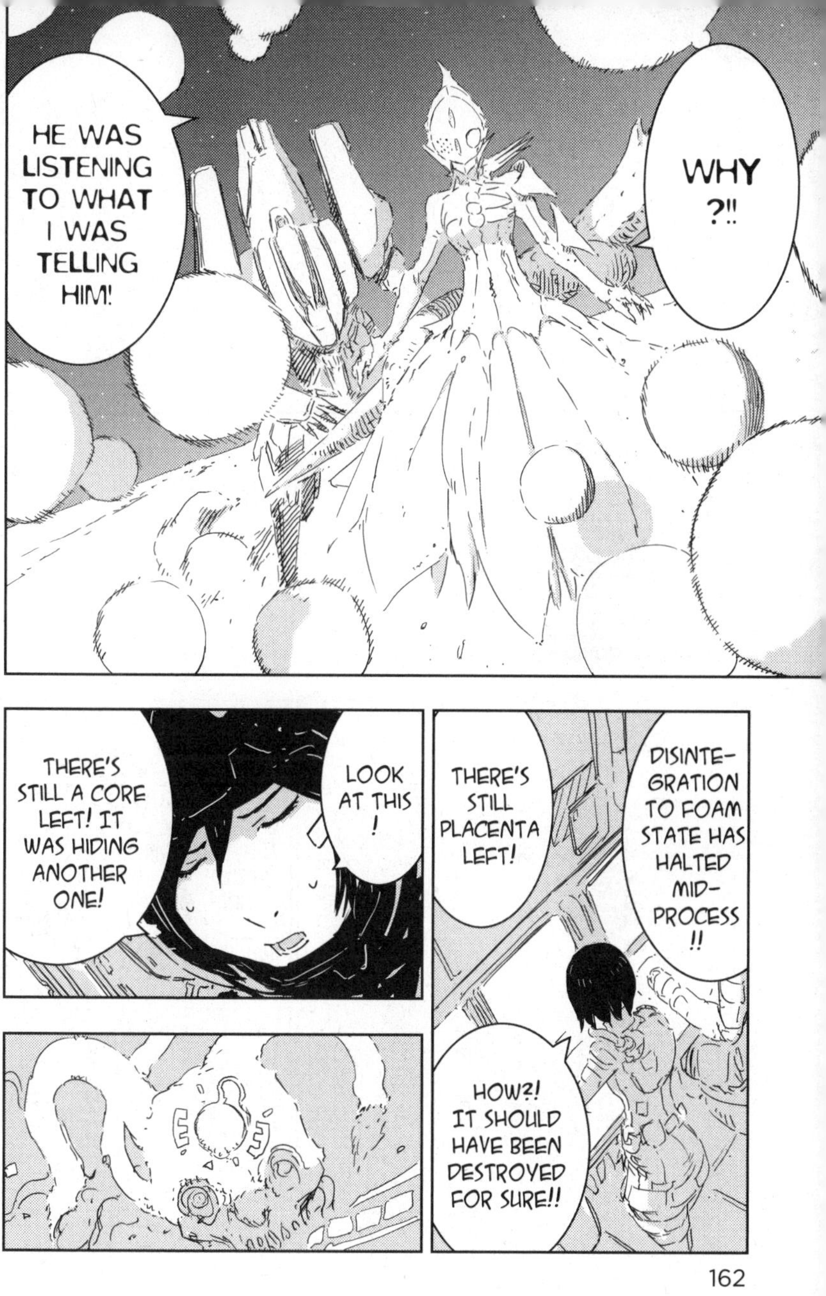
WHY?!!
HE WAS LISTENING TO WHAT I WAS TELLING HIM!
DISINTEGRATION TO FOAM STATE HAS HALTED MID-PROCESS!!
THERE'S STILL PLACENTA LEFT!
HOW?! IT SHOULD HAVE BEEN DESTROYED FOR SURE!!
LOOK AT THIS!
THERE'S STILL A CORE LEFT! IT WAS HIDING ANOTHER ONE!

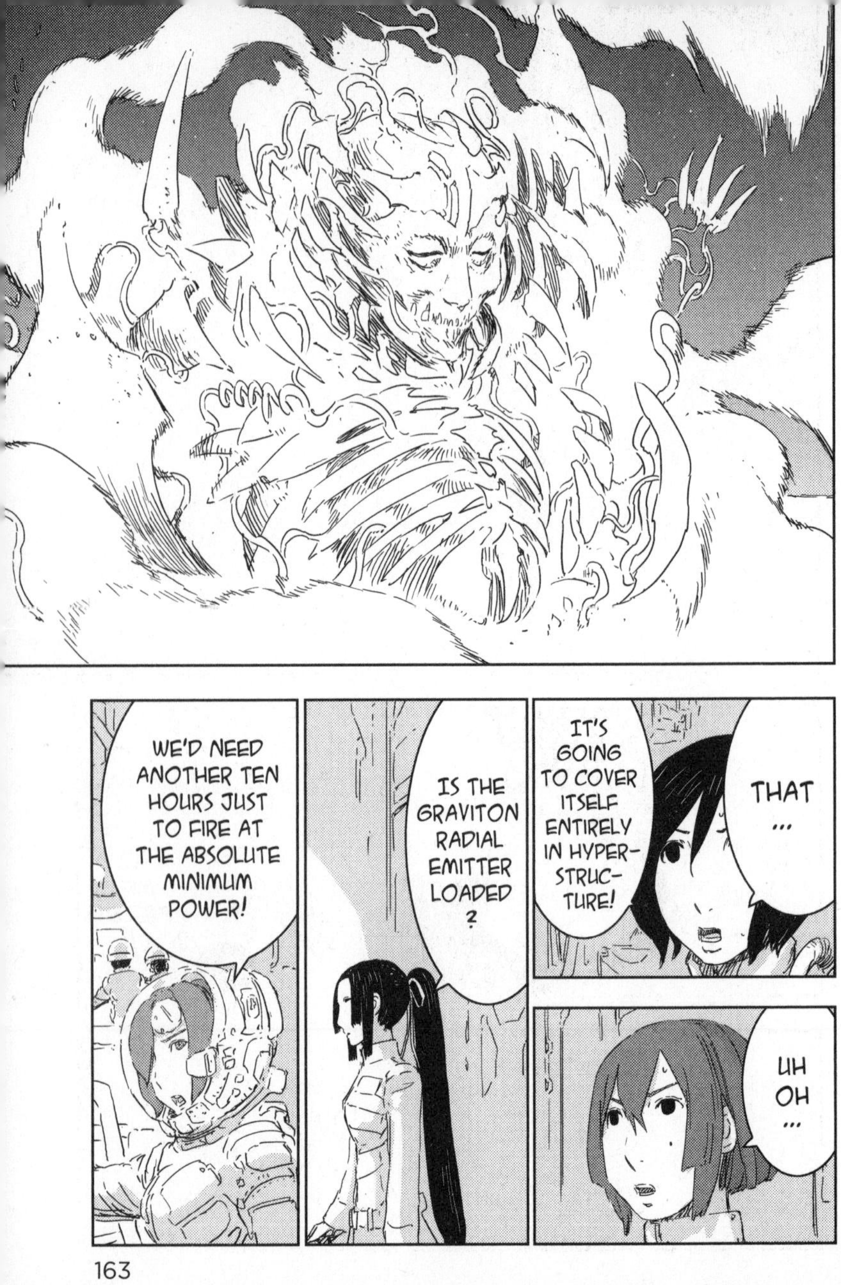
THAT ...
IT'S GOING TO COVER ITSELF ENTIRELY IN HYPER-STRUCTURE!
UH OH ...
IS THE GRAVITON RADIAL EMITTER LOADED ?
WE'D NEED ANOTHER TEN HOURS JUST TO FIRE AT THE ABSOLUTE MINIMUM POWER!

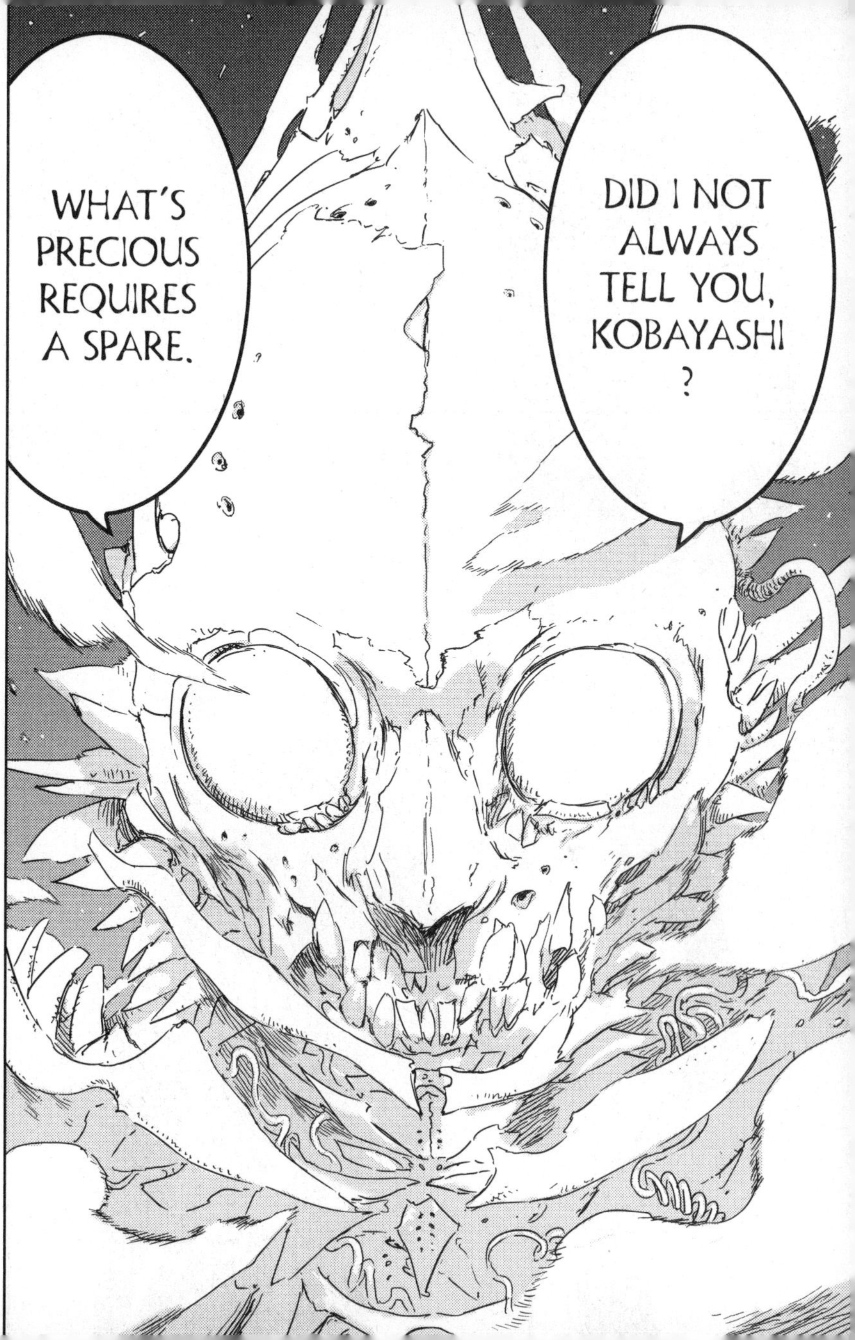
DID I NOT ALWAYS TELL YOU, KOBAYASHI?
WHAT'S PRECIOUS REQUIRES A SPARE.

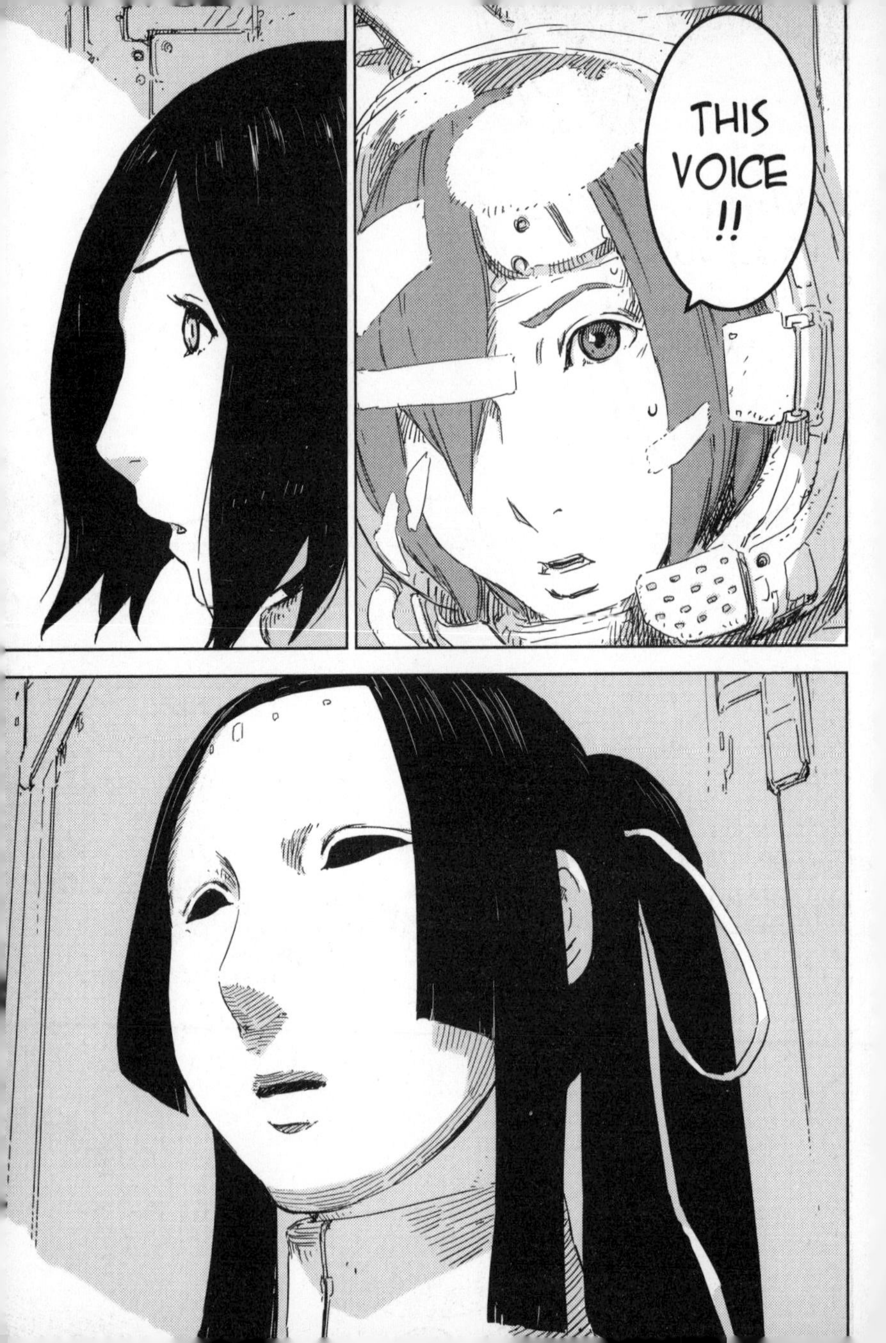
THIS VOICE !!

KNIGHTS OF SIDONIA Volume ⑬ : END

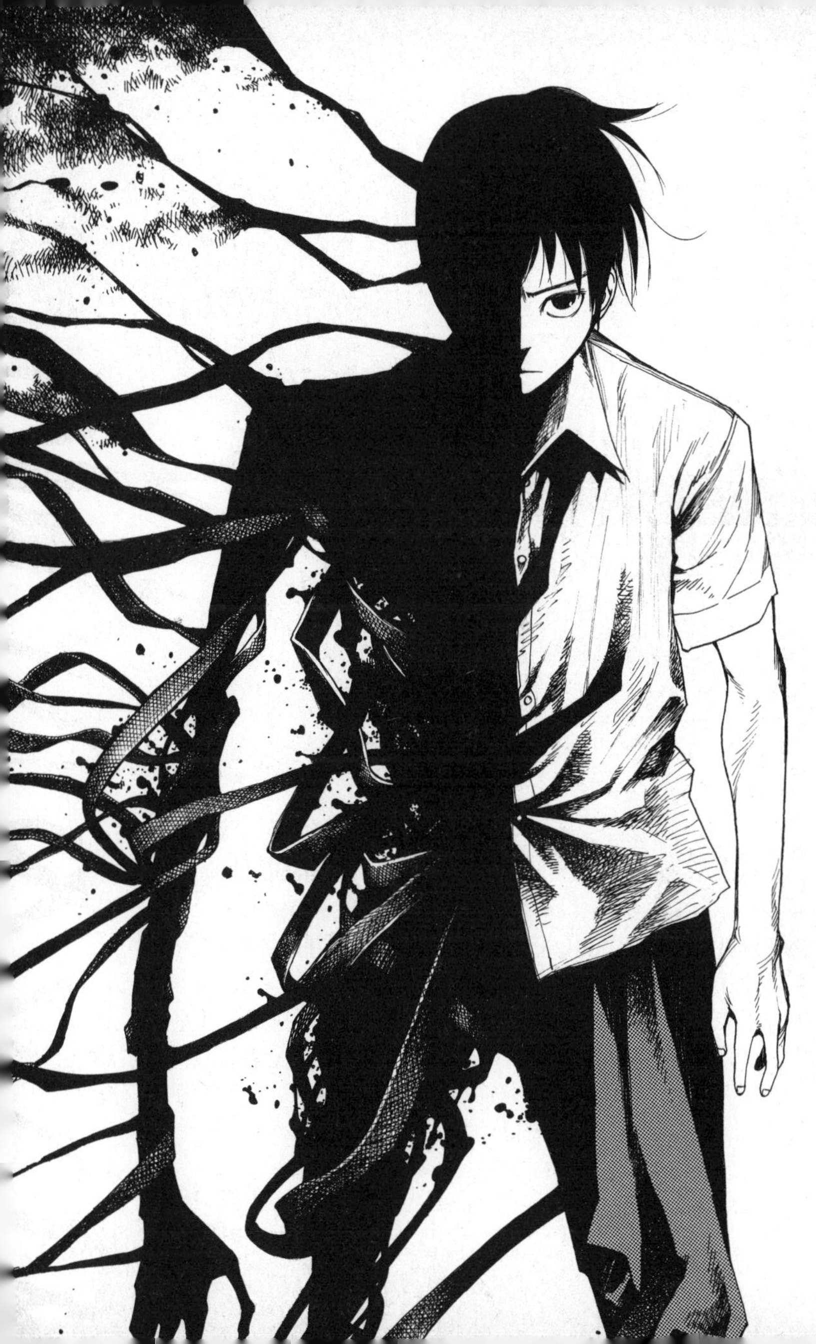

AJIN
DEMI-HUMAN

STORY: TSUINA MIURA
ART: GAMON SAKURAI

SAY YOU GET HIT BY A TRUCK AND DIE.
YOU COME BACK TO LIFE. GOOD OR BAD?

FOR HIGH SCHOOLER KEI—AND FOR AT LEAST FORTY-SIX OTHERS—
IMMORTALITY COMES AS THE NASTIEST SURPRISE EVER.

SADLY FOR KEI, BUT REFRESHINGLY FOR THE READER, SUCH A FEAT
DOESN'T MAKE HIM A SUPERHERO. IN THE EYES OF BOTH THE GENERAL
PUBLIC AND GOVERNMENTS, HE'S A RARE SPECIMEN WHO NEEDS TO BE
HUNTED DOWN AND HANDED OVER TO SCIENTISTS TO BE EXPERIMENTED
ON FOR LIFE—A DEMI-HUMAN WHO MUST DIE A THOUSAND DEATHS
FOR THE BENEFIT OF HUMANITY.

VOLUMES 1-3 AVAILABLE NOW!

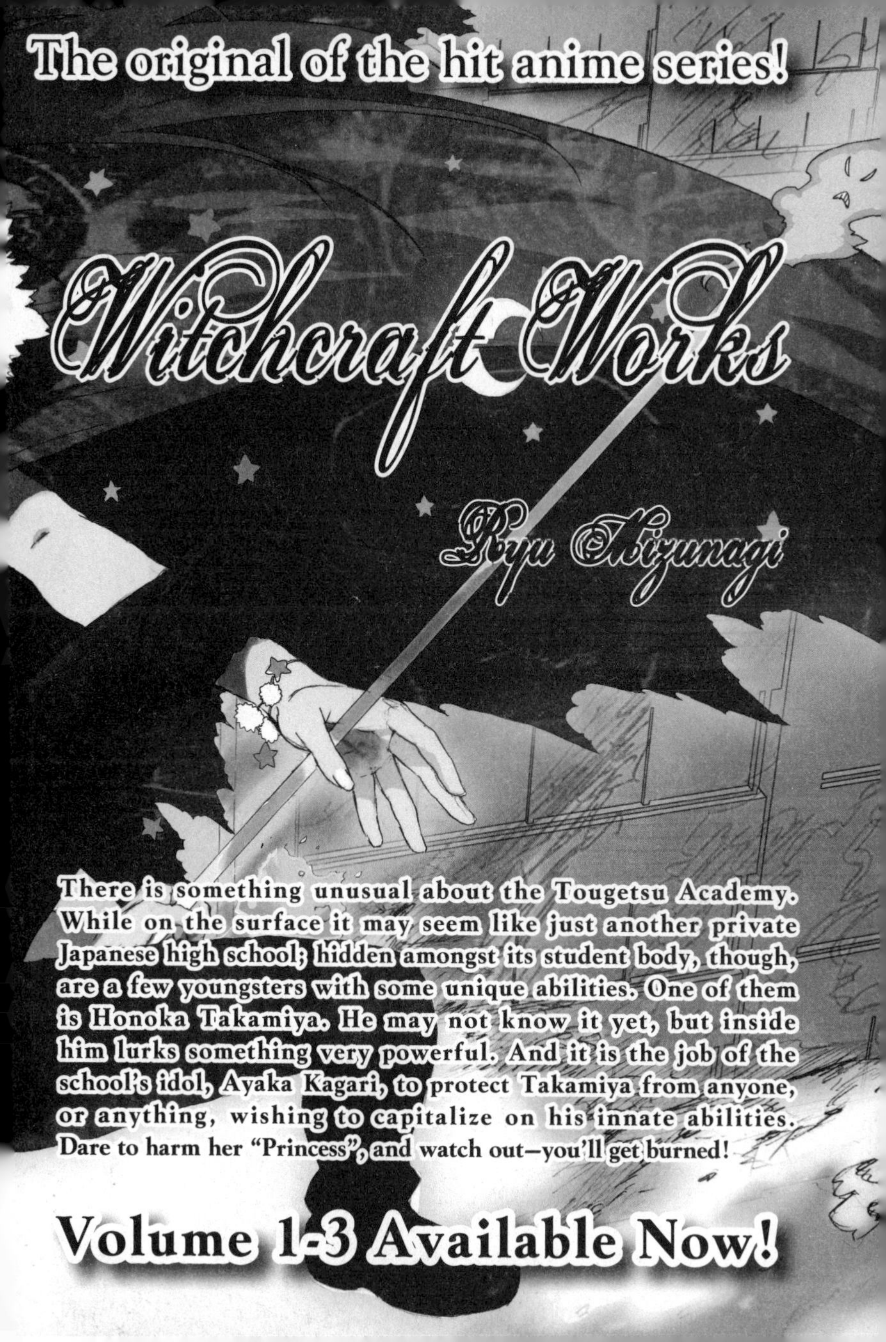
The original of the hit anime series!
Witchcraft Works
Ryu Mizunagi
There is something unusual about the Tougetsu Academy. While on the surface it may seem like just another private Japanese high school; hidden amongst its student body, though, are a few youngsters with some unique abilities. One of them is Honoka Takamiya. He may not know it yet, but inside him lurks something very powerful. And it is the job of the school's idol, Ayaka Kagari, to protect Takamiya from anyone, or anything, wishing to capitalize on his innate abilities. Dare to harm her "Princess", and watch out—you'll get burned!
Volume 1-3 Available Now!

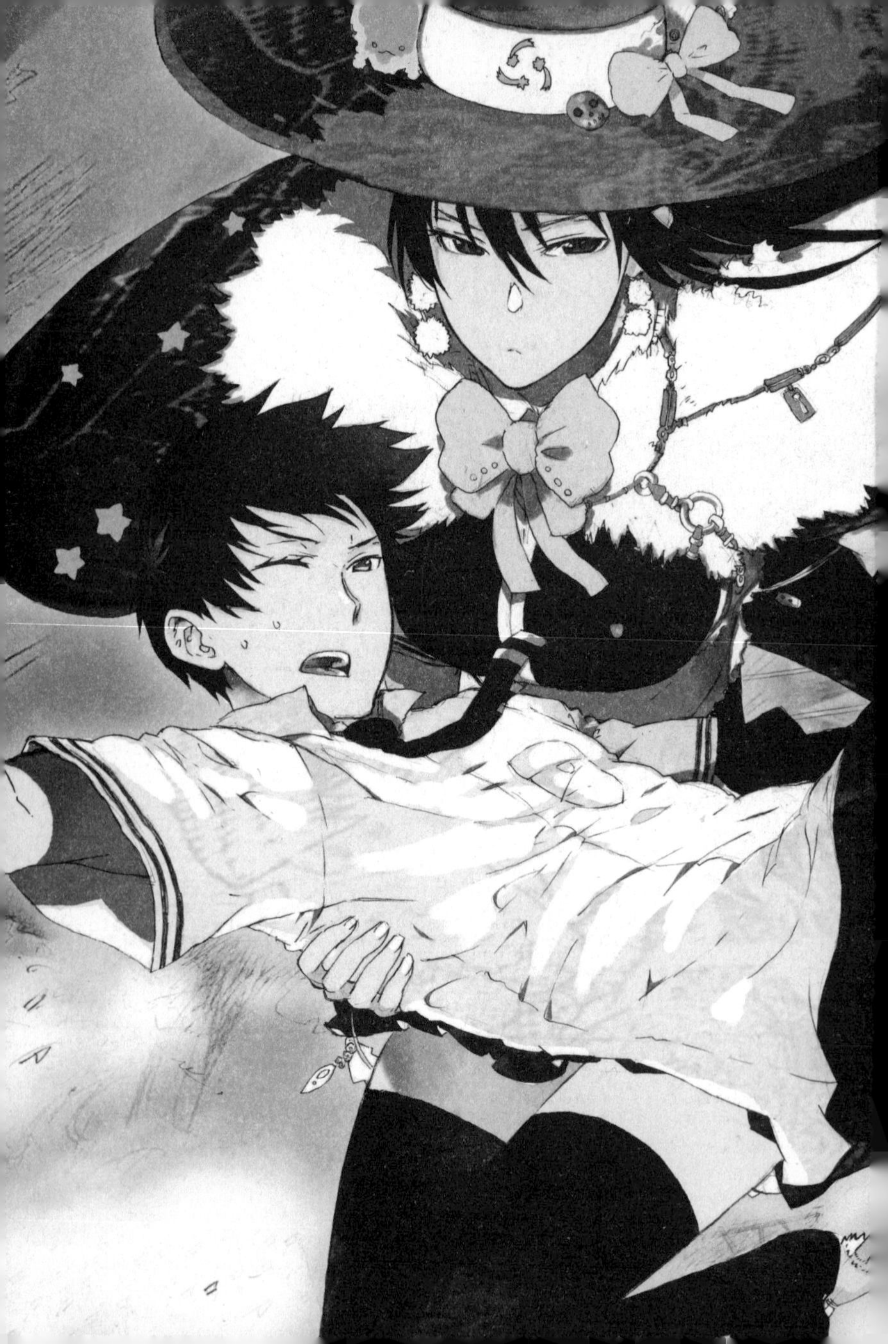

Knights of Sidonia, volume 13

Translation: Kumar Sivasubramanian
Production: Grace Lu
Daniela Yamada
Anthony Quintessenza

First published in Japan in 2014 by Kodansha, Ltd., Tokyo
Publication for this English edition arranged through Kodansha, Ltd., Tokyo
English language version produced by Vertical, Inc.

Translation provided by Vertical, Inc., 2015
Published by Vertical, Inc., New York

Originally published in Japanese as *Shidonia no Kishi 13* by Kodansha, Ltd.
Shidonia no Kishi first serialized in *Afternoon*, Kodansha, Ltd., 2009-2015

This is a work of fiction.

ISBN: 978-1-941220-32-0

Manufactured in Canada

First Edition

Second Printing

Vertical, Inc.
451 Park Avenue South
7th Floor
New York, NY 10016
www.vertical-inc.com